JUDAISM, NATIONALISM, ——· and the ·—— LAND of ISRAEL

JUDAISM, NATIONALISM, and the LAND of ISRAEL

M A R T I N   S I C K E R

Westview Press

BOULDER · SAN FRANCISCO · OXFORD

Copyright © 1992 by Westview Press, Inc.

Published in 1992 in the United States of America by Westview Press, Inc., 5500 Central Avenue, Boulder, Colorado 80301-2877, and in the United Kingdom by Westview Press, 36 Lonsdale Road, Summertown, Oxford OX2 7EW

Library of Congress Cataloging-in-Publication Data
Sicker, Martin.
   Judaism, nationalism, and the land of Israel / Martin Sicker.
      p.   cm.
   Includes bibliographical references and index.
   ISBN 0-8133-8247-5
   1. Jewish nationalism—History.   2. Zionism—History.   3. Jews—
Identity.   4. Palestine in Judaism.   5. Judaism and state.
6. Israel—Politics and government.   I. Title.
DS143.S4754   1992
956.94—dc20   92-11591
                                                                          CIP

Printed and bound in the United States of America

The paper used in this publication meets the requirements of the American National Standard for Permanence of Paper for Printed Library Materials Z39.48-1984.

10   9   8   7   6   5   4   3   2   1

To my late brother-in-law Arnon Fixman,
who would have enjoyed discussing
the thesis of this book with me.
May his memory serve as a blessing.

CONTENTS

INTRODUCTION

An intimate historic as well as intellectual relationship exists between Judaism, Jewish nationalism, and the Land of Israel. This relationship is unique in a number of respects. From biblical days to the present, the Land of Israel has been closely linked to the Jewish religion and to a nationalist understanding of that interconnection. This work will explore these linkages in order to clarify the essential nature of the ideological debate now taking place in Israel and the worldwide Jewish community over the future of the Jewish state and its relation to the Jewish Diaspora.

I should begin by explaining why I refer to "Jewish nationalism" rather than the more familiar term—Zionism. There is good reason for distinguishing between the two concepts. The signal role of the Zionist movement in bringing to realization the idea of a Jewish state only a few decades ago has tended to obscure the proper place of Zionist ideology in the vastly longer intellectual history of Jewish nationalism. Whereas Zionism typically has come to be equated with Jewish nationalism, it would be far more accurate to consider it as a critical aspect or manifestation of that conceptual formulation in modern times. This common misconception about Jewish nationalism has made it particularly difficult for many observers to comprehend the ideological struggle going on in Israel. A case in point is the lack of readiness, or sheer unwillingness, on the part of many to recognize that the era of Zionism, as it has generally been understood for more than a hundred years, is rapidly coming to an end (if it has not already done so). Zionism is yielding its place to other nationalist constructions that, in many essentials, are quite different from, if not alien to, conventional Zionist thinking.

The central purpose of this book is to examine briefly the intellectual history of an extraordinarily powerful concept—the idea of Jewish nationalism—that has effectively conditioned the history of the Jews for more than three millennia. Within this long time span, the historical niche occupied by Zionism, notwithstanding its crucial importance for contemporary Jewry, represents but a brief interlude. To some extent, Zionism might even be legitimately considered as an aberration from the long-standing forms and concepts of traditional Jewish nationalism. Accordingly, this book is not concerned with the history of the Zionist movement, nor does it address the nuances introduced by a wide variety of Zionist thinkers in the ongoing ideological battles between its several schools and tendencies.

Zionism is principally an intellectual product of the second half of the nineteenth century; the idea of Jewish nationalism, however, is probably the oldest nationalist conception known to history. Although there certainly were peoples and nations that preceded the Jews, it seems it was only among the latter that the fundamental concepts that have shaped the history of nationalism were first articulated. Thus, when discussing the origins of modern nationalism, Hans Kohn observed, "Three essential traits of nationalism originated with the ancient Jews: the idea of the chosen people, the consciousness of national history, and national Messianism."[1] The role of these notions in Jewish thought and literature will be the focus of this book.

To set the stage, Chapter 1 opens with an examination of the nationalist dimensions of Judaism, particularly as they are implied within the context of the biblical story of Jewish origins. The linkage between Judaism, nationalism, and the Land of Israel is established clearly in Scripture, as is the national mission of Israel. Having explored the biblical ideal, I turn in Chapter 2 to the realities of Israel's history to show how the threefold relationship was sustained in face of the loss of national independence and the subsequent exile of the people from the Land. In this regard, I shall discuss the prophetic treatment of nationalist themes and aspirations. Following this, Chapter 3 examines how these same themes were addressed by the rabbinic sages of the talmudic era, culminating in the formulation of a quietist ideology designed to suppress nationalism as a vital component of applied Judaism and to relegate it to a distant messianic future. A fundamental ideological split developed over this question, between those who sensed that the suppression of the nationalist aspects of Judaism detracted from its essential relevance and those who considered it imperative that a means be found of vindicating traditional Jewish life in exile once the prospects of a nationalist restoration in the Land of Israel became increasingly remote. The path that this ideological conflict took through the medieval period is the subject of Chapter 4. Particular attention is given to the manifestation of this conflict in the various schools of Jewish philosophy and mysticism.

Chapter 5 deals with the impact of the French Revolution and the era of emancipation on the threefold relationship. During that period the concept of secular Jewish nationalism emerged. The growth of that idea and its offshoot, "territorialism," that is, the possibility of establishing a Jewish national home outside the Land of Israel, is discussed in Chapter 6. Chapter 7 explores the reaction within the Jewish community to the rising prominence of nationalist ideas. The discussion focuses on the emergence of two schools of Jewish thought, religious reform and diaspora nationalism, the former having far greater historic significance. Both schools sought to counter the growth of secular Jewish nationalism as well as a resurgence of traditional Jewish nationalism. Their method was an ideological reformulation of the nature of Judaism and Jewish history that rejected the concept that the Diaspora constituted "exile," thus severing the traditional Judaic nationalist link with the Land of Israel. Next, in Chapter 8, I turn to a consideration of the political Zionism conceived by Theodor Herzl, followed by an examination of the basic modifications made to this formulation of Jewish nationalism by the insertion of socialist concepts into the Zionist agenda.

Finally, I conclude with a brief discussion of the principal intellectual trends touching upon the threefold relationship that were and remain current in the twentieth century. In Chapter 9 I focus on the decline of Zionism as a vibrant nationalist ideology and the renaissance of a vigorous traditional synthesis of Judaism, nationalism, and the Land of Israel. That renaissance is posing an increasingly significant challenge to the secularist interpretation of Israel's past and prospect.

The book draws no conclusions regarding the eventual outcome of the present ideological conflict over the nature and future direction of Jewish nationalism. If it succeeds in clarifying this intellectual struggle, it will have fully satisfied my intent and purpose.

1

The Founding of
the Nation

As is the case with all ancient groups, there is no extant historical evidence of the origins of the Jews as a people and very little concerning their early formative years as a nation. All that we do have of significance in this regard are the stories and references preserved in the earliest literature of the Jews, the Hebrew Bible, most of which, of course, dates from a period when the Jews were already long constituted as the people of Israel. Accordingly, the most appropriate point of departure for this study is Israel's self-conception of its beginning, as it is manifested in the biblical literature, in what may be referred to as its national foundation myth.

I hasten to add that I do not use the term "myth" in the ordinary sense of a fable or imaginary story, something that is a product of pure fantasy. Many myths—particularly political foundation myths—deal with real historical events and people. With respect to such myths, Henry Tudor wrote:

> We may disagree with the account they give of these people and events, but they are not fiction. For the most part, the myth-maker does not invent his facts; he interprets facts that are already given in the culture to which he belongs. What marks his account as being a myth is, not its content, but its dramatic form and the fact that it serves as a practical argument. Its success as a practical argument depends on its being accepted as true, and it is generally accepted as true if it explains the experience of those to whom it is addressed.

The main value of the political myth is in explaining to those to whom it is addressed the particular historical circumstances in which they find themselves. "It renders their experience more coherent; it helps them understand the world in which they live. And it does so by enabling them to see their present condition as an episode in an ongoing drama. . . . It offers, in short, an account of the past and the future in the light of which the present can be understood. And as we would expect, this account is, not only an explanation, but also a practical argument."[1]

THE FOUNDATION MYTH

Let us therefore begin with an examination of the foundation myth of Israel, as it is reflected in the principal source document of Judaism, the Pentateuch. This qualification is essential because many of the elements of the myth are presented in the biblical texts as seemingly disconnected narratives, which require the sympathetic reader to link them in a coherent and meaningful progression. Moreover, from the standpoint of political myth, it makes little if any difference whether one approaches the biblical texts from a fundamentalist or a critical perspective. Whether the Pentateuch was written by Moses at the word of God, as maintained by traditionalists, or whether, as critical scholars argue, it was compiled and edited at some later period in Israel's history is an issue that does not concern us here. Such considerations do not affect the manner in which the received texts have shaped the Jewish national and religious consciousness throughout its long history. In this regard, it should be borne in mind that the traditional approach to the question of biblical authorship would place the origin of the Jewish national idea some thirty-two centuries ago, whereas critical scholarship, at its most extreme position, might reduce that point of origin to some twenty-five centuries ago. I would therefore suggest, from the perspective of the historical significance of the foundation myth, that the difference between the two approaches to the texts is of no practical consequence. Indeed, W. D. Davies in his study of the territorial dimension of Judaism, with specific regard to the divine promise given to Abraham in Genesis 12, observed:

> What is important is not the rediscovery of the origins of the promise to Abraham, but the recognition that that promise was so reinterpreted from age to age that it became a living power in the life of the people of Israel. Not the mode of its origin matters, but its operation as a formative, dynamic, seminal force in the history of Israel. The legend of the promise entered so deeply into the experience of the Jews that it acquired its own reality. What Jews believe to have happened in the Middle East has been no less formative in world history than that which is known to have occurred.[2]

What then is the biblical foundation myth of Israel? It hardly needs mention that the complex narratives of the Pentateuch do not lend themselves to simple summarization and may be interpreted in a variety of ways. What follows is my understanding of the myth that is presented therein, filtered through the prism of traditional Jewish biblical interpretation, which was the only Jewishly relevant and significant approach to the texts until modern times.

In essence, the biblical narrative may be understood as suggesting that, except for his conscious defiance of the divine will, generic man could have lived an idyllic existence in a universal society, something that would have been fully in accord with the divine purpose in the Creation. Given the biblical description of humankind's descent from common ancestors, it would seem quite reasonable that such should have been the case. However, we are told, society had become corrupted. Public immorality was pervasive and was accompanied by a great deal of violence and oppression. It ultimately reached the point where, from the divine perspective, mankind as it was constituted was no longer capable of fulfilling its appointed role in the cosmic scheme. The Creator resolved to bring a cataclysm upon the earth to eradicate almost all of mankind and to begin its repopulation with the family of the one righteous man of the time. Accordingly, after the great deluge had destroyed the world of primeval man, with Noah and his sons and their families the only survivors, "the whole earth was of one language and one speech" (Gen. 11:1). The implication is that, notwithstanding possibly significant differences of personality and character among the Noahides, they were able to communicate with each other linguistically and had a common cultural base. In other words, they had a mutual understanding of their shared experiences as members of a single family, which presumably provided a sound basis for the future development of a cohesive universal society.

The Noahides journeyed in search of a domicile that would serve their purposes and ultimately settled in the land of Shinar (Gen. 11:2). Here they raised their families and developed their primitive economy. Here, too, they began the arduous task of building a new civilization to replace that which had been destroyed in the great flood. However, as time passed and individual subfamilies grew in number, the Noahides began to lose their common identity as members of a single extended family and increasingly identified themselves by their membership in the principal branches of the Noahide family: the Shemites, Japhetites, and Hamites. Over time, even these identities became obscured. Following the precedent already established by their own estrangement from their grand paternal patriarch Noah, the older Noahide patriarchs also forfeited their status as the unifying heads of their respective extended families. Eventually, there would emerge multitudes of distinct groupings of people, with only a faint recollection of their common ancestry and origin.

After preserving the Noahides from the destruction of the deluge, the Creator had specifically instructed Noah and his sons not only to be fruitful and multiply but also to repopulate the earth (Gen. 9:1). Moreover, as originally articulated, the divine scheme called for man to conquer the earth and subdue it (Gen. 1:28); that is, to civilize it. To comply with these imperatives the Noahides had to disperse and begin the spread of their civilization beyond the bounds of their central zone of settlement. It would appear that their leaders clearly understood that for such a civilization-building enterprise to be successful, certain prerequisites had to be met. First, there would have to be a critical mass of people available for the task so that the multiple societies that were to be created would be viable in their struggles with brute nature. Second, stable social institutions would have to be developed in order to forestall a repetition of the failings of the antediluvian world. It would therefore take some time before the instructions of the Creator could be carried out responsibly. In other words, the critical population basis and the fundamental institutional structure of the new civilization would have to be established and developed before it could be replicated successfully elsewhere.

As the generations passed and the population increased significantly, new strains appeared in the social fabric. Vacant arable land presumably became increasingly scarce, as did pasturage for the ever growing numbers of flocks. As the Shinar plain became saturated with settlers, conflicts resulting from these conditions surfaced with ever greater frequency and intensity. Surely the appropriate time for the divine scheme to be implemented had arrived. The human congestion and the attendant problems of adequate food supply and shelter would be alleviated by dispersal of the population. As reasonable as this seemed, it was not a proposition that found many supporters. As a practical matter, it meant abandoning civilization to become pioneers of the unknown. Few if any were prepared to abandon their homes voluntarily, and there was no central institution with the authority to make and enforce such a difficult decision.

The patriarchs of Noahide society feared that the internal strife resulting from the growing population pressures would cause the forced displacement of some of their families. Accordingly, they sought a means of avoiding such a situation, "lest we be scattered abroad upon the face of the whole earth" (Gen. 11:4). Ultimately, they concluded that they would not implement the divine scheme but would take steps on their own to deal with the problems that population dispersion would have solved. They chose to create a countervailing authority to the divine, suggesting: "Come, let us build a city" (Gen. 11:4); that is, they would establish a state, which would be universal in character. This universal city-state would bring peace and order to the land—it would be independent of the influence of any particular patriarch or elder and would represent the will and needs of all the Noahides as a collectivity.

The universal city-state was thus conceived by the Noahides as an alternative to divine authority. To convince the masses to go along with this fundamental social and moral revolution, the Noahides would have to influence the populace to transfer its allegiance from God to the state. This was to be achieved by making a "name" for the city-state. Everything possible would be done to enhance the prestige of the city and its rulers so that, little by little, simple gratitude for peace and security would be transformed into ardent patriotism. As blind loyalty began to overcome the constraints imposed by reason, the Creator would be displaced by the city-state as the source of all moral authority. The construction of the city thus presented a challenge to the authority of the Creator that could not go unanswered.

Accordingly, "the Lord came down to see the city and the tower, which the children of men builded" (Gen. 11:5), that which had been conceived by man as a means for contravening the Creator's intentions for human-kind. Speaking once again in very human terms, the Creator reflects on what he has witnessed. Evidently, the essence of the problem was that "they are one people, and they have all one language; and this is what they begin to do" (Gen. 11:6). The very commonality of language and culture, which would have permitted the city to serve as the basis of a universal moral society, had been exploited by the leaders of the society to pervert their creation into an instrument of defiance of the divine will. Once the city is completed, the leaders will be in a position to carry out their plot against both God and man, "and now nothing will be withhold-en from them, which they purpose to do" (Gen. 11:6). That is, with a dependent and compliant population, there would be no effective source of opposition to the leaders. Under such conditions, the universe of man would once again lapse into the corrupt behavioral patterns of antediluvian society.

The divine response to this challenge went directly to the heart of the matter. The existing commonality of language and culture was intended to serve as the foundation for the development of a universal moral society, one predicated on obedience to the divine will. But if this commonality was to be exploited by men for the purpose of building an essentially corrupt and perverse social order, then that essential facilitating factor would have to be dealt with in an appropriate manner. The divine solution to the problem was to "confound their language, that they may not understand one another's speech" (Gen. 11:7). By causing the emergence of artificial cultural and linguistic differences among the people, the coherence and cohesiveness of the universal society was shattered. The sudden inability of people to communicate with one another disrupted their common enterprise, "and they left off to build the city" (Gen. 11:8). Families and clans gathered around their own standards and split into a multitude of diverse nations, and "the Lord scattered them abroad from thence upon the face of all the earth" (Gen. 11:9), forcing them to carry out the divine intent against their wishes.

One highly significant implication of this episode is that until mankind generally attains a higher moral state, national diversity is an objective historical necessity. The implicit lesson of the biblical saga of the tower of Babel is that even though a universal society may be the ultimate desideratum, it constitutes an inappropriate immediate goal as long as the several national components and their leaders do not reflect the acceptance and adoption of high moral standards; there is no virtue in having a universal society led by an aggregation of villains and moral reprobates. How is the moral stature of the diverse nations and their leaders to be raised to the desired level? The biblical response appears to be that this process was to be assisted through the provision of an operating model of a moral society that could be emulated by the nations of the world. However, since the required exemplar simply was not to be found among the existing nations, an appropriate model would have to be created expressly for this purpose. Accordingly, the biblical narrative proceeds to describe in some detail the processes by which a new and unique nation is fashioned to serve as an instrument of the divine plan for the moral advancement of mankind.

Abraham, a heroic figure endowed with extraordinary moral qualities, is ultimately chosen by God to serve as the human progenitor of the new nation. To prepare him for the task, God must first uproot Abraham from the nation and society into which he was born, severing all social and cultural ties with his past. Thus, God tells Abraham to leave the land of his birth and to break his links with clan and nation. "Get thee out of thy country, and from thy kindred, and from thy father's house, unto the land that I will show thee. And I will make of thee a great nation" (Gen. 12:1–2). He is instructed to go to a distant unspecified land where he will be free to build a new nation and civilization, uninhibited by influences from the old. The land chosen for this purpose has been divinely predetermined, and Abraham will be made aware of it at the appropriate time.

THE MEANING OF HOLY SPACE

At this point, it is necessary to interrupt the recapitulation of the narrative to introduce the Bible's unique theopolitical ideas about sacred or holy space. Generally speaking, in religious conceptions of the universe, space is not homogeneous and undifferentiated. Indeed, some components of space are commonly understood as being qualitatively different from the rest, a distinction that is characterized as constituting "sacred" as opposed to "profane" space. As the eminent historian of religions Mircea Eliade wrote: "It must be said at once that the religious experience of the nonhomogeneity of space is a primordial experience. . . . It is not a matter of theoretical speculation, but of primary religious experience that precedes all reflection on the world."[3] Sacred space is understood to constitute the disjunction in the general spatial homogeneity that has witnessed a specific manifestation of the divine, and to which a transcendent importance is therefore attributed. The patriarch Jacob dreams of a ladder reaching to heaven, with angels ascending and descending it, and hears the Lord declaring: "I am the Lord, the God of Abraham thy father, and the God of Isaac. The land whereon thou liest, to thee will I give it, and to they seed." He wakens in a fright and cries out, "How full of awe is this place, this is none other than the house of God, and this is the gate of heaven." He then marks the spot with the stone that he used for a pillow (Gen. 28:11–19). It is only at that point, where the divine has been manifested, that the connection between the profane and the absolutely sacred is made; it is there that one finds "the gate of heaven," and it is to that place that one directs one's attention when seeking to establish close proximity to the divine. Similarly, the idea of sacred space is also clearly conveyed by the biblical passage describing the burning bush, in which the Lord tells Moses, "Draw not nigh hither; put off thy shoes from off they feet, for the place whereon thou standest is holy ground" (Exod. 3:5).

Taking the matter a step further, Eliade also observed that "every sacred space implies a hierophany, an irruption of the sacred that results in detaching a territory from the surrounding cosmic milieu and making it qualitatively different."[4] Within the bounds of this separated sacred space there is order; outside, one finds only the chaos of undifferentiated profane space. This idea is perhaps nowhere more forcefully and graphically expressed than in the biblical narrative of the events immediately preceding the Exodus. Moses is instructed by the Lord that the "whole assembly of the congregation of Israel" shall prepare for the great event by slaughtering a lamb, "And they shall take of the blood, and put it on the two side-posts and on the lintel, upon the houses wherein they shall eat it. . . . For I will go through the land of Egypt in that night, and will smite all the first-born. . . . And the blood shall be to you for a token upon the houses where ye are; and when I see the blood, I will pass over you, and there shall no plague be upon you to destroy you, when I smite the land of Egypt" (Exod. 12:7, 12–13). The profane space of Egypt is to be swept by catastrophe, but those living spaces of the Israelites that have the blood of the sacrificial lambs smeared around their portals will thereby become temporary sacred spaces, completely differentiated from the profane space outside and therefore safe from the plague that will afflict the latter. Clearly, it is not merely being an Israelite that deflects the plague of death, but rather the act of consciously drawing a boundary that distinguishes between the sacred space within and the profane space outside. Those Israelites who fail to make the required spatial distinction will suffer the same fate as the Egyptians. The act of identifying and associating oneself with the sacred through a demarcation of space becomes in itself an act of consecration, creating a tangible link with the holy.

The biblical idea of sacred space, particularly as concerns that which is to become the Land of Israel, considers the points of the manifestation of the divine as centers from which the sacred may be extended to the geographical and political boundaries of the land. "And the Lord said unto Abraham," who dwelled between Ai and Bethel near the center of the land of Canaan: "Lift up now thine eyes, and look from the place where thou art, northward and southward and eastward and westward; for all the land which thou seest, to thee will I give it, and to thy seed forever. . . . Arise, walk through the land in the length of it and in the breadth of it; for unto thee will I give it" (Gen. 13:14–17). The divine promise and covenant will circumscribe this designated area and bring it all within the bounds of the sacred space that has its center at the point of the theophany. However, the language of the text makes it clear that fulfillment of this commitment is prospective and not imminent; it will take place only when the land is actually occupied and settled by Abraham's descendants. As Eliade observed:

> To settle in a territory is, in the last analysis, equivalent to consecrating it. When settlement is not temporary, as among the nomads, but permanent, as among sedentary peoples, it implies a vital decision that involves the existence of the entire community. Establishment in a particular place, organizing it, inhabiting it, are acts that presuppose an existential choice—the choice of the universe that one is prepared to assume by "creating" it.[5]

The territory selected by God to be the home for the new nation is ideally situated for the mission assigned to it. Since that mission is to serve as a model for other nations, it should be located in a place of great visibility. The land of Canaan, seen within the configuration of the nations of the ancient Middle East, the cradle of civilization, strides some of the major crossroads of the region and is located directly on the land bridge separating Africa from Asia. The future Land of Israel is in fact the volatile and troubled frontier zone that separates the great powers of the ancient world, Egypt and whichever of the nations of Mesopotamia that dominated the region. As a result, Canaan was a veritable no-man's-land and therefore susceptible to the superimposition of a new nation and civilization.

ABRAHAM AND HIS DESCENDANTS

However, it will take time before Abraham and his descendants would be able to establish a solid foothold there for their civilization-building enterprise, because "the Canaanite and the Perizzite dwelt then in the land" (Gen. 13:7). The patriarch is thus informed that although he is to begin the task of nation-building, he will not see its completion in his lifetime. The divine promise made to him is surely eternal and unequivocal but is not to be realized for several centuries. His descendants are destined to undergo a series of formative trials and tribulations during this period, including a long period of exile in an alien land. Then, "in the fourth generation they shall come back hither; for the iniquity of the Amorite is not yet full" (Gen. 15:16). The implications of these statements are clear. The territory is not presently vacant, and Abraham's descendants will be able to take possession of it, in fulfillment of the divine promise, only at such a time when the depravity and corruption of its inhabitants justify their expulsion from the land. In other words, Israel will establish itself in the promised land after dispossessing its current occupiers, but this will occur only at an appropriate moment, the timing of which will be entirely a matter of divine discretion. Thus, it is "for the wickedness of these nations the Lord doth drive them out before thee" (Deut. 9:5), not because of Israel's merit. Divine justice is not arbitrary or capricious. Israel, even though it is intended to fulfill the divine purpose, must wait in exile until the iniquity of the Canaanites justifies their expulsion from the land.

A critical point being made in this narrative is that the land is the Lord's, and he allocates it as and to whom he sees fit, in accordance with his judgment and purpose. A second point of considerable significance is that the nation of Israel will be constituted in exile and only then brought in to possess its promised land. This is implicitly analogous to the biblical teaching that Adam was created outside of Eden and placed in the garden afterwards, presumably so that he should have knowledge of what life outside this special place would be like and therefore be more aware of the conditions that had to be met for his continued residency there. Similarly, the descendants of Abraham would develop a greater appreciation of the freedom and independence they will have in their own land after experiencing a life of subjugation and dependency while in exile. Presumably, this would help them to remain always aware of the purpose for which they were chosen to become a new nation with a land of their own.

The fundamental covenant concluded between God and Abraham is subsequently renewed with the latter's son Isaac (Gen. 26:3–4) and later with his grandson Jacob (Gen. 28:13–15). But as already indicated, the covenanted land was still occupied by nations under the influence of the very civilization from which Abraham was attempting to dissociate. Were the descendants of Jacob to have remained in the land under these circumstances, there is a strong possibility that they might have succumbed to the enticements of the existing well-developed pagan cultures before they were able to exploit the opportunity to establish their own unique national-cultural identity. This made it necessary for the descendants of Jacob, the children of Israel, to form their national identity in isolation from the cultural influences of the surrounding nations. Such a process could only be carried out in Egypt, where the nation would be forged in the throes of adversity. Because the children of Israel were still essentially products of Mesopotamian civilization, even if just language and remote familial connections remained, only in Egypt would they be true aliens. Their constituting an alien element in Egyptian society would significantly reduce the risk of their assimilation into the indigenous culture and of their social integration with the native Egyptians, "because the Egyptians might not eat bread with the Hebrews; for that is an abomination unto the Egyptians" (Gen. 43:32).

Accordingly, a complex series of man-made and natural events soon conspired to cause Jacob and his sons to abandon the covenanted land and to take temporary residence in Egypt, where they settled together in the sparsely populated borderland region of Goshen. There, living in close proximity to one another, their ethnic and cultural distinctions from the indigenous population were increasingly reinforced. It was in Goshen, that their self-awareness, their differentiation from the neighboring Egyptians became manifest. This sense of otherness was reaffirmed by the patriarch Jacob, who in his final testament made it clear that it was not the divine intention that the children of Israel resettle permanently in Egypt. He affirmed that their residence there was intended merely as a temporary expedient, their future lying in the covenanted land. He told his son Joseph, "Behold, I die; but God will be with you, and bring you back unto the land of your fathers" (Gen. 48:21); Jacob charged his sons not to bury him in Egypt, but only in the place that would later become known as the Land of Israel, where Abraham, Isaac, and the matriarchs were interred. This request was fulfilled and was repeated later by Joseph himself, who, as the most powerful person in the country after the king, would seem to have been completely at home in Egypt. Yet when Joseph felt that his end was at hand, he declared to his brethren: "I die; but God will surely remember you, and bring you up out of this land unto the land which He swore to Abraham, to Isaac, and to Jacob . . . and ye shall carry up my bones from hence" (Gen. 50:24–25).

In Egypt, an ever-greater sense of collective identity developed as the Israelites significantly increased their numbers over a period of several generations, evolving from a family to a clan to a people. After some time and a dynastic change in the country, the Israelites' position in Egypt as an alien but tolerated ethnic and cultural minority, as a distinct people, underwent serious erosion. The new ruler, who combined xenophobia with reason of state, adopted a policy of oppression toward the Israelites, whom he correctly perceived as an unassimilable element within Egyptian society. His argument, which has been repeated innumerable times in one form or another throughout the troubled course of Jewish history, was that because the Israelites so steadfastly maintained their ethnic cohesion and culture, their loyalty to the host country was suspect: "Behold, the people of the children of Israel are too many and too mighty for us; come, let us deal wisely with them, lest they multiply, and it come to pass, that, when there befalleth us any war, they also join themselves unto our enemies, and fight against us, and get them up out of the land" (Exod. 1:9–10).

It seemed clear to the Egyptian leaders that ethnic sentiment among the Israelites continued to serve as a vital force for communal self-identity despite their long residence in Egypt. It was commonly believed that the Israelites, at some point, would attempt to uproot themselves and return en masse to their ancestral home in Canaan. At best, as subsequent events were to demonstrate quite conclusively, this was a highly dubious proposition. Most of the Israelites, in fact, were quite prepared to remain in Egypt permanently, notwithstanding their ethnic loyalties. Nonetheless, the popular expectation that they would readily cut their shallow roots in Egypt if but given the opportunity was taken as a certainty. This presented the Egyptians with a dilemma. The Israelites were considered far too valuable an economic asset to allow them simply to rise up and leave the country. However, the Egyptians now also considered them as posing too powerful a threat to the integrity of the Egyptian state to allow them to continue to thrive as a separate community in its midst. The Egyptians resolved the dilemma by deciding to exploit and suppress them simultaneously. As a result, the Israelites were soon transformed from a relatively autonomous ethnic community into a persecuted slave people. The unintended consequences of this change in status were highly significant. The Israelite awareness of their ethnic-cultural distinctiveness was now augmented by a sense of collective historical destiny and a yearning among many of their communal leaders for political freedom and self-determination.

THE EXODUS AND THE COVENANT

The stage was now set for the two most significant and decisive events in the biblical presentation of the protohistory of the Israelites. First, the Exodus consummating the national redemption of the Israelites from their bondage in Egypt, followed by the enactment of the covenant between God and Israel, which established the latter's national ethos and mission. Viewing this aspect of the biblical narrative from the perspective of its implications for universal history, Hans Kohn wrote:

> The act by which the Jews became a people, and at the same time a chosen people occurred at the beginning of Jewish history. It was only through the Covenant that the Jews were constituted a people. Without the consciousness of this fundamental fact, the whole course of Jewish history would become incomprehensible. God chose this people and acted through it in history: the people received the mission to live and to act in history according to God's will. . . . The Covenant concluded between God and the people of Israel formed their gateway into history, a symbolic act of the highest pregnancy, revived three thousand years later as the root of modern nationalism and democracy.[6]

The transformation of the people into a nation demanded an extraordinary leadership, and Moses, a man endowed with the highest prophetic capacity, was divinely chosen for the task. As the minister of the Almighty to the chosen people, he was instructed to deliver the following message of national redemption:

> I am the Lord, and I will bring you out from under the burdens of the Egyptians, and I will deliver you from their bondage, and I will redeem you with an outstretched arm, and with great judgments; and I will take you to Me for a people, and I will be to you a God; . . . And I will bring you in unto the land concerning which I lifted up My hand to give it to Abraham, to Isaac, and to Jacob; and I will give it to you for a heritage. (Exod. 6:6–8)

The process by which the nation of Israel was to come into being was to be unique. Moreover, its independent existence was to reflect a clearly theological-political character. According to the Bible, the nation was forged by God in the adversity of Egypt and "brought forth out of the iron furnace, out of Egypt, to be unto Him a people of inheritance" (Deut. 4:20)—to become the great nation promised to Abraham. The image being portrayed here is that of the people being purified and then formed into a coherent entity in the "iron furnace" of Egypt, the latter thereby fulfilling its assigned role in the divine scheme. Thus, in a dramatic reversal of the usual course of historical development, where the bonds between people living in a given territory naturally evolve into one of nationhood, Israel is first constituted as a nation in alien territory. In biblical terms: "God assayed to go and take Him a nation from the midst of another nation" (Deut. 4:34). Only after its formation is the nation then led to the land that is to serve as its national territory and in which it is to evolve into a nation-state, to apply a modern but nonetheless appropriate term to what emerges at the end of the process.

To further enhance their national distinctiveness, the Israelites are to undergo a fundamental cultural transformation that will effectively separate them completely from their Mesopotamian cultural roots. Unlike the case of Abraham, who because of his towering personality was able to do this autonomously, his descendants will be assisted in the transformation by authoritative prescription. Divine legislation will ordain a way of life that is unique, that is designed to make the children of Israel "a kingdom of priests, and a holy nation" (Exod. 19:6). The nation is to become holy, that is, separate from the commonplace, by virtue of its intrinsic distinctiveness. The nation of Israel is to be dedicated to God's service. As argued by Martin Buber, "However much of the legislation that has come down to us in the Bible may be attributed to later literary accretions, there is no doubt at all that the exodus from Egypt was bound up with the imposing of a law that was taken to be a divine charter and the positive nucleus of all the later developments was essentially the instruction to establish a 'holy' national community in the promised land."[7]

Among the numerous distinctive rules of conduct that were to be observed by the nation are several that were surely designed to dramatically restrict the assimilability of the Israelites into the societies and cultures of the neighboring peoples and nations. Perhaps most notable of these are the injunctions concerning the observation of the Sabbath and the dietary laws, unique regulations that make normal social intercourse with the surrounding nations very difficult. As a practical matter, as long as the Israelites observed these laws faithfully, social and cultural integration with their gentile neighbors would always remain rather problematic.

It is also clear from the biblical narrative that the Israelites were by no means of a single mind with regard to the historic role assigned to them. For many, life in Egypt as a minority, even an oppressed minority, was more acceptable than facing the unknowns of a trek through the desert to conquer a land whose inhabitants were not likely to flee at the approach of the Israelites. This meant protracted war, and they were ill prepared physically and psychologically for such a challenge. The price of independence was to be very high in terms of personal sacrifice, and as would be true of peoples everywhere, not everyone was prepared to pay it. Indeed, there is reason to suspect that the majority, perhaps even the overwhelming majority, of the Israelites were prepared to forgo the chance for freedom and to remain in their current state of subjugation. Upon reflection, this should not be surprising. After all, the Bible tells us that they originally enjoyed an especially privileged position in Egypt on account of Joseph. The subsequent elimination of those privileges therefore would reduce the Israelites to the level of the mass of the Egyptian people, who were by no means free in any meaningful sense of the word. Presumably, even when the Israelites were an oppressed minority, the differences between their quality of life and that of their Egyptian neighbors was probably marginal, and as a practical matter, it would appear that not many were prepared to face the dangers of the desert and war for what might only prove to be a slight improvement in personal status. Of course, they would be free, but it is not clear that they had a clear idea of what freedom really meant: It was not the common experience of humans, then or now.

Because of the ambivalence of many and the opposition of some to abandoning their homes in Egypt, it became necessary to create conditions that would be conducive to a mass exodus, one that would also include those who were naturally reluctant to uproot themselves from the known for the unknown. A series of plagues was inflicted upon the Egyptians because of their leaders' unwillingness to allow the Israelites to go into the nearby desert en masse to worship their God, the initial request made by Moses to test the determination of the Egyptian government to oppose their emigration. There can be little doubt that one principal effect of this was to arouse the anger of the Egyptians against the Israelites, and increase their misery, making it very difficult for the latter to continue their lives as before. Finally, on the night before the Exodus, the Israelites were instructed to sacrifice lambs, an act that the Egyptians considered to be a religious abomination. Indeed, the justification that Moses originally gave to the Egyptian king for his request to allow the Israelites to travel into the desert to worship was precisely that such worship involved the sacrifice of animals, an act that was abhorrent to the Egyptians. Now the Israelites were commanded to commit that very sacrilege in Egypt itself. After this, even those most opposed to leaving the country, including any who refused to participate in the paschal sacrifices, would have little choice but to join the Israelite exodus for fear of what might happen to them if they remained behind.

One particularly significant aspect of the biblical narrative is that it anticipates within the foundation myth of the nation the recognition that liberation movements rarely if ever reflect the explicit or even conscious desires of the majority of the people they propose to free, something that has become a truism of history. It tells us that the Exodus was not the result of a sudden and infectious mass hysteria, but the consequence of careful calculation and the determination of a small group of charismatic leaders, albeit divinely inspired.

As it turned out, the exodus from servitude to freedom was a mixed blessing for many of the Israelites who, uprooted from their homes and transported into the forbidding desert, now had no practical alternative to entering into a unique covenant with heaven at Mount Sinai. Indeed, one of the later rabbinic sages suggested that the biblical text "And they stood under the mount" (Exod. 19:17) should be understood as teaching "that the Holy One, blessed be He, overturned the mountain upon them like an [inverted] cask, and said to them: 'If ye accept the Torah, 'tis well; if not, there shall be your burial.'"[8] Those who imagined that the primary purpose of the Exodus was to give them freedom from the oppression of their Egyptian overlords now discovered that they were brought out of Egypt not to do as they chose but to be free to serve God and his purpose in history as he chose.

The pact that was struck between God and the people of Israel provides that if Israel remains true to its national ethos and mission in all their aspects, then God will assure the continuing prosperity of the nation in its national homeland: "He will bless thee in the land which the Lord thy God giveth thee. The Lord will establish thee for a holy people unto Himself, as He hath sworn unto thee; if thou shalt keep the commandments of the Lord thy God, and walk in His ways" (Deut. 28:8–9). However, if Israel is not true to its national mission, its perfidy will be recompensed by the loss of that homeland and national autonomy. Moreover, "the Lord shall scatter thee among all peoples, from one end of the earth even unto the other end of the earth; . . . And among these nations shalt thou have no repose, and there shall be no rest for the sole of thy foot; . . . And thy life shall hang in doubt before thee; and thou shalt fear night and day, and shalt have no assurance of thy life" (Deut. 28:64–66).

In one sense, perhaps the most distinguishing general feature of this covenant is that it commits Israel to constitutional abnormalcy. As observed by the Moabite prophet Balaam, "Lo, it is a people that shall dwell alone, and shall not be reckoned among the nations" (Num. 23:9). That is, Israel will always remain unique among the nations of the world, constituted and governed in accordance with divine standards and requirements that are not imposed on other nations. It must be different from the others, and should it fail in this, it will be punished in a way that other nations are not. Other nations whose hour has come may be conquered by alien rulers but will generally continue to exist as peoples in their ancestral lands, albeit under foreign domination, and perhaps required to pay homage to other deities. Thus, although the nations as such may disappear, their peoples remain in their lands as before. Israel, in contrast, not only is to forfeit its national patrimony but its people are to be scattered among the nations, denying it normalcy even in defeat.

Consequently, the eternality of the divine commitment with regard to the entitlement to the Land of Israel that was given to Abraham, Isaac, and Jacob does not necessarily assure its unconditional occupation and settlement by their descendants. The promise of actual possession of the land is indissolubly linked with the revelation of the Torah at Sinai. The nation, its land, and its religion thus become one, nationalism and religious faith becoming the two faces of the same coin, whose validity is nullified if there is only one without the other. This linkage is clearly indicated in the statement of Moses, "And the Lord commanded me at that time [the giving of the covenant] to teach you statutes and ordinances, that ye might do them *in the land* whither ye go over to possess it" (Deut. 4:14). This suggests that the basic statutes and ordinances of Judaism were intended to shape the life of the people within the context of a national society rooted in the Land, and that their relevance outside the Land is questionable, a notion so troublesome that only a few in the history of Judaic thought have ever undertaken to give it serious consideration.

The commandments given to the children of Israel prior to their entry into the Land have a twofold nature. On the one hand, they are regulatory in character; that is, they are intended to provide guidance for the sanctification and governance of the Land and the people of Israel. On the other hand, the commandments of the Torah also predicate the conditions that must be met for Israel's continued possession of the Land, "a land which the Lord thy God careth for; the eyes of the Lord thy God are always upon it, from the beginning of the year even unto the end of the year" (Deut. 11:12). Only when the prescriptions of the Torah are observed faithfully are the children of Israel assured uninterrupted occupancy of the territory promised to their ancestral patriarchs. In this regard, the Bible reflects a unique symbiotic relationship between the Land and its inhabitants. Thus, after the long list of prohibited sexual liaisons, an appeal is made to the children of Israel not to defile themselves by participating in such acts of immorality and thereby precipitate a rupture between them and the Land. "Defile not ye yourselves in any of these things; for in all these the nations are defiled, which I cast out before you. And the land was defiled, therefore I did visit the iniquity thereof upon it, and the land vomited out her inhabitants" (Lev. 18:24–25). The implication of this warning is quite clear. The transgressions of the current inhabitants have contaminated the Land itself, which, as God's chosen place, must be purged. If Israel proves to be disobedient to the divine imperatives, it too runs the risk of being ejected from the Land. "Ye shall therefore keep all My statutes, and all Mine ordinances, and do them, that the land, whither I bring you to dwell therein, vomit you not out" (Lev. 20:22).

In his very last words to the nation before his death, Moses reiterated his great concern for the future of Israel in the promised land: "Set your heart unto all the words wherewith I testify against you this day; that ye may charge your children therewith to observe to do all the words of this law. For it is no vain thing for you; because it is your life, and through this thing ye shall prolong your days upon the land, whither ye go over the Jordan to possess it" (Deut. 32:46–47). This caveat was later reaffirmed by Joshua, who warned Israel, "When ye transgress the covenant of the Lord your God, which He commanded you, and go and serve other gods, and worship them; then shall the anger of the Lord be kindled against you, and ye shall perish quickly from off the good land which He hath given unto you" (Josh. 23:16).

ISRAEL AND THE LAND

The relationship of the people of Israel to the Land of Israel, as this connection is presented in the Pentateuch, is thus seen to be quite complex. By virtue of the divine promise to the patriarchs, Israel has inherited an eternal and indefeasible right to possession of the Land. But in accordance with the covenant of Sinai, the nation has been granted only a conditional right of actual occupancy of the Land at any particular time. Its continuing possession of its patrimony remains contingent upon the extent of the nation's general conformity with the stipulations set forth by the Lord, who is the only true proprietor of the Land.

The idea that the Land always remains the peculiar property of the Lord creates a unique relationship between it and the nation of Israel. This special bond is predicated on the proposition that although the people of Israel may be the only legitimate occupants of the Land, they are not its owners. Their proprietary limitations are clearly manifested in the Torah in the form of mandatory land-use regulations that impose significant practical constraints on their freedom to do as they wish with the Land. Most significantly, the occupants may not treat it as personal property, as a commodity to be disposed of at will. This represents a radical departure from conventional views about the nature of landowner-ship, which is normally considered as the recognized possession of land as personal or corporate property. In the biblical view, however, land generally—and the Land of Israel in particular—are not conceived of as real estate that may be treated by its possessors the same as any other commodity.

In the biblical scheme, the Land of Israel is to be allocated among the several Israelite tribes by their component families and may not be permanently reassigned to others at their individual or even collective discretion, because it is not theirs to alienate. This concept is exemplified by the biblical law of the Jubilee, which declares, "The land shall not be sold in perpetuity; for the land is Mine; for ye are strangers and settlers with Me" (Lev. 25:23). This idea is also clearly reflected in the biblical injunction, "Thou shalt not remove thy neighbor's landmark, which they of old time have set, in thine inheritance which thou shalt inherit, in the land that the Lord thy God giveth thee to possess it" (Deut. 19:14). This is traditionally understood to mean that "we are forbidden to alter land boundaries fraudulently, that is, to shift landmarks between ourselves and our neighbours, so as to be able to claim another's land as our own."[9] Indeed, as the law is codified by Maimonides, "If one moves his neighbor's boundary mark and brings some of his neighbor's land inside his own border, even if this be only a finger's breadth, he is deemed a robber if he does so by force and a thief if he moves it secretly."[10] Obviously, even if such alienation of land is done by mutual agreement, it nonetheless remains subject to the requirement of the law of the Jubilee, which precludes it from becoming a permanent transfer of property.

The talmudic sages raised an interesting question with regard to this injunction. As moving someone's landmark without his consent is obviously an act of misappropriation, which is already prohibited by the commandment concerning robbery (Lev. 19:13), what is the significance of the specific injunction against usurping another's land? They concluded that its purpose was to teach that a dual transgression was involved when such usurpation was committed in the Land of Israel. One was guilty not only of misappropriation of another's possession but also of violating the specific allocation of the Land of Israel among the tribes, an allocation that does not confer ownership upon the occupants.[11] Accordingly, to move a landmark in the Land of Israel was not only to rob a neighbor of his rights but also to trespass on those of its divine owner.

In addition to these rules, Israel is instructed with regard to a series of specific divinely ordained regulations that are to govern its tenure on the land and thereby further restrict its "property" rights. For example, Israel is told: "When ye shall come into the land, and shall have planted all manner of trees for food, then ye shall count the fruit thereof as forbidden; three years shall it be as forbidden unto you; it shall not be eaten. And in the fourth year all the fruit thereof shall be holy, for giving praise unto the Lord. But in the fifth year may ye eat the fruit thereof, that it may yield unto you more richly the increase thereof" (Lev. 19:23–25). Also: "When ye come into the land which I give you, then shall the land keep a sabbath unto the Lord. Six years thou shalt sow thy field, and six years thou shalt prune thy vineyard, and gather in the produce thereof. But in the seventh year shall be a sabbath of solemn rest for the land, a sabbath unto the Lord; thou shalt neither sow thy field, nor prune thy vineyard" (Lev. 25:2–4). These regulations, among numerous others, pertain only to the Land of Israel and are not intended as general agricultural rules that apply wherever Israelites live. They are the landlord's specific conditions of occupancy of the Land of Israel. Although the true purpose of these constraints on land use remains unspecified in Scripture, they surely serve to make the people ever conscious of their assigned role in the divine scheme and the place of the Land in that design. As Buber observed, "This land was at no time in the history of Israel simply the property of the people; it was always at the same time a challenge to make of it what God intended to have made of it."[12]

This, then, is the foundation myth of Israel as I find it laid out persuasively in the texts of the Pentateuch. If these interpretations of scripture are valid, and I am convinced that they are, their implications are far-reaching. In sum, according to biblical teaching, Israel is not a natural social phenomenon but a nation that was deliberately brought into existence for a specific universal purpose, namely, to serve as a national model of a moral community worthy of emulation by the other nations of the world. The revelation of the Torah is intended to provide the guidelines for the operation of such a model community, as well as to prepare and discipline the people of Israel for this divinely assigned task, and the Land of Israel is given to them to serve as the provenance within which the national mission is to be carried out.

The accomplishment of its mission by the people and nation of Israel, however, proved to be an extraordinarily difficult and complex assignment. It required nothing less than the establishment of a completely Torah-based society. Consequently, as conditional occupants of the Land of Israel, with a divinely granted contingent right of permanent residency, the nation of Israel was confronted simultaneously by the divine imperative to be different from all other nations and by the practical need to find an acceptable basis for fraternal relations with the nations with which it had to contend for its survival as an independent political entity. In general, finding the acceptable balance between these frequently incompatible requirements turned out to be a task that transcended the abilities of most of Israel's leaders. From the biblical perspective, the failure to strike the appropriate balance underlay much of the tragedy of the nation's history over its long and twisted course.

2

Between the Ideal
and
the Reality

After some initial trials in the desert the Israelites finally stood poised to enter the Land, inspired by the ideals of the Revelation on Sinai and fortified by an unflinching faith in their future as a nation. However, they soon discovered that occupying the promised land would prove to be a far more difficult task than most of the people had imagined. It was not to be handed to them on a silver platter; they would have to continually prove their worthiness to be its occupants, especially as they found themselves enticed by the materialistic cultures of the peoples they were to dispossess.

TAKING CONTROL OF THE LAND

From the moment that the Israelites entered Canaan they had to engage in virtually continual warfare with the many nations and peoples they found there. Initially, the greatest challenges, especially during the period of penetration and conquest that stretched over several centuries, came not so much from the indigenous Canaanites as from the recently arrived Philistines, followed by the Arameans, who both posed a far more potent threat to Israel's political viability in the Land. Despite the enormous difficulties and costs that it entailed, Israel was ultimately able to deal with these challenges successfully. The frequent setbacks were seen as merely temporary in nature and were attributed to Israel's failure to honor the covenant sufficiently; the Israelites were defeated because they had antagonized the Lord by straying from his law.

21

It is important to note that the conduct of the Israelites as individuals was not at issue here. Clearly not all the people were guilty of betraying their obligations under the covenant; it was evidently the collective behavior of Israel as a nation that was being punished. The pervasiveness of the violations of the covenant by the vast majority of the people tainted the nation as a whole. The covenant was principally one between God and the nation of Israel and only secondarily with the Israelites as individuals.

The notion of collective punishment is of course one that is extremely troublesome and repugnant, not only to the modern mind but, as Scripture makes quite clear, to the ancient as well. This is abundantly evident in the biblical story of Abraham's discussion with the Almighty over the fate of the cities of Sodom and Gomorrah. It will be recalled that the sins of these cities were considered to be so great that they were marked for destruction. Abraham, evidently spurred by righteous indignation at the prospect of such collective punishment, challenged the morality of this decision. "And Abraham drew near, and said: 'Wilt Thou indeed sweep away the righteous with the wicked? Peradventure there are fifty righteous within the city; wilt Thou indeed sweep away and not forgive the place for the fifty righteous that are therein?'" (Gen. 18:23–24). After obtaining the Lord's agreement to defer the collective punishment of the cities if there were fifty righteous men to be found therein, Abraham proceeded to negotiate for a lower minimum and finally got the Lord to agree to withhold collective punishment if there were to be found ten righteous men in the city (Gen. 18:32). Abraham did not pursue the issue any further.

We may ask, nonetheless, why should even a single innocent person suffer for the sins of others? The answer implicit in the biblical story is that there must be a critical mass of righteous people present within a corrupt society in order for there to be any prospect of reform, and without such a prospect the society's reason for being becomes invalidated. However, we do not know what that critical number of people is or should be. In the case of Sodom, the number evidently was ten. Because that many righteous men apparently could not be found there, the city was destroyed. In the case of the nation of Israel, knowledge of the critical number needed for moral viability within the divine scheme has not been provided, and the biblical authors and the prophets had no choice but to accept God's judgment on the matter. However, they were not thereby reconciled to the suffering of the innocent, but only to the reality of their inability to fathom the purpose for and the manner in which God acts in history.

It seems clear that, in the biblical view, the number of those who were observant of the covenant fell short of the critical mass needed for Israel's viability as a nation. Accordingly, national atonement and recommitment to the covenant, at least during the early part of Israel's tenure in the Land, could tip the scales in Israel's favor and readily restore the regional balance of power and the nation's political fortunes. But the nation was still far from constituting the ideal society contemplated by the Torah and seemed to be ensnared in an endless cycle of defeat and victory, or punishment and redemption. This recurring pattern in Israel's early history is described by Nehemiah:

> So the children [of Israel] went in and possessed the land, and Thou didst subdue before them the inhabitants of the land, the Canaanites, and gavest them into their hands, with their kings, and the peoples of the land, that they might do with them as they would. . . . Nevertheless they were disobedient, and rebelled against Thee, and cast Thy law behind their back, and slew Thy prophets that did forewarn them to turn back unto Thee, and they wrought great provocations. Therefore Thou didst deliver them into the hand of their adversaries, who distressed them; and in the time of their trouble, when they cried unto Thee, Thou heardest from heaven; and according to Thy manifold mercies Thou gavest them saviours who might save them out of the hand of their adversaries. But after they had rest, they did evil again before Thee. (Neh. 9:24–28)

It seems both reasonable and likely that the Israelites were perceived by the nations they sought to displace in Canaan as an anomaly, not only because of their peculiar religion but also because of their unusual corporate character as a nation. As pointed out earlier, the Israelites were first forged into a covenantal nation outside their country and only afterward brought into the land that was to serve as their national territory. They thus appeared on the scene in Canaan as a nation whose roots were alleged to be in the Land, a territory that they in fact had never seen before actually invading it. Moreover, the Israelites were organized in a manner that seemed rather peculiar. Although they established and lived in permanent settlements, their political structure was more appropriate to a nomadic existence. Thus, the Israelites did not initially form a state of any kind. They remained organized along tribal lines in a loose confederation, without any central leadership, and were essentially connected only by a common religion and ethnic tradition. On occasion, two or more tribes might act in unison, usually under a charismatic leader, when they perceived that a common external threat made such collaboration desirable. More often, the tribes would each go their separate ways, ignoring the plight of their fellow Israelites. This constituted a radical departure from the intrinsic character of the Canaanite and Philistine principalities that the Israelites confronted in the Land. These were established in well-organized city-states, which were only secondarily religious-cultural communities. Thus the Phillistines, even though small in population, were able to control a considerable part of the country for centuries and succeeded in subjugating those Israelites, such as the tribe of Dan, whose biblically assigned territory was in an area under the Philistines domination.

It was not long, however, before the continuing precariousness of the Israelites' grip on the Land brought their elders to the conclusion that they had a dire need to establish a state, in the form of a unitary monarchy, to enable them to compete effectively with the surrounding states. In effect, they sought political normalcy, using the political structures of their neighbors as models. This aspiration was frowned upon by the prophet-judge Samuel (1 Sam. 8:4–7), who evidently did not consider the Israelite tribes to be mature enough religiously and culturally to be able to adopt the political forms of their neighbors without accepting their behavioral norms as well. The prophet's concerns in this regard proved to be prescient, although it took about a century for his fears to become realized.

THE TWO KINGDOMS

Around the beginning of the first millennium B.C.E., a united kingdom was established under the poet-warrior David. However, although competing tribal interests were set aside as a consequence of David's charismatic leadership, the unitary Israelite state was to prove a tenuous and temporary arrangement. The united monarchy lasted only two generations, or some eighty years. After the death of Solomon, David's successor, the state split in two, the northern tribes forming the kingdom of Israel, and the southern tribes, the kingdom of Judah. Although populated by a common people, which occasionally caused them to act as natural allies, the two kingdoms experienced a generally troubled relationship and were often in conflict with each other. This placed an intractable political obstacle in the way of fulfilling the mission assigned to the nation by tradition. A divided house of Israel could hardly serve as a suitable model for the nations. The prophets, men of acute religious and political insight who assumed the responsibility for attempting to improve the moral quality of the society, never seemed to despair of seeking to bring the two entities back together once again, the separation being seen by them as unnatural and inconsistent with the divine intention for the nation of Israel, which remained one despite its artificial division into two distinct states.

The divided nation soon began to reflect significant religious and cultural differences that further exacerbated the problem. In the partition of the country between the two states, Judah gained a distinct religious-cultural advantage over Israel because Jerusalem, and the Holy Temple, fell within its boundaries. This created the unprecedented problem of dual loyalty for many of the people in the northern kingdom: The central shrine of their religion was in Judah, whereas their political center was in Samaria. As a result, the rulers of the northern kingdom attempted to supplant the centrality of Jerusalem and the Temple by establishing alternative cultic sites in the north. To the extent that they succeeded in this effort, their religious practices soon began to vary significantly from the Mosaic tradition followed in the south, spawning a growing prophetic concern over the continued viability of the kingdom in the face of its deviance from traditional Mosaic norms.

This concern over internal cohesion and the growing violations of the covenant was soon intensified by a new external threat, one that made the earlier wars with the Philistines and the Arameans shrink in comparative significance. It was the rise of Assyria, an imperial state so large and powerful that Israel's defeating it was quite inconceivable. This raised the fearful question as to whether the God of Israel, widely conceived in henotheistic terms, that is, as the exclusive deity of the Israelites, was capable of defeating the gods of the Assyrians and their vassals and allies, even when the struggle took place on Israel's own territory, which was the Lord's chosen place. The prospect of Israel's total defeat, and perhaps even its complete loss of the Land at the hands of an external enemy, now had to be faced as a realistic possibility. Indeed, for the first time since the days of Joshua, such an eventuality had become highly probable.

The question of how to reconcile the promise of the covenant with the reality of the Assyrian armies was evidently both highly troublesome and demoralizing. The task of dealing with the resulting crisis of confidence in the nation's future fell to the prophets. In effect, it became necessary for them to think about and expound a broader conception of God than they had traditionally entertained. They abandoned the prevailing notions of henotheism for the universal concept of monotheism, which they considered as clearly implicit if not explicit in the teachings of Moses. It was wrong, they argued, to think of God as the deity of Israel exclusively. On the contrary, the God of Israel was also God of the Assyrians, as he was the God of all other nations and peoples. If the latter persisted in worshipping pagan deities, it was because they were perverse in their understanding of the power of the Lord of the universe. Consequently, if these nations, which failed to perceive the true God, were able to defeat Israel, it was only because they were being used as vehicles by the God of all to punish Israel for its perfidy. Assyria thus became viewed as a divine instrument for chastising Israel. However, because Assyria was but a tool, it was ultimately less significant than Israel in the divine scheme of things. Israel remained the chosen people. Accordingly, if Israel were defeated, it was not that it was intrinsically more evil than the other nations but rather because it was being evaluated by heaven in accordance with a higher standard of conduct: Israel's very reason for being was to serve as an exemplar of morality to the rest of humankind.

The clear articulation of this concept to the people, and their understanding of its implications, were matters of urgency. Absent some dramatic demonstration of national contrition that might evoke divine intervention on behalf of the northern kingdom of Israel, its destruction by Assyria would only be a matter of time. However, the catastrophe looming on the horizon was obscured from the popular view by the ability of Jeroboam II (ca. 786–746 B.C.E.) to reconquer most of the lands previously taken by the Arameans, as well as a substantial part of Syria, making the prophetic forebodings seem unnecessarily alarmist. The booty obtained from these victories resulted in a sudden influx of new wealth into the country. The wealth, which accrued mainly to the priesthood and those close to the royal court, soon resulted in increasing of corruption and social injustice. The prophets saw this development as contributing significantly to the grave danger facing the nation, making its ability to survive in the Land ever more dubious. The growing moral lassitude, and its negative impact on the public, threatened to weaken the state internally just at the moment when it needed to brace itself against the coming onslaught of the Assyrians.

THE PROPHETS AND THEIR MESSAGE

At this time, the prophet Amos became inspired to challenge the complacency of the people in the face of the mounting social decay. In particular, Amos was deeply troubled by the fact that the people, lacking adequate understanding of the political realities of the world in which they lived, seriously misinterpreted the significance of Jeroboam's ability to discomfit the Arameans. They erroneously assumed that the king's victories reflected Israel's intrinsic strength rather than Aramean weakness, a consequence of the unrelenting military pressure being applied against it by Assyria. Amos therefore argued that this sort of political blindness, manifested in an exaggerated and unwarranted self-confidence, was bound to lead to national disaster. He prophesied, "For, behold, I will raise up against you a nation, O house of Israel, saith the Lord, the God of hosts; and they shall afflict you from the entrance of Hamath unto the Brook of the Arabah" (Amos 6:14), that is, across the length of the country. Moreover, he predicted, "And the high places of Isaac shall be desolate, and the sanctuaries of Israel shall be laid waste; and I will rise against the house of Jeroboam with the sword" (Amos 7:9). As far as Amos could see, nothing could prevent the impending disaster for Israel from taking place; it was too late to avert the consequences of the forces that had already been set in motion.

The first of the prophets to leave a written legacy, Amos was also the first who had to deal with the imminent prospect of the actual fulfillment of the biblical warnings of what would occur if Israel failed to observe the terms of its covenant with God. Not only was Israel to be ignominiously defeated by its most formidable enemy, it was also to experience forcible exile and dispersion from the Land, even though it would take a few years before the events he predicted actually occurred. At the same time that he prophesied about the coming national disaster, Amos also sought to reassure the people that the divine promise to the patriarchs remained eternally valid, regardless of the tragedy they were about to experience. At some point in the future, he promised, there would be a national redemption and restoration: "I will turn the captivity of My people Israel, and they shall build the waste cities, and inhabit them; and they shall plant vineyards, and drink the wine thereof; they shall also make gardens, and eat the fruit thereof. And I will plant them upon their land, and they shall no more be plucked up out of their Land which I have given them, saith the Lord thy God" (Amos 9:14–15). It should be noted that although critical scholarship doubts that these passages were actually the work of Amos, suggesting instead that they reflected the concerns of later scribes and were inserted in the text to soften the prophet's harsh stance toward his people, the issue is of little consequence for the purposes of this study. The words of Amos that are significant for the transmission of Israel's nationalist heritage are derived from the received text as we have it, regardless of whether a specific passage is accurately attributed to the prophet or is a later scribal emendation.

A similar message was delivered to the nation by Hosea, who prophesied during the period immediately preceding the destruction of the northern kingdom in 722 B.C.E. As did Amos before him, the prophet warned of the coming catastrophe in unequivocal terms; there was no longer anything that Israel could do to prevent it. He asserted in the name of the Lord, "I will visit the blood of Jezreel upon the house of Jehu, and will cause to cease the kingdom of the house of Israel" (Hos. 1:4). The people would be driven into exile from the Land as punishment for their breach of the covenant and their transgressions against God: "They shall not dwell in the Lord's land" (Hos. 9:3), which they defiled and which must be purged of their transgressions.

But along with his prophecy of doom, Hosea also offered a message of comfort and hope for the nation as a whole, even if not for his individual contemporaries, who were beyond earthly salvation at this point. He provided reassurance that the covenant between God and his people remained in effect. God had not abandoned them completely and permanently; contrition and repentance by the people would still bring about the ultimate redemption of the nation in the Land of Israel. "And it shall come to pass that, instead of that which was said unto them: 'Ye are not My people,' it shall be said unto them: 'Ye are the children of the living God.' And the children of Judah and the children of Israel shall be gathered together, and they shall appoint themselves one head, and shall go up out of the land" (Hos. 2:1–2), that is, the once-more-united nation would leave the lands of its exile and "go up" to the Land of Israel, which is always spoken of in terms of ascension, or *aliyah*.

> And it shall come to pass in that day, I will respond, saith the Lord, I will respond to the heavens, and they shall respond to the earth; and the earth shall respond to the corn, and the wine, and the oil. . . . And I will sow her unto Me in the land; and I will have compassion upon her that had not obtained compassion; and I will say to them that were not My people: "Thou art My people"; and they shall say: "Thou art my God." (Hos. 2:23–25)

Israel was thus to be punished for its sins as a nation but would ultimately be redeemed and restored to its Land.

At the same time that Hosea declaimed against Israel in the north, Isaiah prophesied regarding the kingdom of Judah in the south. Although much of his prophecy dealt with the implications of what he perceived to be a potentially calamitous foreign policy on the part of the kingdom, his principal concern was with the nation's declining faithfulness to God and the impending consequences of its failure to observe the covenant. "Hear, O heavens, and give ear, O earth, for the Lord hath spoken; children I have reared, and brought up, and they have rebelled against Me. The ox knoweth his master, and the ass his master's crib; but Israel doth not know, My people doth not consider" (Isa. 1:2–3). As a result of Israel's defection, "I will ease Me of Mine adversaries, and avenge Me of Mine enemies" (Isa. 1:24). However, once collective punishment for the nation's transgressions was exacted in the tribulations of exile, Isaiah assured his compatriots, there would be a national redemption and restoration in the Land that will recall earlier and brighter days. "And I will restore thy judges as at the first, and thy counsellors as at the beginning; afterward thou shalt be called the city of righteousness, the faithful city. Zion shall be redeemed with justice, and they that return of her with righteousness" (Isa. 1:26–27). Isaiah affirmed that Zion would remain forever the chosen place of God, and that it was there alone that human history, understood as the processes by which mankind is brought to a divinely ordained state of being, would reach its culmination with the fulfillment of the divine purpose. He prophesied: "And it shall come to pass in the end of days, that the mountain of the Lord's house shall be established as the top of the mountains, and shall be exalted above the hills; and all nations shall flow unto it. . . . For out of Zion shall go forth the law, and the word of the Lord from Jerusalem" (Isa. 2:2–3), a teaching that is also included in the prophecy of Isaiah's contemporary, Micah (Mic. 4:1–2). At that time, Israel's mission would be completed and the nations would once again merge into a common universal society, such as existed in primeval days.

In the interim, in the period before history reaches its culmination, Isaiah insisted that the nation of Israel would remain indissolubly linked with Zion and its divinely ordained mission and that Israel would ultimately prevail in the covenanted Land against all who sought to sever that connection. The prophet proclaimed: "Make an uproar, O ye peoples, and ye shall be broken in pieces; and give ear, all ye of far countries; gird yourselves, and ye shall be broken in pieces. . . . Take counsel together, and it shall be brought to nought; Speak the word, and it shall not stand; for God is with us" (Isa. 8:9–10). Despite the adverse prospects facing the nation in the short term, Isaiah remained completely confident in an ultimately favorable outcome for his people if only they would return to their faith in God. "Therefore thus saith the Lord God: Behold I lay in Zion for a foundation a stone, a costly cornerstone of sure foundation; he that believeth shall not make haste" (Isa. 28:16). That is to say, one who has true faith will remain steadfast in his trust regardless of how long it takes for the national redemption and restoration to be realized, for it will surely come.

Micah too foresaw the catastrophe that was to engulf the nation and prophesied concerning the forthcoming destruction of Jerusalem and the dispersion of the people from the Land: "Therefore shall Zion for your sake be plowed as a field, and Jerusalem shall be become heaps, and the mountain of the house as the high places of a forest" (Mic. 3:12). Nevertheless, there was always the promise of eventual national redemption. "I will surely assemble, O Jacob, all of thee: I will surely gather the remnant of Israel" (Mic. 2:12) and renew the kingdom of Judah. Micah was confident that the nation of Israel would ultimately reestablish its proper relationship to God: "He will again have compassion upon us; He will subdue our iniquities; and Thou wilt cast all their sins into the depths of the sea. Thou wilt show faithfulness to Jacob, mercy to Abraham, as Thou hast sworn unto our fathers from the days of old" (Mic. 7:19–20). There can be little doubt as to what Micah is alluding to by invoking God's promises to the patriarchs; it is the promise of national restoration and independence in the Land.

In essence, the identical message was proclaimed by Jeremiah at the turn of the sixth century, although formulated in somewhat sharper terms. Israel would suffer the destruction of its state and the exile of its people because of its transgressions. But national redemption and restoration would surely come at some point in the future. Jeremiah affirmed this in the name of the Almighty:

> Behold, I will gather them out of all the countries, whither I have driven them in Mine anger, and in My fury, and in great wrath; and I will bring them back unto this place, and I will cause them to dwell safely; and they shall be My people, and I will be their God. . . . Men shall buy fields . . . in the land of Benjamin, and in the places about Jerusalem, and in the cities of Judah, and in the cities of the hill-country, and in the Lowland, and in the cities of the South; for I will cause their captivity to return, saith the Lord. (Jer. 32:37–38, 44)

This theme regarding the eventual restoration of Israel to the Land is repeated numerous times by the prophet (Jer. 12:15, 16:15, 24:6, 29:14, 30:3, 31:9–11, 31:22, 33:7).

EXILE AND DIASPORA

As prophesied, the kingdom of Judah in 586 succumbed to conquest by the Babylonians. The Temple was destroyed, Jerusalem lay in ruins, and most of the elite elements of the population were deported into exile in Mesopotamia. Ezekiel, who was among the exiles, was the first of the major prophets to confront the realities of the dispersion and the question of the possibility of an authentic Jewish existence outside the Land. It is clear that many, if not most, of the exiles were fully prepared to reconstruct their lives, both individually and communally, in the lands of their dispersion. Indeed, Babylonia in particular seemed to lend itself to this. By contrast with Egypt, which was a relatively homogeneous society, Babylonia was an empire that encompassed a wide diversity of peoples and religions, and it was quite conceivable that Israel could thrive there as an autonomous ethnic-religious group as long as it remained loyal to the state. The critical question was whether there was reason to uphold the covenant if one was no longer directly concerned about achieving national redemption in the Land and was content to be but a member of one religious cult among the many that existed within the bounds of the Babylonian empire. In other words, could a denationalized Judaism, which effectively nullified the significance of the covenant as depicted in Scripture, remain a meaningful expression of the unique relation between God and the people of Israel?

Ezekiel forcefully and categorically rejected the notion that the Diaspora might serve as an acceptable and normal mode of existence for the chosen people of God. Indeed, against those who were prepared to sacrifice their unique national identity for the sake of a peaceful existence in an alien land, Ezekiel contended that such a position directly contravened the divine purpose and scheme in history. It was surely the divine wish that a chastened nation of Israel thrive in the Land of Israel, where it was to become an example of proper national life for the other nations of the universe. Accordingly, invoking the language and imagery of the story of the Exodus, he prophesied:

As I live, saith the Lord God, surely with a mighty hand, and with an outstretched arm, and with fury poured out, will I be king over you; and I will bring you out from the peoples, and will gather you out of the countries wherein ye are scattered, with a mighty hand, and with an outstretched arm, and with fury poured out; and I will bring you into the wilderness of the peoples, and there will I plead with you face to face. Like as I pleaded with your fathers in the wilderness of the land of Egypt, so will I plead with you, saith the Lord God. And I will cause you to pass under the rod, and I will bring you into the bond of the covenant; and I will purge out from among you the rebels, and them that transgress against Me; I will bring them forth out of the land where they sojourn, but they shall not enter into the land of Israel; and ye shall know that I am the Lord. . . . For in My holy mountain, in the mountain of the height of Israel, saith the Lord God, there shall all the house of Israel, all of them serve Me in the land; there will I accept them. . . . And ye shall know that I am the Lord, when I shall bring you into the land of Israel, into the country which I lifted up My hand to give unto your fathers. (Ezek. 20:33–38, 40, 42)

Ezekiel's message is unequivocal. Israel has a special task to perform in human history, and that can only be accomplished by an Israel that is constituted as an autonomous nation in the Land of Israel. Its mission cannot be carried out by isolated groups of Jews in the Diaspora. Therefore, regardless of the wishes of the people, there will ultimately be a divine intervention in the course of history that will result in the reconstitution and rededication of the nation in accordance with the fundamental covenant between God and Israel. Indeed, the prophet was so certain of the coming national restoration that he stipulated how the Land was to be redistributed among the returning tribes, thereby establishing the basis for land tenure in the future (Ezek. 47:15–48:35).

It is perhaps ironic that this fervently nationalistic position was, in much later times, taken out of context and interpreted as suggesting that the return to the Land should take place *only* when there is a divine intervention, and that no attempt should be made to precipitate the restoration by human hands. Thus Ezekiel's prophecy was read as one of pious complacency rather than as a challenge to those Israelites who were prepared to reach a permanent accommodation with life in the Babylonian Diaspora.

It is noteworthy that even in the case of the prophet conventionally known as Second Isaiah, or Deutero-Isaiah, whose prophecies generally deal with themes that are more universal in character than those of his predecessors, national redemption and restoration are seen as prerequisites of Israel's universal mission. Prophesying at the time of the destruction of the neo-Babylonian empire by Cyrus of Persia and the subsequent return of some of the Israelite exiles to the Land of Israel, he declared, "Yea, He saith: It is too light a thing that thou shouldest be My servant to raise up the tribes of Jacob, and to restore the offspring of Israel; I will also give thee for a light of the nations, that My salvation may be unto the end of the earth" (Isa. 49:6). That is, it was not enough that Israel merely be reconstituted as a nation; Israel was also to serve as an exemplar for the other nations of the earth. It would be difficult to understand the prophet's meaning in any other sense. After all, what example could a failed nation present for emulation by others? Only a restored Israel, rededicated to its ancient faith, could serve as a beacon of social justice and public morality. This conception seems to be made abundantly clear in Isaiah's prophetic assertion: "For Zion's sake will I not hold My peace, and for Jerusalem's sake I will not rest, until her triumph go forth as brightness, and her salvation as a torch that burneth. . . . Thou shalt no more be termed Forsaken, neither shall thy land any more be termed Desolate; but thou shalt be called, My delight is in her, and thy land, Espoused; for the Lord delighteth in thee, and thy land shall be espoused" (Isa. 62:1, 4). Israel does indeed have a universal mission, but it can only be achieved through national reconstitution in Zion.

LIVING IN THE DIASPORA

Notwithstanding the efforts of these exilic and postexilic prophets to imbue the people with a commitment to the restoration of the nation in anticipation of eventual redemption, the rapid and increasing "normalization" of Jewish life in the Diaspora had become a fact that could not be ignored. For the first time since the days of Moses, the possibility of such an existence outside the Land was accepted by the majority of the exiles who were simply not prepared to uproot their lives once again in order to return to what they correctly saw as a historically troubled land. Many enjoyed a relatively comfortable existence in Mesopotamia, where they had a substantial measure of communal autonomy; they were reluctant to face the comparative hardship of life in the Land of Israel, which had been ravaged by war and was now overrun by the local enemies of the nation. As a consequence, only a relatively few were prepared to take advantage of Cyrus's edict of 538 B.C.E., which authorized the return of the Jews from exile to their ancient homeland.

To justify their unwillingness to return to the covenanted land, it became necessary for those who remained behind in Babylonia to develop an alternative religious ideology to that which placed central importance on the Land and the Temple of Jerusalem, which could now be rebuilt. Their approach to doing this was to diminish the religious significance of actually living in the Land, to stress instead the central importance of keeping the community of the covenant intact, regardless of the place where this was achieved. In effect, the ancient biblical portrayal of the Land as the ultimate sacred space, which was an inextricable part of the covenant between God and Israel, continued to be revered, but only as a mythological abstraction that had little relation to the real world of the Jews. Biblical Judaism, which was two dimensional in the sense that it contained both temporal and spatial elements, was now reduced to a single dimension for all practical purposes. Notwithstanding the national restoration in the Land that was in process, from this point onward Israel in the Land would have to compete for national primacy with Israel in the Diaspora. Because the majority of those in the Diaspora, the greater part of the nation, adopted this stance, it became a practical necessity for even the most ardent traditionalists to accept this view as a legitimate expression of Judaism. At the same time, however, many religious leaders continued to seek to instill in the people a love of the Land and a yearning for it as the only truly appropriate and permanent place for the people and nation of Israel. An example of this is the well-known and unequivocally nationalistic psalm that subsequently became part of the synagogue liturgy: "If I forget thee, O Jerusalem, let my right hand forget her cunning. Let my tongue cleave to the roof of my mouth, if I remember thee not; if I set not Jerusalem above my chiefest joy" (Ps. 137:5–6).

THE RETURN AND THE SECOND COMMONWEALTH

Nonetheless, it seems that many among those who did return to the Land, as well as the descendants of those who were able to avoid exile in the first instance, were disenchanted by the problems that had perennially accompanied Israel's national independence in the Land. Accordingly, there apparently were a substantial number of Israelites in the Land who sought to reestablish their lives there on an ethnic-communal basis but demonstrated little interest in a national restoration. This tendency reflected the desire to escape the responsibilities of ethical nationhood, to borrow Mordecai Kaplan's phrase. Thus, many were ambivalent about or even opposed to the reconstruction of the Temple as the religious and political center of the nation, a crucial step on the road to a reconstitution of the Israelite commonwealth. The postexilic prophets therefore challenged those settlers' complacency and indifference with regard to the matter of national restoration in the Land. Haggai declaimed: "Thus speaketh the Lord of hosts, saying: This people say: The time is not come, the time that the Lord's house should be built. Then came the word of the Lord by Haggai the prophet, saying: Is it a time for you yourselves to dwell in your ceiled houses, while this house lieth waste? . . . Go up to the hill-country, and bring wood, and build the house; and I will take pleasure in it, and I will be glorified" (Hag. 1:2–3, 8). The message was clear, the time for the restoration to take place was when the opportunity to do so presented itself. The notion that the process of restoration had to await a moment of divine intervention or the advent of a divine messenger, a Messiah, was quite alien to the prophet.

Although the prophets had indeed alluded to the day of the coming of the Messiah as the event that would alter the course of all human history, it was evident that the restoration that was in fact taking place was necessarily nonmessianic in character. For one thing, the number of those who returned to the Land was quite small, only about forty thousand people. Second, and perhaps even more significant, the return was achieved as a result not of the manifest expression of the collective will of the nation of Israel but rather of a Persian political decision probably intended to help secure a reliable base in Palestine for a planned invasion of Egypt. Presumably, a grateful Jewish population in Palestine would lend unselfish support to the Persian armies. The return from Babylonia was thus a very different sort of affair from the first return from Egypt, when Israel entered the Land by force and began the process of conquest against considerable odds, a struggle that lasted for generations. The second entry into the country came, as Joseph Grunblatt wrote, "not with a bang but a whimper, a low-key, limited reunion of the land and the people." Moreover, the very prosaic character of the return from exile and the subsequent restoration of the Temple suggests "that the theory of Return is not inexorably tied in with the doctrine of the Messiah in the actual historical process, that a Return may take place on its own ground rules, and that the Messiah must wait for his arrival on his ground rules."[1]

Perhaps because of the lackluster nonmessianic character of the return from the Babylonian exile, the process of national restoration, which focused principally on the reconstruction of the Temple, was impeded by the strong opposition of both internal and external forces. The former sought to delay the process ostensibly on theological grounds, whereas the latter sought to prevent it entirely for partisan political reasons. In rejoinder, the prophet Zechariah tried to convince the people that the restoration was indeed in accordance with the divine wish. "For thus saith the Lord of hosts: As I purposed to do evil unto you, when your fathers provoked Me, saith the Lord of hosts, and I repented not; so again do I purpose in these days to do good unto Jerusalem and to the house of

Judah; fear ye not" (Zech. 8:14–15). There was no question at the time that a restoration of Israel as a sovereign nation in the Land would be opposed by the states of the region and that military assaults on the fledgling state of Judaea were to be expected. However, the prophet assured the people, their opponents would be defeated. "In that day will I make the chiefs of Judah like a pan of fire among wood, and like a torch of fire among sheaves; and they shall devour all the peoples round about, on the right hand and on the left; and Jerusalem shall be inhabited again in her own place, even in Jerusalem" (Zech. 12:6). That is, the siege of Jerusalem, the symbolic essence of the reconstituted state, would be broken, and the city would emerge victorious once again as the national center of the people of Israel.

The restoration of the Temple, however, did not bring in its wake the anticipated political independence. The reconstituted community of Judaea had a good deal of local autonomy and was ruled by its high priests without too much direct outside interference in communal affairs, but it nonetheless remained subject to heavy taxation and economic exploitation by its Persian overlords. This situation was lamented by Nehemiah:

Behold, we are servants this day, and as for the land that Thou gavest unto our fathers to eat the fruit thereof and the good thereof, behold, we are servants in it. And it yieldeth much increase unto the kings whom Thou hast set over us because of our sins; also they have power over our bodies, and over our cattle, at their pleasure, and we are in great distress. (Neh. 9:36–37)

With the subsequent defeat of the Persian empire by Alexander the Great in the late fourth century, the situation did not improve for Judaea. Dominion over the Land passed to the Greeks, and the area became a pawn in the regional conflict between the Ptolemaids of Egypt and the Seleucids of Syria. That conflict raged for a century and a half after the death of Alexander and the partition of his empire. The unrelenting tribulations suffered by the Land and its people during this long period posed a significant ideological problem for the intellectual and spiritual leaders of the nation. Indeed, an entirely new and unprecedented situation had developed. The Temple had been restored, but the anticipated concomitant national independence failed to follow. As a practical matter, the Judaeans were free to worship as they chose as long as they rendered fealty to their Greek masters. The continuing subjugation of Israel to foreign rulers in the Land came to be understood as yet another phase of the punishment inflicted by God on the people for the transgressions perpetrated by their ancestors. As a consequence, the Jews generally accepted their condition with equanimity.

This situation persisted until the first part of the second century B.C.E., when for reasons of state, the Seleucids attempted to weld the disparate religions and national groups to be found within their far-flung empire into a cohesive mass, with unquestioning and unquestionable loyalty to the ruling house. The Seleucids sought to achieve this in part by demanding universal conformity to a state religion based on Hellenistic practices. This posed an awesome challenge to the Jews of the empire, threatening their very existence even as a primarily religious community. The leaders of the people in Judaea, seemingly caught in an insoluble dilemma, determined to oppose these demands by passive resistance, coupled with a readiness to accept martyrdom rather than yield to the Seleucid demands. They rejected active opposition as inappropriate because their oppressors were believed to be acting as the divine instruments of their collective punishment; active opposition would therefore constitute defiance of heaven. Moreover, it was not considered proper for Israel to attempt to escape the consequences of its transgressions against the covenant. In other words, the leaders argued that national salvation was in God's hands and would come at a time determined by heaven and not by man.

This passive position was opposed by Mattathias, the aged patriarch of the Hasmoneans, a minor clan of priests. Mattathias appears to have proposed the radical thesis that the extreme adversity being experienced by the Jews at the hands of the Seleucids was not necessarily a result of God's wish to further chastise his people. There was, he seems to have suggested, the distinct possibility that the Seleucids might be persecuting the Jews out of their own arrogance and for purposes unrelated to God's concern for the people of Israel. If this were indeed the case, it would surely be permissible, if not mandatory, for the Jews to actively oppose such impositions against the faith of Israel.[2] In other words, as there was no way of knowing whether the Seleucids were really serving as the rod of God's anger, to be certain that martyrdom was truly in accord with the divine wish, it made little sense to acquiesce. Indeed, as the threat to the Jews was imminent and unequivocal, it was surely appropriate to take positive action to avoid needless transgressions of God's specific laws. Pursuing the logic of this argument, Mattathias stirred up a rebellion against the Seleucids that soon led to a full national restoration and political independence under his sons.

The Hasmonean kingdom lasted for about a hundred years before it became so weakened by internal conflicts, religious, social, and political, that it quickly succumbed to Roman intervention and domination and its own subsequent dissolution. Nonetheless, the Jews managed to maintain some semblance of communal religious, if not political, autonomy for much of the next century. Then, following a dramatic upsurge in Jewish nationalist sentiment, a major revolt broke out against Rome that culminated in 70 C.E. in the destruction of the Temple, the last vestige of Jewish national autonomy.

It is beyond the scope of this study to examine the proximate historical reasons for the termination of Jewish political autonomy in the Land of Israel and the demise of the Second Commonwealth. Nonetheless, viewing the pattern of events described in this chapter from a national religious perspective, as Grunblatt suggested:

> an almost frightening hypothesis seems to emerge from the experiences of the First and Second Commonwealths: that we cannot survive in the land unless it becomes messianic. If we insist on remaining historical . . . we cannot make it. And "let us be like all nations" need not mean being pagans or even being corrupt. It may mean just trying to be "normal." We cannot be "normal" and "make it," because we are not a normal people. Either we become redemptive or we become self destructive.[3]

3

Coping with Exile
and
Powerlessness

Writing of the Jews as a nationality, Bernard Joseph observed:

> Despite the frequent discord amongst the Jews whilst they lived their national
> life in their homeland, the sentiment of nationality was already so highly
> developed at the time of the extinction of their political life in A.D. 70 as to
> be the marvel of succeeding generations of historians. They had succeeded
> in imbibing the sentiment of nationality so deeply and of evolving a
> communal life which was so thoroughly nationalistic, that they were enabled
> to endure as a nationality for centuries after their dispersion. . . . They
> contrived to live, in the spirit, the nationalistic life which they had previously
> lived in Palestine, maintaining their national exclusiveness and unity.[1]

That the Jews were able to succeed in doing this, despite the overwhelming
odds, is a lasting tribute to the sustaining power of the Jewish national
idea as it confronted and overcame the vicissitudes of history.

JERUSALEM DESTROYED
The destruction of the Second Commonwealth by the Romans left the
nation of Israel in a state of almost total disarray, politically, economically,
and socially. The Temple was destroyed and Jerusalem lay in ruins, soon
to be rebuilt as a Roman city. This left the religious leaders—the sages, or
rabbis, of the postdestruction period, the heirs of the prophets—with the
awesome task of reconstituting the national community despite the people's political powerlessness.

The sages sought to mitigate the despair of the people by convincing them that, notwithstanding the catastrophe, there was continuing meaning to their lives as Jews. The sages also spoke with confidence about a national restoration in the Land in the not-too-distant future. To lend credence to their teachings, it became essential for the sages to provide a cogent and plausible explanation of why such a national disaster had struck the Jewish nation a second time if the constitution of the Jews as an independent people in their own state in the Land of Israel was indeed an integral part of the divine scheme of things.

To deal with this problem, the sages offered a unique interpretation of the nation's history, one that completely discounted all external factors: "Why was the first Sanctuary destroyed? Because of three [evil] things which prevailed there: idolatry, immorality, bloodshed."[2] They thus asserted that the destruction of the First Commonwealth did not take place because of the overwhelming power of Israel's enemies. Instead, it occurred because of the removal of the protective shield of the divine presence over the nation owing to its neglect of the covenant. It was therefore Israel's faithlessness, exemplified by the pervasiveness of the enumerated transgressions within the ancient society, which permitted the political forces at work in the region to engulf the kingdom of Judah. This argument was not intended to suggest that the majority of the nation had actually indulged in these heinous practices, but rather that the nation as a whole was held accountable for permitting such violations of the Torah to become commonplace, even if carried out only by a small minority of the people. That is, the nation had failed to meet its collective responsibility for upholding the moral standards for the society ordained by the Torah, in accordance with the national covenant with God. The destruction of the commonwealth was therefore to be understood as divine punishment for this failure.[3]

It should be noted that the sages considered these particular transgressions to constitute the most reprehensible of all possible violations of God's law. Indeed, they were considered so heinous as to outweigh even the most fundamental natural law of self-preservation. The sages taught, "With regard to the transgression of all the precepts that are in the Torah, if it is said to a man: Transgress and be not killed, he should transgress and not be killed except for [the transgressions of the prohibitions against] idolatry, illicit sexual relations, and bloodshed."[4] In other words, the frequency and pervasiveness of these cardinal sins reflected such a flagrant disregard of the most critical requirements of a moral society that the destruction of the state and the Temple on their account was held to be fully justified.

Since the destruction of the First Commonwealth, it was suggested, there had been a radical transformation of mores among the people. The sages asserted that the people had indeed absorbed the intended lesson from the horrendous experience of the destruction of the first Temple. As a result, the moral standards and ethical practices of Jewish society during the Second Commonwealth period had reached a much higher degree of conformity with the requirements set forth in the Torah. But if such were the case, the sages asked, "Why was the second Sanctuary destroyed, seeing that in its time they were occupying themselves with Torah, [observance of] precepts, and the practice of charity?" The response the sages offered to this question was, "because therein prevailed hatred without cause. That teaches you that groundless hatred is considered as of even gravity with the three sins of idolatry, immorality, and bloodshed together."[5] That is, even though the transgressions that brought down the First Commonwealth were not characteristic of the Second Temple period, the vitality of the nation had been sapped by unwarranted internal discord and social strife to the extent that the state collapsed under Roman pressure.

In addition to the obvious importance assigned by the sages to the maintenance of social cohesiveness, as reflected in this teaching, the latter also contains certain broader implications that merit careful consideration. After all, the pervasiveness of "hatred without cause" is being offered by the sages as the principal justification for the eradication of all semblance of Jewish national autonomy, the destruction of the Temple, and the dispersion of the people. This would appear to be a rather extreme approach to making a moral point. It therefore seems evident that the less-obvious point that they were making is that the debilitating effects of the prevailing social disharmony had not only undermined the stability of the society and the state but had actually made the continued existence of the Second Commonwealth superfluous. Presumably, its viability as a state had declined to such an extent that it was no longer capable of even prospectively fulfilling the nation's historical mission, and if this were the case, then it no longer served any purpose. Accordingly, the teaching implied, Israel had to learn another traumatic lesson from this second national catastrophe, namely, that of the essential need for tolerance of reasonable differences between persons and groups within the society. This lesson would have to be fully absorbed if the people were to be prepared for the ultimate national redemption and restoration that was still to come. Of the latter the sages had no doubt, and they made it their task to keep this expectation alive among the people as well.

A leading role in this effort was played by the principal popular religious leader of the period immediately following the destruction of the Temple, the sage R. (Rabbi) Yohanan ben Zakkai. Recognizing the futility of continued resistance to the overwhelming power of Rome, he had abandoned Jerusalem during the last phase of its siege in order to begin the task of rebuilding the community of scholars that was critical to the survival of the nation. He also undertook to bolster the confidence of the people in an ultimate national renaissance. Toward this end, he introduced a number of religious enactments that were intended both to keep the memory of the destroyed Temple alive among the people and to evoke a yearning for a restored Jerusalem.[6]

Similarly, his renowned and ardently nationalistic disciple, R. Akiba, added the following benediction to the liturgy of the Passover Seder:

> Therefore, O Lord our God and the God of our fathers, bring us in peace to the other feasts and festivals which are coming to meet us, while we rejoice in the building-up of thy city and are joyful in thy worship; and may we eat there of the sacrifices and of the Passover-offerings whose blood has reached with acceptance the wall of thy Altar, and let us praise thee for our redemption and for the ransoming of our soul. Blessed art thou, O Lord, who has redeemed Israel.[7]

This prayer clearly reflects the conviction that Jerusalem would soon be rebuilt and the Temple restored, something that was conceivable only if the Romans were driven out of the country and an independent Jewish state were reestablished.

Owing in part to the efforts of these and other inspired religious teachers, the nationalist spirit among the Jews of the Land was kept alive, notwithstanding the desire of the Romans to eradicate it completely. Indeed, it remained so strong that, a major, but vain, rebellion against Roman domination erupted about sixty years after the destruction of the Temple and lasted for three years. It was only after that rebellion, the Bar Kokhba revolt, was finally suppressed in 135 C.E. that the sages felt the pressing need to reorient their conceptual approach to the question of a national restoration. They were compelled by events to accept reluctantly the idea that the restoration of the Jewish state was not going to be realized at any time in the foreseeable future. Given the decimation of the population by war and outmigration, the sages now had to shift their focus to the means by which to cope with the decline of the Land of Israel as the primary center of Jewish national-religious life and the emerging importance of the diaspora communities, particularly in Mesopotamia (Babylonia), as decentralized and self-contained centers for the Jewish people.

The approach of the sages was basically twofold. On the one hand, they continued to acclaim, indeed some sought to magnify, the importance of the Land of Israel in the divine scheme for mankind, and consequently in the nation's future history. The people, they argued, should not submit to unrelenting despair, because a new dawn awaited the nation, which would prosper in its now-subjugated land. Thus, R. Jose ben Dormaskit taught: "In the future the Land of Israel will expand on all sides like a fig that is narrow below and broadens upwards, so that in the future the gates of Jerusalem will reach as far as Damascus. . . . And the returning exiles will come and settle therein."[8] On the other hand, the sages also began to give clearer expression to the messianic hopes and expectations in which the people had found consolation in times of adversity since the days of the prophets.

Challenged especially by the growth of the Mesopotamian Jewish community as a counterpoise to the declining community of the Land of Israel, and the prospect that the latter would therefore diminish in importance in the eyes of the people, the sages deemed it necessary to continue to remind their fellow Jews everywhere that "the Land of Israel is holier than all other lands."[9] They reaffirmed that the Land of Israel remained the center of the universe and that, as argued by R. Simeon b. (ben) Yohai, of all the lands in the world the only one that God considered suitable for Israel was indeed the Land of Israel.[10] In this regard the sages insisted: "no land was so precious as the Land of Israel. Said the Holy One, blessed be He, to Moses: 'The Land, surely is precious to Me'. . . and Israel are precious to Me . . . I shall,' said the Holy One, blessed be He, 'bring Israel, who are precious to Me, into the Land that is precious to Me.'"[11] Notwithstanding their determined efforts in this regard, the sages were unable to prevent the changes they feared. As pointed out by Joseph Klausner: "The leadership in Judaism passed gradually from Palestinian to Babylonian Jewry, so that the Jews became more and more remote from their native soil and from the source of their political life. Consequently, the clear and more or less realistic desires for political and moral redemption inevitably gave way to new, mystical-religious fantasies."[12]

MESSIANIC EXPECTATIONS

In the absence of a serious expectation of a national restoration anytime in the readily foreseeable future, there emerged an understandable tendency on the part of some to project their messianic expectations to the posthistoric world of the future, thereby enabling them to come to terms with the present world in which they lived. This approach proved theologically and religiously satisfying to many, perhaps even most, Jewish religious and communal leaders of the period, who could now direct their efforts to restructuring their individual and communal lives as a religious sect in the lands of the Diaspora, but it marked a major crossroads in the history of Jewish nationalism. For one thing, it presaged the end of all active concern with the historical role of the nation. Moreover, it placed in jeopardy the fundamental ideas and precepts of the covenant and the

Torah, many of which were directly predicated on the autonomous existence of the nation in the promised land.

To counteract the negative consequences to the national idea of this approach to the problem of exile and political powerlessness, the great Babylonian sage Samuel (early 3rd cent.) attempted to keep the people focused on the central role of the Land in the life of the nation as well as on the forthcoming national restoration in the Land. He asserted that the traditional messianic teachings about redemption and restoration referred to events that were to take place in *this* world, the world of human history, and not in some future posthistorical world to come. Samuel taught, "There is no difference between this world and the days of the Messiah except [that in the latter there will be no] bondage of foreign powers."[13] Therefore, the restoration of Jewish national autonomy in the Land of Israel would in itself signal the onset of the messianic age, the period in which Israel would at last fulfill its historic mission. Another sage went even further and suggested the possibility that "the Temple would be rebuilt before the reconstitution of the kingdom of David," that is, before the arrival of the Messiah, as it had been once before upon the return of the Jews from the Babylonian Captivity.[14]

To further emphasize his conviction that the restoration would indeed come within historical time, even though it seemed so unlikely, R. Hanina taught: "From the year 400 after the destruction onwards, if one says unto you, 'Buy a field that is worth one thousand denarii for one denar'—do not buy it."[15] That is, the onset of the messianic age was expected to occur within the next several generations, and it would surely incorporate the rehabilitation and restoration of Israel in its land. Because of this, R. Hanina suggested that it was in the long term interest of the Jews of the Diaspora to recognize that their life in exile was only temporary, and that it would not be prudent for them to continue to invest their capital in property that they or their heirs would have to abandon when they returned to the Land from their exile.

There was, however, a serious danger inherent in such predictions regarding the actual date of the beginning of the messianic age or, even worse, of the coming of the Messiah and the inauguration of the long-awaited national restoration. When the predicted time arrived, but the Messiah did not, the effects on those who awaited him with great anticipation could be traumatic, leading to depression and loss of faith and hope in the Jewish future. Accordingly, the rabbis subsequently discouraged attempts to calculate the end of days and the arrival of the Messiah. One sage, R. Samuel b. Nahmani, went so far as to declare: "Blasted be the bones of those who calculate the end. For they [the people] would say, since the predetermined time has arrived, and yet he has not come, he will never come."[16]

Nonetheless, the widespread expectation that the messianic era would be inaugurated sometime during the fifth century remained very high. Not only did the period coincide with that predicted by R. Hanina, but there was also an ancient tradition that predicted that the Messiah would arrive in the eighty-fifth Jubilee of the creation, or the second half of the fifth century. One consequence of the popular enthusiasm generated by such messianic expectations was the emergence of the first of the considerable number of false messiahs and precursors who were to appear during the next twelve hundred years. Thus, a certain Moses of Candia (Crete), which had a substantial Jewish community, declared himself to be the Messiah at that time. He was deemed to be so credible that normal life in the community came to a virtual standstill as he promised to lead them, like Moses, through the waters to the promised land. Apparently, large numbers of men, women, and children followed him toward the sea. At his promise that the waters would part for them as they had for the Israelites under Moses, these people threw themselves off a cliff into the sea, and many died.[17] It has been suggested that it was as a direct result of this incident that R. Ashi, one of the last of the sages of the talmudic period, reinterpreted the tradition of the eighty-five Jubilees from creation to the Messiah, in an effort to mitigate the effects of such exaggerated expectations on the people.[18] He asserted flatly, "Before that, do not expect him; afterwards you may await him."[19] That is, the Messiah will most assuredly not come before the conclusion of the eighty-fifth Jubilee and may well delay his arrival until long thereafter. In other words, he was not to be expected in the near future and might not come until the far distant future.

As part of their effort to affirm unequivocally the centrality of the Land of Israel in Judaism, some of the rabbis proceeded to evolve a series of legends and homiletic interpretations of the biblical texts that focused on the notion that the Land of Israel constituted *the* ultimate sacred space in the world of creation. The sacred center of that world was the city of Jerusalem, the center of which is the site of the Temple, the center of which is the site where the Holy of Holies was located, the place at which the principal interface between the human and the divine occurred. Accordingly, the very spot where Jacob had his dream of the ladder, the point of the sacred break in the continuity of profane space, was considered to correspond to the exact site upon which the Temple was later to be built. In one such homily, it was taught:

Jacob rose up early in the morning in great fear, and said: The house of the Holy One, blessed be He, is in this place, as it is said, "And he was afraid, and said: How full of awe is this place! this is none other than the house of God" (Gen. 28:17). Hence thou canst learn that every one who prays in

> Jerusalem is [reckoned] as though he had prayed before the Throne of Glory, for the gate of heaven is there, and it is open to hear the prayers of Israel, as it is said, "and this is the gate of heaven." (Gen. 28:17)

Then, in a flight of the mythological imagination, that same sacred site is transformed back in time to be the very center of creation. The homily continues:

> And Jacob returned to gather the stones, and he found them all (turned into) one stone, and he set it up for a pillar in the midst of the place, and oil descended for him from heaven, and he poured it thereon. . . . What did the Holy One, blessed be He, do? He placed [thereon] His right foot, and sank the stone to the bottom of the depths, and He made it the keystone of the earth, just like a man who sets a keystone in an arch; therefore it is called the *foundation stone*, for there is the navel of the earth, and therefrom was all the earth evolved and upon it the Sanctuary of God stands.[20]

The common mythic notion of the *omphalous*, the navel of the earth, was thus drawn into service by the classical midrashic homilists to enhance the sense of the sacredness of the Land, from which the creation of the world was thought to have begun. "The Holy One, blessed be He," they taught, "created His world in the same way as a woman gives birth, beginning from the navel and stretching here and there; in this way did the Holy One, blessed be He, create all the world. He began from the place of the Holy Temple and from there stretched out to encompass the whole world. Therefore it is known as the 'foundation stone,' for from it all the world was set."[21] Another midrashic homily is even more elaborate in this regard, suggesting that "the navel is Jerusalem, and the [center of the] navel itself is the altar," which stands on the "foundation stone."[22] Moreover, the site of the "foundation stone" was considered to be the very spot where Adam, the first human, was brought into being on the sixth day of creation.[23] The sacredness of the place, by extension, was also believed to radiate throughout the area within the boundaries of the Land of Israel, thus enabling R. Anan to teach: "Whoever is buried in the Land of Israel is deemed to be buried under the altar."[24] This latter notion, which linked the deceased of Israel directly to the gates of heaven, was to become a concept of particular significance throughout most of the early and later medieval period.

The site of the Temple, which was built over the "foundation stone," was also conceived as the center of the entire universe, from which the primordial light radiates throughout the world. This is reflected in the teaching of R. Berekiah that "light was created from the place of the Temple."[25] Accordingly, tradition records that the architectural plan of the

Temple was designed in part for this specific purpose, that is, to shed its light on the universe. "R. Levi explained: In the way of the world, when a man builds himself a grand house, he has the openings for the windows made narrow on the outside but broad on the inside in order to have the greatest amount of light enter it. But the windows in the Temple were made otherwise: they were narrow on the inside and broad on the outside in order to send forth light into the world."[26] There is some disagreement among the sages over the nature of the light that was thus transmitted, some taking the statement literally and some figuratively. Thus, in a discussion between R. Hiyya and R. Jannai about the meaning of the name "Moriah," the site of Abraham's binding of Isaac, also identified by tradition as the site of the "foundation stone" and the Temple, "one said: The place whence *orah* [light] goes forth to the world; while the other explained it: The place whence *yirah* [religious reverence] goes forth to the world."[27] However, both views clearly affirm the centrality of the sacred place, with the second expositor attributing even greater religious importance to it than the first.

The Temple site was also seen as the principal if not exclusive locus of Israel's channel of communication to God. In this regard, the sages taught:

> If one is standing outside Palestine, he should turn mentally towards Eretz Israel. . . . If he stands in Eretz Israel he should turn mentally towards Jerusalem. . . . If he is standing in Jerusalem he should turn mentally towards the Sanctuary. . . . If he is standing in the Sanctuary, he should turn mentally towards the Holy of Holies. . . . In this way all Israel will be turning their hearts toward one place.[28]

A FOCUS ON THE LAND

The sages were not satisfied merely with homiletic treatment of the theme of the cosmic centrality of the sacred space of the Land. They also drew halakhic or legal distinctions with regard to the status of the Land of Israel as compared to the other places where Jewish communities were to be found. Thus, R. Ahi son of R. Josiah interpreted the biblical command, "Thou shalt not deliver unto his master a bondman that is escaped from his master unto thee" (Deut. 23:16), to have application only in a case where the slave of a Jew fled to the Land of Israel.[29] That is, in his view, the very provenance of the Land of Israel is considered as having redemptive qualities that cannot be found elsewhere. The extraordinary merit of the Land is also reflected in the teaching of R. Judah b. Dosithai, "that if a fugitive from Palestine went abroad, his sentence is not set aside; from abroad to Palestine, his sentence is set aside, on account of Palestine's prerogative."[30] Once again, the Land itself provides a form of sanctuary.

Going further, the sages taught that hymns of praise (*Hallel*) are not recited for miracles that occurred outside the Land of Israel after it was settled.[31] This view is explained as resulting from the halakhic position that the hymns of praise are only recited when the community has been saved from destruction and that the community of Israel is considered to exist, as a communal entity for halakhic purposes, only in the Land of Israel. Accordingly, miracles that are performed on behalf of Jews living outside the Land, such as that which is commemorated by the festival of Purim, do not engender the recitation of the appropriate psalms in the festival liturgy celebrating the event. The rationale behind this ruling is that the saving act under consideration is deemed to have been performed exclusively for the sake of those individuals who directly benefited from it rather than for the community as a whole.[32]

Similarly, the sages argued that the Land itself had redemptive attributes that limited the halakhic significance of time spent outside the Land, at least for certain purposes. One example of this concerns the general halakhic rule that in the event that a man does not have children by his wife within ten years of their marriage, he is obligated to seek alternative means of fulfilling the obligation of propagation. Yet it seems quite clear from the biblical text that Abraham, who is traditionally considered to have been observant of the precepts of the Torah even before they were revealed to Moses, was married to Sarah for a longer period than ten years before he took Hagar the Egyptian to be his wife, an event that took place "after Abram had dwelt ten years in the land of Canaan" (Gen. 16:3). Here was an apparent discrepancy that demanded explanation. The rabbis resolved the issue by arguing: "This teaches you that the years of his stay outside the Land were not included in the number."[33] That is, with specific regard to the rule under discussion, the calendar only tolled the time Abraham actually spent in the Land of Israel.

At the same time that the sages extolled the sanctity and centrality of the Land of Israel, it also became essential for them to explain and justify Israel's forcible alienation from its sacred patrimony. For this purpose they made reference to the biblical admonition, "Ye shall therefore keep all My statutes, and all Mine ordinances, and do them, that the land, whither I bring you to dwell therein, vomit you not out" (Lev. 20:22). This passage, among others, was presented by them as a clear forewarning of the fate that had awaited the nation and that had indeed befallen it, as a consequence of its neglect of the covenant, the reason for which the Land was granted to Israel in the first place. The nation had been awarded the Land with the specific understanding that it should build its unique society there. It was not the divine intent that Israel make use of the promised land to become a nation like those that surrounded it.

The sages categorically rejected the popular aspiration for national "normalcy." They considered such to be equivalent to a negation of the national mission, which required that Israel remain fundamentally different in character from, rather than become the same as, the other nations. The sage Rav is traditionally considered to have given classic expression to this concern in the *Aleinu* prayer, which became a major feature of the liturgy of the High Holy Days and which was subsequently made an integral part of the three daily prayer services. "It is for us to praise the Lord of all, to proclaim the greatness of the Creator of the universe for he has not made us like the nations of the world, nor positioned us like the families [tribes] of the earth; He has not made our portion as theirs, nor our destiny as that of all their multitude." The prayer affirms most explicitly that it simply was not in the intended scheme of things for Israel to be a "normal" nation or for the Jews to be a "normal" people.

Because Israel failed not only to accomplish its assigned mission under the covenant but also to achieve even the minimum necessary preparation for it, its loss of national sovereignty was considered appropriate and its alienation from the Land fully justified. Accordingly, the sages taught: "The land . . . cannot tolerate men of transgression. It is to be compared to the son of a king, whom they made to eat food that was indigestible, which he is compelled to vomit out."[34] This idea too was incorporated into the liturgy of the High Holy Days and the festivals in the form of a public acknowledgment of the justice of the expulsion and exile from the Land, a self-indictment that remains part of the traditional prayer service to this day: "Because of our sins, we were exiled from our land and far removed from our country."

Indeed, the rabbis went further and emphatically acknowledged that, in any case, the Land of Israel was not really theirs to do with as they pleased. It was ultimately the special property of the Lord, who alone would determine who might occupy it at any particular moment in history. In this regard, R. Isaac taught that Scripture began with the story of creation rather than with the recitation of the divine law to indicate clearly to all that the earth in its entirety ultimately belongs to God, who created it and awards it to whomsoever he chooses.[35] Nevertheless, R. Hiyya, who evidently could not reconcile himself theologically to the idea of Israel's loss of the Land, offered a homiletic interpretation of the prophecy of Ezekiel, concerning the justification for the dispersion of the Jews from their land, that suggested that even God despaired over what had happened to his people. The prophet had vindicated the exile because "when the house of Israel dwelt in their own land, they defiled it by their way and their doings" (Ezek. 36:17). But R. Hiyya pictured God as saying, "Would that the children of My people were in the Land of Israel, even though they defile it."[36]

The faith of the sages in the divine promise of national redemption remained unshakable, and they looked forward with eager anticipation to the day when it would inevitably come and encouraged the people to prepare for it constantly. From their places of exile, they exalted the idea of living within the sacred precincts of the Land and taught, "One should always live in the Land of Israel, even in a town most of whose inhabitants are idolators, but let no one live outside the Land, even in a town most of whose inhabitants are Israelites; for whoever lives in the Land of Israel may be considered as one who has a God, but whoever lives outside the Land may be regarded as one who has no God."[37] That is, the threat of the loss of national identity, leading to cultural and religious assimilation, is deemed to be so great in the Diaspora that it is reasonable to expect that the exiles will eventually succumb to it. Within the sacred precincts of the Holy Land, however, the redemptive qualities of the Land itself make the fear of such a total rejection of the covenant comparatively unrealistic.[38] Other sages suggested that any Jew who lived in the Land, by virtue of that circumstance alone, was to be considered as one who "accepted the kingdom of Heaven."[39] In this latter regard, they also taught that the kingdom of heaven itself would be incomplete as long as Israel remained in exile.[40]

Some rabbis of a particularly nationalistic bent went as far as to teach, "Living in the Land of Israel is equal in weight to all the mitzvot of the Torah."[41] In view of the consideration that a commandment to live in the Land could at best be but one of the 613 mitzvot (precepts) of the Torah, the statement is remarkable to say the least and a clear reflection of the cosmic importance attributed to the Land by the sages. It should be noted parenthetically that, of the traditional count of 613 precepts, some 315 have application only within the confines of the Land of Israel.[42]

Living in the Land was deemed so important by the sages as to justify halakhic modifications to facilitate it. Thus, although it is improper, as a rule, to ask a gentile to perform work for a Jew on the Sabbath, it was permissible to do this if it involved having one prepare a deed for the purchase of a home in the Land of Israel. As explained in the Talmud, "The Rabbis did not maintain this prohibition in this case on account of the welfare of the Land of Israel."[43] That is, reestablishing the Jewish presence in the Land of Israel was considered to be of such overriding importance as to justify an exception to the general regulatory injunction.

Notwithstanding the intense concern of the sages with the Land of Israel, and their acknowledgment of its great and irreplaceable religious significance, the elements of the internal ideological conflict over the nature of the forthcoming redemption of Israel—a conflict that continues even today—had already become increasingly evident during the later years of talmudic era. As the prospects of a restoration of Jewish sovereignty over the Land diminished with time, and as the Jewish communities in the Diaspora increasingly prospered, especially in Mesopotamia, where they thrived under relatively permissive Persian rule, the problem of reconciling the longing for Zion with the facts of exile became one of increasing concern to the rabbis, who were split among themselves on how to deal with the issue.

The difference of views on this matter is clearly reflected in the discussion recorded in the Talmud concerning the desire of R. Zeira, in the latter part of the third century, to leave Mesopotamia, against the wishes of his mentor, R. Judah bar Ezekiel, the dean of the Pumbeditha academy, and to settle in the Land of Israel. R. Zeira's decision to emigrate was in itself unexceptional; a small but steady stream of rabbis and their disciples had been returning to the Land from Mesopotamia, beginning with the sage R. Nathan the Babylonian about a decade after the end of the Bar Kokhba revolt in 135. However, attitudes toward such emigration had begun to change significantly during the following century. Although R. Judah bar Ezekiel clearly articulated his devotion to the Land of Israel, he was at the same time adamantly opposed to the emigration there of scholars from Mesopotamia. His objection reflected a sincere concern that such migrations would detract from the acknowledged competence of the Mesopotamian talmudic academies as the intellectual centers of the Jewish Diaspora. Given that there was no early prospect of any national redemption and restoration in the Land of Israel, he deemed it essential that priority be given to strengthening the religious foundations of the existing Jewish communities in the lands of their exile, even if this meant impeding the emigration of scholars to the Land. This position was quite difficult to square with the traditional views regarding the theological centrality of the Land and the precept requiring one to live there. It thus became necessary for R. Judah bar Ezekiel to base his argument on some ground other than the practical needs of the Mesopotamian Jewish community. Accordingly, he embraced an exegetical position that seemed to vindicate his objection to emigration to the Land, a stance that other sages found to be very troubling.

As recorded in the Talmud: "R. Zeira was evading Rab Judah because he desired to go up to the Land of Israel while Rab Judah had expressed [the following view]: Whoever goes up from Babylon to the Land of Israel transgresses a positive commandment, for it is said in Scripture, 'They shall be carried to Babylon, and there shall they be, until the day that I remember them, saith the Lord'" (Jer. 27:22). That is, the prophetic text was understood by Rab Judah as constituting an admonition against taking any unilateral initiative toward a national restoration in the Land without a clear sign from heaven that the appropriate hour for such was at hand. Accordingly, the Jews were instructed to remain passively in their exile until such time as there was a divine intervention on their behalf. Those who supported R. Zeira's position apparently dismissed the relevance of the text cited by R. Judah bar Ezekiel to the issue under discussion on the basis that it had been taken out of context.

To offset this criticism, the advocates of R. Judah bar Ezekiel's position resorted to an alternative biblical text, "I adjure you, O daughters of Jerusalem, by the gazelles, and by the hinds of the field, that ye awaken not, nor stir up love, until it please" (Cant. 2:7). The implication of this text, in their view, is that the Jews were supposed to remain patiently in their exile until it pleased God to intervene and bring them back to the Land of Israel. The supporters of R. Zeira rejected this interpretation and countered that the true intent of the admonishment was "that Israel shall not go up [all together as if surrounded] by a wall."[44] That is, Israel should not go up to the Land en masse and by force, as a nation; but it was quite permissible, even desirable, to emigrate there on an individual basis in fulfillment of the Torah's precept concerning residence in the Land. Accordingly, they considered it as completely acceptable for Jews to abandon their places of exile and return to the Land as private persons, and to prepare themselves thereby for the moment of the coming national restoration.

THE TIME TO RETURN

Rejecting this argument, R. Judah bar Ezekiel and his disciples remained unalterably opposed to voluntary emigration to the Land of Israel, even of individuals. Given their position on the issue, how then did they deal with the numerous teachings of other and earlier sages that emphasized the religious centrality and sanctity of the Land of Israel as opposed to the profane lands of the exile, as well as the religious obligation to dwell there? R. Judah responded to the challenge indirectly by dramatically elevating the religious status of the Diaspora. In what amounted to a revolutionary doctrine, he taught: "Whoever lives in Babylon is accounted as though he lived in the Land of Israel; for it is said in Scripture, 'Ho, Zion, escape, thou that dwellest with the daughters of Babylon'" (Zech. 2:11).[45] In his interpretation, the text draws a parallel between Babylon and Zion, suggesting that Zion is portable and not necessarily tied to the Land, at least for as long as it pleased God to keep Israel in dispersion. Because Israel was exiled as a nation from the Land as punishment for its collective failure to live up to the covenant, the individual members of the nation were not to be held personally accountable for failing to fulfill the precept requiring residence in the Land, and continuing to live in the Diaspora even though it was possible for them to return to it. Consequently, R. Judah argued, as the Jews were not under any current religious obligation to return to the Land as individuals, it was desirable that they remain in the Diaspora and patiently await the redemption of the nation as a whole.

It is not clear whether R. Judah bar Ezekiel was deliberately constructing an ideology of exile; His primary concern was with preventing the abandonment of the communities of the Diaspora by its religious scholars. But the net effect of his teaching was to elevate national quietism and passivity to a religious principle.

The views of R. Judah bar Ezekiel and his disciples were widely accepted for the next millenium and a half as the dominant traditional perspective on the matter and the authoritative source for religious arguments against all attempts at nonmessianic redemption and restoration of the nation in its land. These views were articulated most unequivocally in what became known as the doctrine of the three oaths or adjurations [of Cant. 2:7, 3:5, 5:8]: "What was the purpose of those three adjurations? One, that Israel shall not go up [all together as if surrounded] by a wall; the second, that whereby the Holy One, blessed be He, adjured Israel that they shall not rebel against the nations of the world; and the third is that whereby the Holy One, blessed be He, adjured the idolators that they shall not oppress Israel too much."[46] In effect, this doctrine precluded the acceptability of any premessianic attempt to restore the Land to Jewish control, "for if they do, why should the King Messiah come to gather the exiles of Israel?"[47] It required the Jews to suffer the tribulations of exile with equanimity and implied that the gentile nations were somehow bound by a divine obligation not to make those trials too onerous.

In what may perhaps be described as a desperate effort to counteract the influence of R. Judah bar Ezekiel's ideological affirmation of the Diaspora, the advocates of voluntary resettlement in the Land of Israel were able to mount one further argument that posed an exceptional challenge to their opponents, primarily because of its impact on the popular imagination. They invoked the powerful eschatological argument, based on the teaching of the respected sage R. Eleazar, that the final resurrection of the dead would take place exclusively in the Land of Israel. R. Eleazar had stated unequivocally, "The dead outside the Land will not be resurrected," a position that was bolstered by the subsequent teaching of "R. Jeremiah b. Abba in the name of R. Johanan, that whoever walks four cubits in the Land of Israel is assured of a place in the world to come."[48] By implication, those who did not had no such assurance.

These teachings therefore placed a very high premium on emigration to the Land of Israel, even if it were only to die there. This notion regarding the exclusive resurrection of the dead in the Land of Israel was soon extended to include the burial there of those who died in exile. In this regard, we are told that

Rabbi [Judah the Prince] and R. Eliezer were once walking by the gates outside of Tiberias, when they saw the coffin of a corpse which had been brought from without the Land to be buried in Eretz Israel. Said Rabbi to R. Eliezer: What has this man availed by coming to be buried in Eretz Israel when he expired without the Land? I apply to him the verse, "Ye made My heritage an abomination"—during your lifetime—"And ye defiled My Land" (Jer. 2:7)—in your deaths. Yet since he will be buried in Eretz Israel, God will forgive him, he replied, for it is written, "And His land maketh atonement for His people." (Deut. 32:43)[49]

The teaching of R. Eleazar, which went undisputed by his colleagues and therefore was deemed authoritative by later generations, presented a very troubling problem for those who accepted the doctrine of the three oaths, particularly because it provided no exception for the righteous of Israel who died and were buried outside the Land. What would happen to the scholars and other pious men who remained and died in the Diaspora, in accordance with the teachings of R. Judah bar Ezekiel? Would they be denied ultimate resurrection because of their displacement from the sacred center?

It appears that acceptance of the notion of the Land of Israel as the ultimate sacred space, the very gate of heaven, was so strong in the popular consciousness, and the consequent impact of R. Eleazar's view so powerful, that it became necessary for the advocates of remaining patiently in the exile to devise a fantastic solution to the problem of the resurrection of the righteous who died in the diaspora. Thus, R. Elai taught: "[They will be revived] by rolling [to the Land of Israel]. R. Abba Sala the Great demurred: Will not the rolling be painful to the righteous?—Abaye replied: Cavities will be made for them underground."[50] That is, they avoided directly challenging R. Eleazar's teaching by providing a means by which the righteous who died outside the Land would be miraculously transported there for their resurrection. According to R. Simon, God "makes cavities like channels for them in the earth, and they roll along in them until they reach Eretz Israel, when the Holy One, blessed be He, will infuse in them a spirit of life and they will arise."[51] In this manner, their graves in the Diaspora will be directly linked with sacred earth of the Land of Israel. Even so, R. Simeon ben Lakish taught that those who died in the Land of Israel would be resurrected first.[52]

The concern over the question of ultimate resurrection evidently took such hold of the popular imagination, that even those who fundamentally disagreed with R. Eleazar and who held that the righteous would be resurrected wherever they were to be found nonetheless felt it necessary to vindicate their position in terms of R. Eleazar's teaching. Moreover, they had to deal with some biblical passages that seemed to be directly supportive of R. Eleazar's position. For example, the patriarch Jacob, before his death in Egypt, instructed his sons not to bury him there but to take his body back to the Land of Israel (Canaan) for interment. It became necessary for those who disagreed with R. Eleazar to explain this in terms of the theories of R. Elai and Abaye. Thus, one sage was led to remark: "Our father Jacob well knew that he was a righteous man in every way, and, since the dead outside the Land will also be resurrected, why did he trouble his sons? Because he might possibly be unworthy to [roll through] the cavities."[53] The similar instructions of Joseph to the children of Israel, to remove his body to the Land when they returned there from Egypt, was explained in the same manner. The argument, however, does not strike one as very potent, as it tends to place both the patriarch and Joseph in the position of hedging their bets rather than appearing convinced of their ultimate resurrection even in Egypt. The issue of where the resurrection would take place continued to play a prominent role in the religious thought of the medieval period, with some vestiges of the argument lingering into modern times.

4

The National Question in Medieval Jewish Thought

The problem of reconciling the traditional devotion to the Land of Israel with the realities of Jewish life in the Diaspora became ever more troublesome during the Middle Ages. This was especially the case after the rise of Islam and the subsequent Muslim conquest of the entire Middle East, making the prospect of a Jewish national restoration in the Land appear increasingly less likely at any time in the foreseeable future. As a consequence, the controversy regarding the legitimacy of Jewish existence in the Diaspora, which had already received dramatic formulation and expression during the talmudic era, took on new dimensions that affected the character of the subsequent treatment of the issue.

LIFE IN THE DIASPORA

One significant factor affecting the renewed flowering of Jewish cultural life in the Diaspora, at least in the East, was the increased tolerance shown to the Jews by their Muslim rulers, beginning with the reign of the fourth caliph, Ali (656–661). He extended formal recognition to the relative autonomy of Mesopotamian Jewry by authorizing the establishment of two major communal institutions, an exilarchate under Bustenai, which assumed administrative responsibility for the community, and the gaonate under Mar Isaac, which saw to the community's internal religious needs.

Under the authority and influence of the gaonate, rabbinic law and lore began to undergo a renaissance of exposition and development, thereby reaffirming the importance of the Diaspora community as the effective religious and cultural locus of Jewish existence. At the same time, however, the religious authority of the gaonate began to be challenged by a growing number of persons who, perhaps inspired by their engagement in the newly emerging intellectual environment being promoted by the caliphate, increasingly questioned the biblical basis and authority for much of rabbinic legislation. This ultimately led to a schism in the community and the emergence of the Karaites, generally held to have been founded by Anan (ca. 760). The Karaites rejected talmudic law entirely and acknowledged only the validity of biblical law, precipitating an internal struggle within Judaism that was to last for centuries, with some vestiges of this religious conflict remaining evident even in contemporary times.

As a consequence of this and some less significant schismatic tendencies, as well as of other social and cultural perturbations, the centuries immediately following the close of the talmudic period witnessed the emergence of a number of pseudomessiahs and messianic movements that proposed radical changes to traditional Judaism. It is of particular interest that these would-be saviors often displayed an extreme nationalistic fervor that was manifested in a readiness to attempt to conquer the Land of Israel even against insuperable odds, ostensibly in order to restore the nation to its pristine prerabbinic state in its own natural environment. Among these were the messianic movements initiated by Abu Isa al-Isfahani (ca. 680) and Serenus of Babylonia (ca. 720) and that of Judah Judghan of Hamadan (ca. 800).

What was it that drove these movements to nationalist activism while the traditional communities of rabbinic Judaism remained placid, apparently content to await an unequivocal sign from heaven concerning the redemption and restoration of Israel? Joseph Klausner suggested that once these schismatic movements broke with traditional Judaism, they found themselves without communal roots. Therefore, they sought to ground themselves in the ancient soil of Israel, which alone seemed able to offer the promise of a normalized existence for the people.[1] In this regard, it is important to note that the Jews of the Diaspora were unique among groups that had been displaced from their ancient homelands in that the Jews never became fully integrated into the societies of their host lands. Indeed, it was virtually impossible for them to become integrated to any great extent into the environment within which they lived, especially in the religion-dominated societies of the Middle Ages, both Muslim and Christian. They remained a separate and essentially unassimilable nation, nurturing a sentimental attachment to the Land of Israel even though they no longer entertained any serious expectations of an early restoration there.

To counter the messianic arguments and pretensions of these schismatic movements and sects, in particular, the Karaites, as well as those who became so demoralized by the Diaspora as to deny that there was any longer a basis for belief in the coming of the Messiah, Saadia Gaon (892–942) sought to articulate the traditional belief in the Messiah in terms acceptable within the prevailing intellectual currents of his time. He asserted, "Our Master, magnified and exalted be He, has informed us, the congregation of the children of Israel, that He would deliver us from our present state, and gather our scattered fragments from the east and the west of the earth, and bring us to His holy place and cause us to dwell therein, so that we might be His choice and peculiar possession."[2] With regard to when the restoration would take place, he said: "God has set two different limits to our state of subjection. One is the limitation produced by repentance, whereas the other is that occasioned by the end. Whichever of these happens to come first will draw after it the redemption."[3] That is, sincere repentance on the part of the people would induce heaven to act favorably on Israel's behalf in advance of the time already set for its ultimate redemption.

A century later, in North Africa, Hananel ben Hushiel (ca. 980–1056) gave voice to clearly nationalist sentiments as he sought to explain the nature and significance of the phenomena of earthquakes in terms that made them a manifestation of divine concern over the sufferings of Israel in exile. He wrote that earthquakes served to remind "Israel that the Holy One blessed be He has not abandoned or forgotten them, but will some day restore them. In this way their heart will be strengthened lest they despair of redemption, and they will suffer all inflictions until the fulfillment of the time set by the Lord for their life in Exile, just as He announced in advance about their first exile [in Egypt], 'And they shall afflict them four hundred years' [Gen. 15:13]." Hananel insisted that even though the duration of the earlier exile was known, whereas that of the present exile was not, it was nonetheless definitively set to come to an end at some point in time. "That is why the Lord gives certain signs in His world to demonstrate that He encounters some difficulty because of Israel's living a migratory life under foreign domination, but that His mercy has not abandoned them and that some day He will restore them to their pristine glory."[4]

Within the traditional community of rabbinic Judaism, it also became necessary for the advocates of acceptance of the relative normalization of Jewish life in the Diaspora to deal with the ever-troublesome teaching of R. Eleazar regarding the exclusivity of resurrection in the Land of Israel. Perhaps even more important, something had to be done about the fantastic solution to the dilemma proposed by those opposed to voluntary return to the Holy Land, namely, the rolling of the skeletons of the righteous through underground tunnels (*gilgul ha-mehillot*) from the lands of exile to the sacred soil at the time of the resurrection. Although that notion retained a strong grip on the popular imagination, it was clearly an embarrassment to the new generations of Jewish rationalist thinkers that emerged in Spain during the "golden age" of that community.

One of the first to challenge openly the conception of the *gilgul ha-mehillot* at the time of the resurrection was the philosopher Abraham bar Hiyya (d. ca. 1136), who rejected the notion entirely and proposed a radical alternative in its place. Instead of the bones of the dead being miraculously transported to the Land of Israel, he postulated that at the time of the resurrection the Land of Israel would in effect come to the dead in the Diaspora. Implicit in this proposition was the transformation of the notion of the "Holy Land" from constituting the physical sacred center of the Jews to the idea that it represented a conceptual center of sacred space that was not indissolubly linked to a specific and tangible geographic provenance. In this way, by disembodying the conception of the promised land, he proposed to eliminate the deeply rooted yearning for the Land of Israel that had successfully prevented the full normalization of Jewish life in the Diaspora.

Abraham bar Hiyya suggested that during the process of the resurrection, everyone in the world except the righteous would perish: "Then all the dead of Israel in every country will rise from their graves, according to their lot, and will occupy the places of their dwellings, after the disappearance and destruction of the Gentiles from all the lands, and not even one of the wicked of the nations will remain, and risen Israel will inherit the dwellings of the nations." The resurrection of the righteous will thus take place wherever they are to be found, and not only in the Land of Israel, as taught by R. Eleazar.

But Bar Hiyya was not satisfied merely to have made this dramatic assertion. He evidently wanted to create an ideology of exile that would entirely eliminate the centrality of the Land of Israel in Judaism and Jewish national existence, at least in a physical sense, by transforming the notion into a purely spiritual conception. In pursuing this approach, he went even further and effectively declared that the Diaspora was not a punishment for the sins of Israel, as had been taught for more than a millennium, but rather that it had always been an intrinsic element of the divine plan for the world. "For this reason has God dispersed Israel among the nations in every settlement of the earth, to enable them in the future, when they are to rise from their graves, to dwell in their places and to inhabit all the dwelling-places of the earth, and all the lands of the earth will be called 'Land of Israel.' The Land of Israel will then be greatly expanded, so as to fill the entire world."[5]

In Bar Hiyya's view, then, Israel becomes transformed from a national community to a spiritual community that is destined to become universal at the time of the resurrection. He grounds this rather revolutionary doctrine in the controversial prophetic teaching of Jeremiah: "Behold, the days come, saith the Lord, that I will make a new covenant with the house of Israel, and with the house of Judah; not according to the covenant that I made with their fathers in the day that I took them by the hand to bring them out of the land of Egypt" (Jer. 31:30–31). The original covenant was principally concerned with the possession of the Land of Israel, in fulfillment of the promises made to the patriarchs. But that covenant was broken by the children of Israel, when they failed to observe the commandments of the Lord, even though they were given every opportunity of doing so while in possession of their own land. As a consequence, the nation was driven into exile. However, in the postexilic stage, the prophet tells us, the Lord will enter into a new and different covenant with the children of Israel. Jeremiah states, "But this is the covenant that I will make with the house of Israel after those days, saith the Lord, I will put My law in their inward parts, and in their heart will I write it; and I will be their God, and they shall be My people" (Jer. 31:32). Gone is any articulated concern with the promise of the Land. The renewed covenant is thus interpreted as no longer concerned with the well being of the nation in the political sense but only in the purely spiritual sense. As Bar Hiyya observes:

> It does not mention the form of the old spirit, which is removed and replaced with a new spirit . . . because the spirit acquired by the heart in this world did not exist in it at the time of its creation but came from without and is acquired by teaching and training. You can say that it existed potentially, and that it is actualized by training and education; and that, at the time of redemption, God brings out the spirit. . . . And all who will be in the world at that time—namely Israel and all associated with them, as we have learned above—will be united in faith and fear and they will observe all the commandments enshrined in their hearts and uttered by their mouth, and all the world will be upright.[6]

The national focus is replaced entirely by the universal in this formulation.

Indeed, in thus establishing the spiritual legitimacy of the Diaspora, Bar Hiyya even implies that it is spiritually superior to the Land of Israel, whose inhabitants may be considered as further removed from spiritual salvation than those Jews chastened by the exigencies of life in the lands of their exile. "Thus salvation will come immediately after the repentance of Israel in its exile, namely in their hearkening to the voice of the Lord."[7] Moreover, Bar Hiyya proposed that the very concept of exile should now be understood in spiritual rather than national terms. Accordingly, true redemption from the anguish of exile also should not be conceived in a political or geographic sense, but rather as being strictly spiritual in nature: "A man can acquire the world for very little and it is easy to do and involves no effort; it is a question of suppressing your desires so that you should hate the vain pleasures of this world, which cause exertion and sorrow. In this way you will free yourself from the burden of this world and go out from Exile to attain salvation and the Kingdom of God."[8]

Bar Hiyya thus effectively disestablished the Land of Israel as the focus of Jewish national sentiment, substituting for it a spiritual conception of the nation that blends entirely into universality upon its redemption at the appointed hour of repentance and salvation. The Land of Israel is thus spiritualized by him out of tangible existence as an object of national yearning and purpose.

JUDAH HALEVI

A diametrically opposed position on this issue was taken by the great medieval poet and philosopher Judah Halevi (ca. 1075–1141), who was by any measure an outstanding territorial nationalist. Halevi wrote:

> Is it well that the dead should be remembered,
> And the Ark and the Tablets forgotten?
> That we should seek out the place of the pit and the worm,
> And forsake the fount of life eternal?
> Have we any heritage save the sanctuaries of God?—
> Then how should we forget His holy Mount?
> Have we either in the east or in the west
> A place of hope wherein we may trust,
> Except the land that is full of gates,
> Toward which the gates of Heaven are open—
> Like Mount Sinai and Carmel and Bethel,
> And the houses of the prophets, the envoys,
> And the thrones of the priests of the Lord's throne,
> And the thrones of the kings, the anointed?
> Unto us, yea, and unto our children, hath He assigned her.[9]

In sharp contrast to the views of Abraham bar Hiyya, his contemporary, Halevi emphasized the traditional notion of the Land as the ultimate sacred space, the very gate of heaven. He noted that according to tradition, Adam lived and died there. Moreover, "it was also the first object of jealousy and envy between Cain and Abel, when they desired to know which of them would be Adam's successor, and heir to his essence and intrinsic perfection; to inherit the Land, and to stand in connexion with the divine influence."[10] He further envisioned the Land of Israel as the only place where it was possible for the Jews to achieve spiritual perfection, both individually and as a nation, and saw residence there as a necessary goal for every true son of Israel. "Was not Abraham also, and after having been greatly exalted, brought into contact with the divine influence, and made the heart of this essence, removed from his country to the place in which his perfection should become complete?"[11]

Perhaps paraphrasing the stance taken by Abraham bar Hiyya, Halevi asked rhetorically, "What can be sought in Palestine nowadays, since the divine reflex is absent from it, whilst, with a pure mind and desire, one can approach God in any place?"[12] Halevi's response drew a significant distinction between the two aspects of the divine presence, or Shekhinah, which he characterized as the visible and invisible, or spiritual. "The visible Shekhinah has, indeed, disappeared, because it does not reveal itself except to a Prophet or a favoured community, and in a distinguished place." But tradition had taught that one could attain to prophecy only on the sacred soil of the Land of Israel or with regard to it. "Whosoever prophesied did so either in the Land, or concerning it, viz. Abraham in order to reach it, Ezekiel and Daniel on account of it."[13] It was only there that the nation could constitute the favored community, because it was only there that the nation could carry out the divine charges directed to it. "As regards the invisible and spiritual Shekhinah, it is with every born Israelite of virtuous life, pure heart, and upright mind before the Lord of Israel."[14] But the continued presence of the spiritual Shekhinah in no way compensates for the temporary disappearance of the visible divine presence. This means that Israel must strive not to find a way of living without the visible Shekhinah but rather to labor for its return.

Halevi stated, "Palestine is especially distinguished by the Lord of Israel, and no function can be perfect except there." Indeed, a good deal of the divine legislation is devoted exclusively to those who reside within the bounds of the Land. Moreover, "heart and soul are only perfectly pure and immaculate in the place which is believed to be specially selected by God. If this is true in a figurative sense, how much more true in reality." Indeed, for one who wishes to atone fully for his past transgressions, presence in the Land of Israel is essential, as it is only there that one may bring the sacrifices required by the Torah as part of the processes of atonement for one's intentional as well as unintentional sins. Of course, as a practical matter, one is effectively precluded from participating in such a vicarious atonement rite in the absence of the Temple. Nonetheless, as taught by the sages, the tragedy of exile itself may constitute such atonement,[15] "especially if his exile brings him into the place of God's choice."[16]

Halevi concluded his argument with regard to the central importance of the Land of Israel with the affirmation that

This sacred place serves to remind men and to stimulate them to love God, being a reward and promise, as it is written: "Thou shalt arise and have mercy upon Sion, for the time to favour her, yea, the time is come. For thy servants take pleasure in her stones and embrace the dust thereof" (Ps. 102:14). This means that Jerusalem can only be rebuilt when Israel yearns for it to such an extent that they embrace her stones and dust.[17]

For Halevi, then, the redemption of the Land depends principally on the commitment and determination of the Jews themselves to transform it back into their true religious-national center.

MAIMONIDES

Maimonides (1135–1204), the most influential thinker in medieval Jewish history, appears to have been somewhat ambivalent about the the contemporary relevance of the issue. On the one hand, he seems inclined to understate the significance of the need to return to the Land, perhaps a reflection of the practical constraints on the life of the Jew of his time. On the other hand, he strongly reaffirmed the traditional belief in an ultimate restoration of a sovereign Jewish state in messianic times. In this latter regard, Maimonides adopted and restated the position taken by the sage Samuel to the effect that the messianic age would take place within the context of human history. He wrote that the messianic age "would be a time when dominion would be restored to Israel, and they shall return to the Land of Israel." The restoration of which he spoke would clearly be political in nature, with the power and glory of the new commonwealth exceeding even that of King Solomon. "And there will be no change in the order of reality from that which presently exists except that sovereignty shall be restored to Israel."[18] In another place, Maimonides wrote further: "King Messiah will arise and restore the kingdom of David to its former state and original sovereignty. He will rebuild the sanctuary and gather the dispersed of Israel. All the ancient laws will be reinstituted in his days; sacrifices will again be offered; the Sabbatical and Jubilee years will again be observed in accordance with the commandments set forth in the Law."[19]

It is noteworthy that in his codification of the Jewish law, Maimonides, virtually alone among the codifiers, took pains to deal with the entire body of Jewish law that would be applicable only in the Land of Israel, in a sovereign Jewish state, and at a time when there was a restored Temple, conditions that had not existed for more than a millennium at the time that he wrote. Finally, conspicuous by its absence is any reference in the work of the great philosopher and rabbi to the doctrine of the three oaths. Maimonides apparently rejected its validity as a binding doctrine and therefore excluded it from his codification and restatement of the halakhah.

Nonetheless, the doctrine of the three oaths continued to be widely accepted, deferring any hope of national restoration to the messianic age. Some thinkers, such as David Kimhi (ca. 1160–1235), sought to reinterpret the doctrine in a manner that brought it back into the realm of history. Kimhi agreed that only God can bring salvation to man. But, he argued, since it is not within man's capacity to rescue his fellow man from adversity unless such is the wish of God, God evidently exercises his will through man. Therefore, "just as He contrived to bring about the redemption from the Babylonian Exile by means of Cyrus, so will He in the future bring about the redemption of Israel by means of the kings of the nations, who will be inspired to send them [away from their lands to the Land of Israel]."[20] Kimhi thus saw the restoration coming in what would appear to be a natural rather than a providential manner. It would, however, take place through the intervention of the gentile nations, rather than through any overt efforts on the part of the Jews themselves, thereby remaining consistent with the doctrine of the three oaths.

THE KABBALISTS

The emergence of the mystical kabbalist movement at about this same time introduced elements of a new ideology of the Land of Israel that was more in line with the traditional nationalist views expressed by Judah Halevi. In one early kabbalistic work, inquiry is made regarding the meaning of the prophetic phrase, "the whole earth is full of His glory" (Isa. 6:3). The response given is: "This is the earth that was created on the first day. It is on high, filled with God's glory and paralleling the Land of Israel."[21] In this passage we see once again the traditional focus on the role of the Land as sacred space. Some of the early kabbalists, such as Jacob ben Sheshet of Gerona (mid-thirteenth century), invoked the classic view that "the land of Israel lies in the middle of the world, the very navel of the world."[22] Others envisioned the geographical Land of Israel as the physical counterpart of the Shekhinah, calling to mind Halevi's views of the division of the Shekhinah into its spiritual and visible aspects. Some went further and formulated a geosophy, according to which the Land is organically connected to the absolutely divine, which is its exclusive ruler, unlike the other lands, each of which is ruled by an angel. In this approach, the Land of Israel is linked specifically to the divine emanation (sefirah) of Malkhut, or the Kingdom. Gershom Scholem observed:

> The kabbalists of Gerona held that for as long as the exile continues the Sefirot [emanations] do not function normally; as they are withdrawn toward the source of their original emanation, Israel lacks the power to adhere to them truly by means of the Divine Spirit, which has also departed for above.

. . . When the Jewish people still lived in its own land, on the other hand, the divine influx descended from above to below.[23]

Nonetheless, even among the kabbalists of Gerona, attempts were made to dilute the imminent religious significance of the Land of Israel in favor of coming to terms with the reality of the Diaspora. According to R. Ezra of Gerona (d. 1238 or 1245), "Nowadays, the Jews are already exempt from the obligation of dwelling in the Land of Israel, and it is like an atoning altar for them when they suffer, for the love of God, the [vicissitudes] of Exile, and afflictions and the subjugations."[24] In this view, suffering in the exile becomes a surrogate for living in the Land of Israel. Ezra of Gerona does not suggest that the link between the Land of Israel and heaven is severed; only that the fulfillment of the obligation to live in the Land is deferred until the time of the Messiah. Moreover, he held that even after the coming of the Messiah, the Jews must await permission of the gentile rulers in order to emigrate to the Land; they may not do so at their own initiative.

NAHMANIDES AND HIS FOLLOWERS

A far more activist approach to the matter was taken by Nahmanides (1194–1270), who was one of the few major figures among Spanish Jewry actually known to have gone to the Land of Israel for the purpose of settling there. In explaining why, according to the biblical narrative, God destroyed Sodom and Gomorrah but not other equally evil societies, Nahmanides wrote, "You should know that the judgment visited upon Sodom was because of the unique distinction of the Land of Israel as 'the inheritance of the Lord' (II Sam. 20:19), which does not tolerate people who do abhorrent things." That is, Nahmanides maintains, the Sodomites were singled out for divine punishment on account of the distinctiveness and sanctity of the Land, which was destined to be the place of the Holy Temple and which they contaminated by their moral corruption and decay.[25]

By contrast with Ezra of Gerona, who gave the Jews a blanket dispensation from observance of the precept regarding residence in the Land, Nahmanides considered it an unconditional obligation upon the Jew to settle in the Land of Israel because it was only there that one could observe all the mitzvot, which were commanded in order to establish the basis and pattern of Israel's existence in the Land.[26] He saw this as the unequivocal intent of the biblical text: "And ye shall drive out the inhabitants of the land, and shall dwell therein; for unto you have I given the land to possess it" (Num. 33:53).[27]

Nahmanides went further and reaffirmed the eternality of the bond that existed between the Land and the people of Israel. He categorically rejected the notion that this bond could be severed even during the periods when Israel was in exile. Accordingly, he understood the biblical text, "And I will bring the land into desolation; and your enemies that dwell therein shall be astonished at it" (Lev. 26:32), as a message of reassurance for all the communities of the Diaspora, one that assured them in effect

> that their land will never accommodate their enemies. This also constitutes an explicit assurance to us that there is not another land in the whole world that is as good and as blessed as ours, even though it now lies in ruins. [The reason for this is that] since we have left it, the Land has never sustained any other nation or people, many of which have tried to settle it, but all have found it beyond their ability to do so.[28]

In his view, then, the Land of Israel is the unique patrimony of the Jews and rejects all others.

The importance attached by Nahmanides to the possession of the Land is also clearly reflected in his stance in the theoretical halakhic controversy with Maimonides over the nature of the biblical obligation to conquer the Land. Whereas Maimonides took the position that the original conquest under Joshua was carried out for the primary purpose of eliminating the seven Canaanite nations that inhabited the Land, Nahmanides argued that the primary purpose of the conquest was the occupation of the Land itself.

The halakhic principle at issue in this controversy concerns the implications of the biblical obligation to offer peace terms before prosecuting a war. In Maimonides' view, as the purpose of the original conquest was principally to destroy the paganism of the peoples of the Land, if the latter had responded positively to a call for peace, that is, if they had accepted the conditions that would effectively eliminate paganism, then the Israelites would have been prepared to share the Land with them. Nahmanides, in contrast, insisted that the principal purpose of the conquest was the effective occupation of the Land. Therefore, even if the Canaanites had agreed to abandon their paganism for the sake of peace, it would have had no effect on the obligation to take complete and unequivocal control of the Land. In other words, if one were to apply modern categories to this dispute, Maimonides may be understood as adopting the position of cultural nationalism, which seeks cultural domination within a given territory, whereas Nahmanides' perspective reflects an ardent political and territorial nationalism. Indeed, Nahmanides insisted that Maimonides' enumeration of the 613 precepts was deficient because he omitted inclusion of a precept requiring the Jews to reclaim the Land itself, in addition to eliminating the seven Canaanite nations. Moreover, whereas Maimonides qualified the continued applicability of the precept regarding the destruction of the seven nations by characterizing it as no longer operational, Nahmanides insisted that the precept calling for effective occupation of the Land of Israel by the people of Israel has eternal validity and therefore imposes a continuing requirement that every Jew is obligated to fulfill.[29]

Nahmanides also addressed the troubling issue of whether the actions of men to advance the process of national redemption constituted unwarranted meddling in the divinely ordained scheme of things. In his view, such endeavors in no way suggested a lack of faith in the ultimate messianic redemption and restoration. In fact, he asserted, "Although redemption will come as a miracle, man is yet enjoined to contribute his own share and then leave the rest to Heaven." In addition, in what will strike some as clearly prophetic of what would take place in modern times, Nahmanides suggested: "Thus the beginning of Israel's deliverance will come about by means of royal dispensations allowing for a partial ingathering of the Exiles. Only thereafter will the Almighty speed the process along."[30]

The concept of the singularity and centrality of the Land in Judaism is also reflected quite clearly in the work of Nissim Gerondi (ca. 1310–ca. 1375), who wrote in the tradition of Nahmanides. For Nissim too, the spiritual efficacy of the Land was beyond compare. He explained the talmudic teaching that one who lives outside the Land is similar to one who has no God, as meaning that all lands other than the Land of Israel were under the influence of the constellations, whereas the Holy Land alone was directly governed by God himself. As a consequence, anyone who lived outside the Land thereby removed himself from the direct and unmediated influence of the Lord. Consistent with this position, Nissim maintained that the efficacy of prayer outside the Land was necessarily diminished.[31]

The attribution of ultimate theological significance to the Land of Israel is also found in the major theosophical work of kabbalah, the *Zohar*, where the Land is linked directly with the divine in such a manner that, as suggested by Moshe Idel, "the act of dwelling in the Land in the geographical sense bears overt ritualistic significance as a mystical participation in the infra-divine processes."[32] In the *Zohar*, the teaching of the *gilgul ha-mehillot* is restated with approval, further emphasizing the crucial importance of the Land, and is applied in interpretation of the prophetic statement, "Thus saith the Lord God: Behold I will open your graves, and cause you to come up out of your graves, O, My people; and I will bring you to the land of Israel" (Ezek. 37:12). How will this be done? According to the *Zohar*, at the time of the resurrection, "the bodies of the dead outside of the Land of Israel will be formed and will then roll underground to the Land of Israel, where they will receive their souls, but not outside the Land."[33] Moreover, it teaches that the resurrection will take place in the Land of Israel forty years earlier than in the Diaspora, another reflection of the Land's superior status in the eyes of heaven.[34]

The tangibly physical aspect of the Land that is emphasized in the theosophical kabbalah is transmuted into pure spirituality in the school of the ecstatic kabbalah. In the mystical concept of Abraham Abulafia (1240–ca. 1291), the Land of Israel, the only dwelling place of prophecy according to the traditional rabbinic teaching, is effectively equated with the human body, which is itself the actual recipient of prophecy. The idea of the Land of Israel is thus spiritualized completely and removed from any physical and geographical context. In the ecstatic kabbalah, the actual Land of Israel no longer plays a central role in the nation's eschatological future. It is somewhat ironic that Abulafia's teachings seem to have had their greatest influence among those kabbalists who in fact lived in the Land of Israel.

We thus see the consolidation of views in the medieval period on both sides of the issue of the centrality of the Land of Israel, as a practical religious matter as well as from a more abstract and theoretical perspective. However, given the harsh realities of Jewish existence during this period, it should not be surprising that the perspective that realized the greatest following was that which affirmed the validity of Jewish life in the Diaspora. Nonetheless, powerful nationalist voices continued to emerge, forcefully reminding the people of the irreplaceability of the Land as the foundation of the nation. One such advocate of emigration and settlement in the Land, in the tradition of Nahmanides, was Simeon ben Zemah Duran (1361–1444), who made a point of noting that his illustrious predecessor had identified the commandment to live in the Land of Israel as one of the precepts of the Torah that remained eternally valid and operational at all times.

He exploited the occasion of an inquiry directed to him concerning "whether a person who goes to the Land of Israel and enters it is absolved of all his light or serious sins by repentance; and whether in the case of a person who dies on the way to the Land of Israel, his intention atones as if he actually lived in the Land," to articulate his position. In his responsum, Simeon ben Zemah wrote, "A person who wants to repent his sins and wants to go to the Land of Israel, although it is repentance that absolves him, going to the Land of Israel speaks in his favor and saves him from sin all his life." Moreover, he assured his inquirer that even if one did not manage to reach the Land, "a good intention is considered by God as a good deed." In emphasizing the sacral qualities of the Land, Simeon ben Zemah invoked the traditional beliefs regarding the uniqueness of the sacred space of the country. Thus, he noted that "being buried in the Land of Israel is likened to being buried under the altar," a reference to the site of the "foundation stone" and the navel of the earth. He also indicated that the Land "is called 'the beateous land of the living' because people die there without the agony of rolling through tunnels," at the time of the resurrection.[35]

In a similar vein, an anonymous disciple of Nissim Gerondi wrote, commenting on the patriarch Jacob's burial instructions to his sons: "One should always try to be buried in the Land of Israel. . . . And this is because, without doubt, the Land of Israel represents a higher value than all other lands."[36] Moreover, the Land of Israel is unquestionably superior to all other lands "with regard to the matter of the resurrection, and this is because those who die outside the Land attain life through the process of *gilgul ha-mehillot*, but with regard to the Land of Israel it is written: 'And may they blossom out of the city like grass of the earth' (Ps. 72:16)."[37] Indeed, he asserted in another place, "the singular virtue of the Land of Israel over all other lands is that it is only there that the soul is prepared to cleave to the higher light."[38] This concentration on the special character of the Land is also reflected in the work of Isaac Aboab (14th–15th cent.), who wrote:

> The choice place for hearing one's prayers was Jerusalem, when Israel was established on its land, as we learned in the *Pirke de Rabbi Eliezer* [chap. 35] . . . that every one who prays in Jerusalem is reckoned as though he had prayed before the Throne of Glory, for the gate of heaven is open to hear the prayers of Israel. And now, since because of our transgressions we are dispersed in exile, in every place where we offer our prayers we must turn our faces toward the Holy of Holies. And in this land, where we stand to the west of Jerusalem, we must turn our faces to the east toward the Western Wall of the Temple, where the Shekhinah rests.[39]

Thus, even though it may be necessary to reconcile oneself to the temporary reality of exile, it is clearly only by vicarious association with the sacred soil that one can truly establish the link with heaven.

THE LURIANIC KABBALISTS

A rather different approach to the matter is reflected in the work of the Lurianic kabbalists, beginning in the second half of the sixteenth century. Whereas Abraham bar Hiyya had argued that Israel's inheritance of the world was to be the result of the resurrection of the dead, the Lurianic kabbalists went a step further and made this notion an integral aspect of everyday life. Although themselves centered in the Land of Israel, they envisioned the Diaspora not only as a punishment or a curse, but also as a challenge to be met. They drew a direct linkage between the exile of Israel and the original sin of Adam. That transgression had cosmic consequences, causing the diffusion of holy sparks both from Adam's eternal soul and the divine presence, or Shekhinah. Consequently, the gathering together of these holy sparks wherever they were to be found is an essential step in paving the way for the ultimate redemption. This mission was assigned to Israel, which was similarly scattered. Accordingly, as Hayyim Vital (1542–1620) put it, "the ingathering of the exiles itself means the gathering of all the sparks that were in exile."[40]

The Diaspora, because it was regarded as the main arena in which the forces of evil are at work, was to become, even more than the Land of Israel, the battleground for the confrontation between the kabbalists and the *sitra aharah* (the other side). Isaac Luria (1534–1572) taught, "Israel ought to be in Exile in each and every nation, in order to collect the roses of the holy souls which were dispersed among those thorns."[41] This view transformed the necessity of exile into a virtue, endowing the Diaspora with divine significance. The essence of this teaching is given further articulation by Luria's disciple Menahem Azariah da Fano (1548–1620), who stated, "Happy are the penitents, for it was in order to preserve life that God sent them to purify the places to which they have been scattered."[42] As described by the Lurianic kabbalists, the exile begins to take on a new and unprecedented universalist dimension. This is also reflected in the teaching of another Lurianic kabbalist, Naftali Bacharach (17th cent.), who held that the study of Torah purifies the air of the lands in which the Jews live so that, in the future, the whole world will become as pure as the Land of Israel.

The universalist notion of Israel's divinely appointed role in the Diaspora, an idea that has been given new ideological significance in modern times, was perhaps best summarized by the contemporary writer, André Neher:

The *Shekinah* resides with every exiled fragment of the Jewish people. In every particle of land trodden by a Jew in exile the presence of God is revealed. Far from being an outward road leading the Chosen People farther and farther away from the centre of their election, the Exile is for Israel a mission, each stage of which strengthens the bonds between the Jew and the God who accompanies him. It is a mission of the heart; for the universe would be lacking in shape unless Israel were omnipresent, making the Divine sap pulsate through the organism of the cosmos like blood through the body. It is a mission of maintaining God's time; for on the dial of the centuries, each of which marks a different human hour, Israel alone marks the permanent hour of God. Finally it is a mission of *Redemption*; for every land that is reached by the Jew in Exile is also reached by the God who accompanies him; and thus in each field of his Exile the Jew places the seeds, which will one day all together bring forth the Divine harvest throughout the whole earth.[43]

MAHARAL OF PRAGUE

At the same time that the Lurianic kabbalists were propounding a universalist justification of the Diaspora, an antithetical position was being argued by the renowned Judah Loew ben Bezalel (ca. 1525–1609), better known as the Maharal of Prague. He applied the conventional medieval notion of "natural place" to the history of the Jews, with remarkable results. The idea of "natural place" asserted that every object in existence has a particular place that is natural to it. Any such object may temporarily be forced out of its natural place, but eventually it must reassume its natural position or risk total disintegration. Using this concept as a basis, Maharal proceeded to argue that every nation also has its natural place and that the natural place of the Jews is the Land of Israel. Accordingly, the exile and dispersion of the Jews from their ancient homeland is necessarily unnatural. "There is no doubt," he asserted, "that the Diaspora is an aberration from the order established by God, who arranged each nation in its appropriate place, and placed Israel in the place appropriate for them, which is the Land of Israel." Moreover, the dispersion of Israel among the nations must be seen as unnatural because the Jews constitute but a single nation, and it is therefore appropriate for them to be found together, in the same way that we find that other natural phenomena are unified and not segmented. Consequently, Maharal argued, it is only right and proper that the nation of Israel be reunified.

Furthermore, he insisted not only on the reunification of the Jewish people in their land but also on their right to independence and self-determination. He wrote: "It is improper that one nation should be subjected to another, to have a heavy yoke placed upon it, because God created each nation independently. . . . Accordingly, it is proper that each nation, because of its independent creation, should not have the authority of another over it."[44] As for Israel, "when they are in exile, they are like a sick person who is abnormal, because it is unnatural and inconsistent with the processes of the world that one nation should be subjected to another."[45]

Maharal reaffirmed his belief that the Diaspora was but a temporary situation and that the nation of Israel still had the latent power to bring about its own national restoration in the Land of Israel. In his view, the prevailing situation of the Jewish people was extraordinary and could not persist interminably.[46] "There is still the power of unity within Israel even in their exile, and they have not been entirely divided; and because of this residual unifying power, they will yet unite! . . . Indeed, there is a power to unify Israel from out of their Diaspora, and it is because of that unifying power that Israel shall return from its exile."[47]

It is noteworthy that Maharal evidently discarded completely the long-standing doctrine of the three oaths, with which his own position was totally incompatible. This suggests further that the doctrine tended to be invoked by those who wished to affirm the legitimacy of Jewish existence in the Diaspora and rejected by those who wished to reaffirm the importance of the Land of Israel as the natural locus of Judaism and the mission of Israel in history.

5

The Beginnings
of Modern
Jewish Nationalism

The eighteenth century bore witness to a good deal of intellectual ferment in the Jewish community, much of it focused on the notion that the time was arriving for the reconnection of the people of Israel with their ancient homeland in the Land of Israel. It was a period of intense messianic speculation, one that was still reeling from the unsettling effects of the Sabbatean movement of the preceding century, which, as was the case with the schismatic movements of early medieval times, sought a restoration of Jewish sovereignty in Palestine. Beginning early in the new century, a small but steady stream of the followers of Israel Baal Shem Tov (ca. 1700–1760), the founder of modern Hasidism, began making their way to the Land of Israel in order to fulfill the commandment of living in the Land. There they managed to establish a number of communities despite the enormous difficulties they had to overcome in the process.

RENEWED NATIONAL STIRRINGS

It also was during this period that the powerful voice of Jacob Emden (1697–1776) raised the vexing question of why the current exile of the Jews from their homeland had endured for such a protracted period as compared to the nation's earlier experiences of exile. He concluded that the present exile was being prolonged because the Jews had found themselves in a relatively comfortable position in the countries of their domicile and had all but forgotten their connections to the Land of Israel and Jerusalem. From this perspective, the exile endured because the Jews did little to bring it to an end. Moreover, he feared that as the Jews became more accepted in the societies of Europe, the chances of their assimilation and integration would increase dramatically. Consequently, he became a staunch advocate of emigration to the promised land. "What is there for us to do, we poor and downtrodden who reside near the north pole, where the light of the *Shekhinah* never shone, and who are remote from the Holy Land and the holy tongue; we must make every effort and ascend by whatever means of transportation to the lovely country, and neither rain nor snow should prevent us from going to the place of the Service."[1]

In making his case, Emden also rejected the common argument made by the religious leaders of the day that such emigration should be prohibited because it involved significant dangers, and that one should not consciously place his life in jeopardy. Of course there were risks involved, but, in his view, that did not justify complacency. There were often equal risks in remaining in the Diaspora. In effect, Emden called for the Jews to take their destiny as a people in their own hands. In the introduction to his prayerbook, he wrote:

> I am ever amazed that Israel, so stringent with themselves with respect to the minutiae of mitzvoth, which they go to great lengths and expense to observe as perfectly as possible, yet belittles and is indolent with regards this delightful mitzvah, the pin upon which the entire Torah is suspended . . . it behooves every Jew to make a determined resolution to go up and dwell in Eretz Yisrael, at least if he is able to make some kind of a living there.[2]

Additional stirrings of Jewish nationalism took place in the latter half of the eighteenth century, inspired in part by the great rabbi Elijah, the Gaon of Vilna (1720–1797). Most significantly, he laid the basis for a reassertion of the ancient view that the essence of the Jewish religion was intimately related to the Land, and that the possibility of a full Jewish life in the Diaspora was mere illusion. He taught, "The essential fulfillment of the precepts is dependent on the Land, but everyone is obligated to study and become familiar with the performance of the precepts that will be required practice when they come to the Land."[3] That is, the intended context for the observance and performance of the precepts of the Torah was that of the nation dwelling in its own land. In the Diaspora the precepts principally serve an educational and preparatory purpose: The people must learn by practice what will be expected of them when the restoration takes place. Accordingly, it made little sense to seek to legitimize the Diaspora for the sake of the Torah, when it was clear that the Torah was intended to be the constitution of an autonomous Jewish community within the bounds of its own land.

It seems that the very advent of the Gaon appeared to his followers as a sign of the beginning of the messianic age and the restoration of the Jews to the Land of Israel. The Gaon himself made an aborted attempt to emigrate to Palestine in his later years but was forced to turn back because of the hardships entailed in the journey. His dream was subsequently realized by five of his six leading disciples, who emigrated from Eastern Europe to Palestine in the first half of the following century, along with some five hundred followers. This development represented a frontal challenge to the continued validity of the traditional doctrine of the three oaths, the injunctions against hastening the redemption and forcing Israel's way back into its Land.

EMANCIPATION

At about the same time that the Gaon's teachings, and those of his disciples, were stirring the traditional communities of Eastern Europe, an even more dramatic process was placed in motion in the West by the French Revolution of 1789. When the Declaration of the Rights of Man was voted into law by the Revolutionary Assembly in Paris on August 27, 1789, it triggered a sequence of events that was to transform radically the character and direction of Jewish history over the next two centuries.

The declaration, which was to form the ethos of the new France, set forth the basic proposition that all men are born free and equal. However, at the time of its proclamation, this proposition was not conceived as extending to the Jews. The question of its applicability to the Jews was first raised in debate in the assembly on December 21, 1789, and was subsequently tabled by Mirabeau, one of the main proponents of Jewish emancipation, because he could not get enough support at the time to assure a favorable vote on the matter. Nonetheless, the proponents of Jewish emancipation subsequently succeeded in obtaining a favorable outcome after a very unruly debate on January 28, 1790, when civil equality was granted to the Sephardic Jews of France and to the Jews of the Papal States. Equivalent status was not extended to the Ashkenazic Jews of France until September 27, 1791. Following this, the emancipation of the Jews took place as a matter of course wherever the armies of France set foot and, as a consequence of the wars that ensued, it soon extended to much of Western Europe.

Emancipation, however, was not greeted at first by all the Jews of France as a blessing. Many of the Ashkenazim from the communities of Alsace and Lorraine saw in it a clear threat to the internal communal autonomy they had long been granted. Indeed, some of the troublesome implications of emancipation were to be seen reflected in the arguments that had been set forth several years earlier by the philosopher Moses Mendelssohn. In

1781, Mendelssohn had undertaken to refute the stance taken by opponents of the right of the Jews to emancipation and equality of civic status. They took the position that as long as the Jews continued to entertain the hope of an eventual restoration to Zion their loyalties to the country of current residence were justifiably suspect.

Mendelssohn sought to overcome this argument by asserting that it was controverted by the facts. He insisted: "Our hoped-for return to Palestine, a concept so troublesome to Mr. M. [Michaelis, a critic of calls for Jewish emancipation] has no bearing whatever on our attitude to the government. This has been proved by experience, at all times and in all places where Jews have enjoyed a measure of tolerance. It is simply man's nature to love the land where he fares well." Mendelssohn then adduced the traditional doctrine of the three oaths as further evidence that there were no realistic grounds for questioning the alleged dual loyalty of the Jews. He asserted: "Our Talmudic sages had the foresight to emphasize again and again the prohibition to return to Palestine on our own. They made it unmistakably clear that we must not take even a single step preparatory to a return to Palestine, and a subsequent restoration of our nation there, unless and until the great miracles and extraordinary signs promised us in Scripture were to occur."[4]

However, Mendelssohn's restatement of the traditional response to the question of Jewish nationalism failed to satisfy those critics who insisted on seeing unacceptable nationalist implications in Judaism. To deal with this continuing challenge to Jewish emancipation, Mendelssohn radically altered his approach to the issue in his "Jerusalem or On Religious Power and Judaism," which appeared two years later, in 1783. In this essay, he argued forcefully for the principle of separation of church and state. He drew a distinction between the Torah conceived as the constitution of the Jewish state and Torah understood as a set of rules governing the conduct of the individual Jewish life. He conceded that once the Jewish state had ceased to exist, the political functions of the Torah were no longer applicable. In contrast, the precepts of the Torah governing man's personal conduct of life remained in full effect. But if the political aspects of the teachings of the Torah were no longer operational, what was the meaning of the concept of messianic redemption that played such a prominent role in Jewish belief? Mendelssohn responded to this challenge by imputing new content to the messianic concept. In his view, the idea of a messianic restoration was henceforth to be understood not in Jewish nationalist terms but rather as the realization of that diaspora condition wherein the Jews would be permitted to enjoy full civic rights and religious freedom in the lands of their residence. In effect, emancipation itself was now conceived as the redemptive messianic act, without any reference to the idea of an ultimate restoration in the Land of Israel.

Mendelssohn thus sought to resolve the problem of dual loyalty by striking what he evidently considered a fine balance between the traditional messianic expectation of national redemption and the need to find an acceptable modus vivendi for the Jews among the nations during the interim period. However, as a practical matter, his approach seemed to redefine the former out of existence in order to facilitate the latter. Moreover, emancipation on the basis of Mendelssohn's formulations regarding the separation of church and state and the denial of Jewish nationality also meant the undermining of the internal Jewish communal authority that had helped the people survive as Jews through centuries of adversity. Who could say for certain, that once Jewish communal cohesiveness and internal autonomy were uprooted, a new wave of anti-Semitism might not bring an end to Jewish emancipation, leaving the people more exposed and vulnerable than ever? Furthermore, who could predict with confidence the effects of emancipation on the religious culture and practices of the Jews, that is, once they were no longer living within the context of a relatively autonomous communal structure? Acceptance of emancipation was thus seen by many as a desperate gamble, not as something to be taken lightly or as a matter of course. The experience of the ages urged caution.

When the Jewish question was under discussion in the National Assembly in Paris in 1789, Stanislas Clermont-Tonnerre, one of the protagonists of Jewish emancipation, declared: "The Jews must be refused everything as a nation; they must be granted everything as individuals. . . . They must constitute neither a political body nor an order within the State. They must be citizens individually. . . . One cannot accept a society of noncitizens within the State and a nation within a nation." In his view, it was reasonable that the Jews be considered as members of a religious confession, something that did not negate their being loyal Frenchmen in all other respects. However, Abbe Maury, speaking for the opposition, based his arguments against emancipating the Jews on the conviction that "the name Jew denotes not a religious sect but a nation" and that a Jew who remained faithful to his national traditions could not be a Frenchman. Both liberals and conservatives were thus in agreement that the Jew had to renounce his nationality in order to be entitled to equal civic rights. He could be permitted to remain a Jew in religion if he became a Frenchman by nationality. The only significant difference between the two positions appears to have been that the liberals believed that such national assimilation was possible and they therefore felt vindicated in their demand for equal rights for the Jews, whereas the conservatives did not believe that it was possible that the Jews would truly abandon their traditional national aspirations. As a result, the conservatives remained adamantly opposed to granting full emancipation to the Jews.

As already suggested, this dichotomy of views regarding the implications of Jewish emancipation was also reflected within the Jewish community itself. The Ashkenazic Jewish leaders of Alsace-Lorraine, for example, were particularly reluctant to lend their wholehearted support to the drive for emancipation. They found themselves torn between their anticipation of the positive civic benefits that were to be derived from emancipation and their fear of its unforeseen consequences for the coherence and viability of their communities. As a result, many sought to limit the degree of emancipation; they wanted a compromise arrangement that would acknowledge the validity of the traditional national aspects of Judaism and therefore leave the existing autonomous communal structures intact. A petition to this effect was submitted to the assembly on August 31, 1789, in the name of the Jews of eastern France. However, such equivocation on a matter of fundamental principle was deemed quite unacceptable; the National Assembly had little inclination to accord any degree of civic legitimacy to what amounted to a nation within the nation. If and when granted, emancipation was to be complete and unequivocal, as was the loyalty to the French nation that was expected in return.

In some respects, the worst fears of those Jewish leaders who were hesitant about supporting complete emancipation were soon to be realized. As the walls of isolation came down, the pillars of communal authority were toppled as well and the Jewish community underwent a traumatic culture shock. The sudden transition from a situation in which the Jews had no civic rights at all to a condition of full citizenship brought on a wave of assimilation that threatened to engulf most of emancipated Jewry. At the same time, as the French conservatives had feared, many tradition-oriented Jews simply failed to draw the desired distinctions between the national and religious elements of Judaism. They thus sought to conceal their national sentiments under the guise of the religion, for example, continuing to avoid intimate social contact and intermarriage with their Gentile neighbors, a situation that aroused the ire of French nationalists, both liberal and conservative. The latter were determined not to permit the Jews to get away with this sort of equivocation for very long.

The issue of Jewish nationhood thus continued to be a matter of serious public contention, and in 1806, Napoleon Bonaparte decided to bring the matter to a head. He convened an assembly of Jewish notables for the purpose of clarifying the national and religious status of the Jews once and for all. The assembly that was brought into being in conformity with the Decree of May 30, 1806, included some of the most prominent spokesmen for the various tendencies and segments within the Jewish community and consisted of both religious and lay leaders.

In accordance with Napoleon's specific instructions, a list of twelve questions was presented to the assembly, most of which dealt with matters of marriage, the rights and jurisdiction of the rabbinate, the professions forbidden by Jewish law, and the permissibility of the practice of usury. However, of particular importance were the fourth, fifth, and sixth questions, which were clearly intended to address the issues of Jewish nationality, although this was not stated explicitly. They were as follows: "In the eyes of Jews are Frenchmen considered as brethren or as strangers? In either case what conduct does their law prescribe towards Frenchmen not of their religion? Do the Jews born in France, and treated by the law as French citizens, acknowledge France as their country? Are they bound to defend it? Are they bound to obey the laws, and to follow the directions of the civil code?"[5]

Napoleon's approach to dealing with the Jewish question was quite different from that of the National Assembly, which had granted the complete emancipation of the Jews in 1791. The assembly had been interested primarily in the status of Jews as individuals within French society. Napoleon, in contrast, conceived of the Jews principally as a national entity and was concerned about defining the relationship of the Jewish nation to France. In his view, emancipation had not fundamentally changed the national character of the Jews. His primary interest, therefore, was not in whether Jews, as individuals, were good citizens but whether the existence of the Jewish nation in France was compatible with French national interests. The real issue was whether Jews, as members of the Jewish nation and notwithstanding their affirmative protestations, could be loyal citizens of France. There was evidently little question in Napoleon's mind that the Jews constituted a distinct nation. Thus, as noted by Franz Kobler:

> The Notables were not asked whether the Jews considered themselves a separate nation but whether their supposed national existence could be reconciled, according to the valid Jewish law, with the exigencies of an immediate and all-embracing participation in the life of a non-Jewish nation. The question of whether the Jews regarded Frenchmen as their brethren or as aliens did, therefore, by no means concern the feelings of single Jewish men and women. It was a question of supranational law and politics referring to the Jews in general, not merely to the French Jews.[6]

The questionnaire was given to the assembly of Jewish notables on July 29, 1806, and a response was provided several days later, drafted primarily by Rabbi Joseph David Sinzheim of Strasbourg. The assembly's response succeeded in allaying Napoleon's concerns by asserting that Jews considered France their fatherland and Frenchmen their brethren. In the words of the response, "At the present time, when the Jews no longer form a separate people, but enjoy the advantage of being incorporated with the

Great Nation, (which privilege they consider as a kind of political redemption) it is impossible that a Jew should treat a Frenchman, not of his religion, in any other manner than he would treat one of his Israelitish brethren."[7] Moreover, it was asserted that those Jews who were citizens of France had no loyalties to any other state, and their relation to fellow Jews in England, for example, in no way impinged on their loyalty and patriotism as Frenchmen.

The emperor may have been satisfied with the Jewish professions of loyalty, but he did not change his views with regard to the central issue of Jewish nationhood. There is a certain irony in the fact that although Napoleon insisted that the Jews were a nation, many Jews took pains to deny it unequivocally. Nonetheless, Napoleon proceeded to deal with the Jews under the assumption that they were indeed a distinct nation. In consonance with his dream of a universal empire centered in Paris, he conceived of a grandiose scheme in which he himself played the role of a new Moses, destined to bring the dispersed nation of Israel under a common head, his own. For this purpose he wished to see the French capital serve as the New Jerusalem, the political and cultural center of the reconstituted Jewish nation. There, in emulation of the great lawgiver, he would undertake to issue a new dispensation for the Jews of the new era that he would initiate. Accordingly, on August 23, 1806, Napoleon decreed that a Great Sanhedrin be convoked to enact legislation that was to govern the lives of the Jews of France, Germany, Italy, Portugal, and Spain. Napoleon had it made clear to the members of the assembly of notables "that I desire to employ all means in order to bring it about that the rights which have been restored to the Jewish people may not become illusory and finally to make them find Jerusalem in France."[8]

Delayed by the outbreak of war, the Great Sanhedrin was finally convened in Paris in February 1807. Notwithstanding Napoleon's desires with regard to the future of the Jewish nation, the Sanhedrin, which survived as an institution for little more than two years, took a radically different approach to the matter. Its members declared that "from now on the Jews are no longer a nation since the honor had been bestowed on them to become part of the great [French] nation and they see in this their full political liberation." Thus, instead of becoming a proponent of Napoleon's plans to revitalize the Jewish nation, the Sanhedrin adopted what had become a typical polemical argument during the era of emancipation; namely, it characterized Israel exclusively in terms of being merely a common religious community rather than a single people, let alone a distinct nation. Similarly in the other Western European countries, the Jews achieved their emancipation either through comparable open renunciations of their nationality or by a silent though tacit acquiescence in its denigration.

For a large segment of the Jewish masses, however, emancipation was seen not as a legitimate righting of long-standing wrongs perpetrated against the Jewish people, but rather as a privilege granted by the Christian nations in return for Jewish national self-destruction. As a result, many among the first generation of emancipated Jews accepted their new nationality in name only and persisted in maintaining their traditional Jewish national identity in private. However, the attractions of integration into the surrounding society were such that, among subsequent generations, assimilation increasingly came to be considered as a desirable practical option, even though many continued to lead dual lives as they struggled to suppress their own national individuality in favor of that of the host nation. As Simon Dubnow pointedly remarked:

> "Assimilation" of this kind was but a change in form—and a morally inferior one—of the previous state of bondage of the Jews. The Jew of the Middle Ages bent only his back before his oppressors, but he never dealt falsely against himself nor did he ever renounce one iota of his national rights. The modern Jew, however, who had been given the opportunity to become a proud member of the society of peoples, bartered away his soul and perverted his national type so that he could be like the ruling nationality. This is nothing but a change in the form of servitude, the substitution of inner for external humiliation.[9]

IN THE UNITED STATES

At the same time that Western European Jewry was struggling to shed its national traits, Napoleon's perception of the Jews as a nation rather than merely as a religious sect struck a responsive chord across the ocean, in the United States. Perhaps arrogating to himself Napoleon's aspiration to be the new Moses, according to some critics, the prominent American Jewish leader Mordecai Manuel Noah (1785–1851) spoke of the future of the Jewish nation in a "Discourse Delivered at the Consecration of the Synagogue Shearith Israel" in New York on April 17, 1818. Recognizing that it would take some time before the nation could be restored in its ancient homeland, he proposed, as an interim step, that Zion be temporarily reestablished in the United States. "Until the Jews can recover their ancient rights and dominions, and take their ranks among the governments of the earth, this is their chosen country; here they can rest with the persecuted of every clime, secure in person and property, protected from tyranny and oppression, and participating [in] equal rights and immunities." He took note that the seven million Jews of the world in his time represented a greater number than at any earlier period of Israel's history and possessed greater wealth, influence, and talents than any equivalent body of people to be found on earth. He saw in them the instrument of their own national salvation as well as that of Europe itself. "The signal for breaking the Turkish scepter in Europe, will be their emancipation; they will deliver the north of Africa from its oppressors; they will assist to establish civilization in European Turkey, and may revive commerce and the arts in Greece; they will march in triumphant numbers, and possess themselves once more of Syria [Palestine], and take their rank among the governments of the earth." Noah assured his listeners that all this was well within the realm of real possibility and not mere fancy. He was confident that the Jews of Europe and North Africa were ready for such a step. "They hold the purse strings, and can wield the sword; they can bring 100,000 men into the field. Let us then hope that the day is not far distant when, from the operation of liberal and enlightened measures, we may look towards that country where our people have established a mild, just, and honorable government, accredited by the world, and admired by all good men."[10] This was indeed a far cry from the traditional notion of messianic redemption and restoration.

Noah soon conceived of a plan to prepare the Jews for a renewal of their national existence by establishing a Jewish colony in New York State. At the beginning of January 1820, Noah requested that the state government authorize the sale of Grand Island, in the Niagara River, near Buffalo, for the purpose of establishing a settlement to be named "Ararat." That was to be the base from which the newly revitalized nation would emerge. Although Ararat was subsequently established formally on September 15, 1825, it never took hold and the project soon collapsed, after receiving a generally hostile reception from the leaders of European Jewry. Nonetheless, Noah stands out as the first proponent of a modern Jewish state in the nineteenth century. Moreover, in sharp contradistinction to many advocates of the Jewish state idea that arose later, Noah's conception was based not on the idea of finding a solution to the problem of oppression and persecution of the Jews but rather on an inner recognition that the future of Israel demanded a political restoration of the nation in Palestine.

In 1837, Noah asserted: "Our learned Rabbis have always deemed it sinful to compute the period of the restoration; they believe that when the sins of the nation were atoned for, the miracle of their redemption would be manifested. My faith does not rest wholly in miracles—Providence disposes of events, human agency must carry them out." He opposed the classic passivity of the Jews regarding their own destiny. "The Jewish people must now do something for themselves; they must move onward to the accomplishment of that great event long foretold—long promised— long expected; and when they do move, that mighty power which has for thousands of years rebuked the proscription and intolerance shown to the Jews, by a benign protection of the *whole* nation, will still cover them with his invincible standard." He was convinced that the time was ripe for the reconstitution of the nation in the Land. The Ottoman Empire was in dire political and financial straits, with the pasha of Egypt, Muhammad Ali, making claims on both Syria and Palestine. Noah was confident that a deal could be struck with the latter whereby "Syria will revert to the Jewish nation by *purchase*." He asserted that "the facility exhibited in the accumulation of wealth, has been a providential and peculiar gift to enable them, at a proper time, to re-occupy their ancient possessions by the purse-string instead of the sword." Once this initial step was taken, the ingathering of the exiles would occur as a matter of course. "Once again unfurl the standard of Judah on Mount Zion, the four corners of the earth will give up the chosen people as the sea will give up its dead, at the sound of the last trumpet."[11]

It is interesting to note that Noah, a man of affairs with practical political experience, saw the time as ripe for a restoration of the Jewish state with the support of Great Britain and France on explicitly geopolitical grounds. He observed that Turkey was under continuing pressure because of the growing power of Russia, at a time when Muhammad Ali was extending his sway over the Red Sea region. These encroachments clearly threatened the security of the British Empire in Asia. Accordingly he argued:

An intermediate and balancing power is required to check this thirst of conquest and territorial possession, and to keep in check the advances of Russia in Turkey and Persia, and the ambition and love of conquest of Egypt. This can be done by restoring Syria to its rightful owners, not by revolution or blood, but as I have said, by the purchase of that territory from the Pacha of Egypt, for a sum of money too tempting in its amount for him to refuse, in the present reduced state of his coffers. . . . Under the co-operation and protection of England and France, this re-occupation of Syria within its old territorial limits, is at once reasonable and practicable.[12]

Noah's increasingly secular nationalist orientation is perhaps nowhere better demonstrated than in his "Restoration Discourse" of 1844. The Damascus affair of 1840, involving a blood libel followed by a pogrom, had elicited worldwide expressions of concern about the fate of the Jews. However, the new focus being placed on the Jews generated concerns within the stricken community that there would be a renewed effort by the Christians to remove the cause of Jewish persecution through religious conversion. Noah sought to allay such fears by arguing that there was little danger from this source, but that "there is danger I admit—danger not from Christians, but from ourselves. Danger from apathy, from indifference—danger from a want of nationality." He insisted that the general

Jewish indifference to religion precluded it from being able to inspire Jews to make significant sacrifices for it. From that point of view, he was perhaps the first major advocate of secular Jewish nationalism, although it would take another generation before his message was picked up and further developed in Europe. In a remarkable statement, Noah laid out the rationale for the Jewish national political movement that was to emerge toward the end of the nineteenth century.

> The Jews want *nationality*; you cannot rally them on any given point; you cannot inspire them either with faith or enthusiasm. We pray fervently and constantly to be restored to Zion; we believe in the coming of the Redeemer, and pray earnestly for his coming; and yet talk to the mass of our people on the Restoration—on their return to Jerusalem—and they express no confidence in it; few would be willing to go; and the coming of our Redeemer— the advent of our Messiah—seems to give them no trouble, no solicitude at all. They pray for him from habit, and have no faith in what they pray for. What is the cause of all this discrepancy between assertion and belief? The want of nationality, I again repeat: we are a sect, not a nation. The Greeks remained two thousand years in slavery, and yet they arose and redeemed their country. Why should not the Jews do the same? Christians would honor us even if we failed. Nothing therefore in my opinion will save the nation from sinking into oblivion but *agitating this subject of the Restoration*. We should pass the word around the world—"Restoration of the Jews"— "Justice to Israel"—"the Rights and Independence of the Hebrews"—"Restore to them their country"—"Redeem them from captivity."[13]

REACTIONS IN EUROPE

In the meantime, the question of Jewish nationality became a major issue within the European Jewish community as the emerging Reform movement sought to purge Judaism of its nationalistic contents, including the belief in the Messiah and redemption in the form of national restoration (see Chapter 7). In an attempt to bridge the gap between the national implications of traditional messianism and the promise of emancipation, Samson Raphael Hirsch (1808–1888), the founder of neo-Orthodoxy, argued in 1836 that it was not necessary for the Jews to deny themselves the opportunities for civic advancement in order to retain their ancient faith in its traditional forms. On the contrary, he asserted, "It is our duty to join ourselves as closely as possible to the state which receives us into its midst, to promote its welfare and not to consider our well-being as in any way separate from that of the state to which we belong." In his view, this was perfectly consistent with the spirit of Judaism: Even when Israel had its own sovereign state, political independence was never an end in itself but only a means by which to fulfill Israel's spiritual mission.

Accordingly, he argued, "Land and soil were never Israel's bond of union, but only the common task of the Torah; therefore, it still forms a united body, though separated from a national soil; nor does this unity lose its reality, though Israel accept everywhere the citizenship of the nations amongst which it is dispersed." He held that the concept of the nation of Israel, at least until the ultimate national redemption took place in the messianic age, was devoid of temporal political or territorial significance and was entirely spiritual in content. Moreover, although Jews continue to pray for the long-awaited day when "the Almighty shall see fit, in His inscrutable wisdom, to unite again His scattered servants in one land, and the Torah shall be the guiding principle of a state, an exemplar of the meaning of Divine Revelation and the mission of humanity," they remained enjoined by the doctrine of the three oaths from taking any steps to realize such a goal on their own initiative. "Actively to accelerate its coming [would be] sin, and is prohibited to us."[14]

Nonetheless, the enthusiasm that was generated as an outcome of the general sprouting of nationalism in Europe infected some traditional rabbinic thinkers as well, forcing them to reexamine the premises of their long-standing faith in messianic redemption in the light of contemporary social and political realities. As noted earlier, this process was initiated at the beginning of the century by the disciples of the Vilna Gaon. In what was perceived at the time to be a revolutionary doctrine, they asserted that the coming redemption would not be entirely miraculous in nature and would require human assistance. Thus, Judah Halevi Edel wrote in 1819 that because no overt miracles had occurred during the restoration of the Second Commonwealth, there was no reason to expect any to take place during the third period of redemption either. Instead, he asserted, "in the future, the matter will be carried out in a natural way, without miracles."[15] Moreover, Aviezer of Tykocin argued some years later that the longtime prohibition against accelerating the redemptive process did not apply during "favorable periods"; at such times one was not only permitted but actually obligated to do so to the extent possible. A somewhat different rationale was offered by Israel of Shklov, who argued that the traditional prohibitions against hastening the redemption were conditioned on the prior agreement of the gentile nations with God not to treat the people of Israel too harshly. As these nations clearly violated their part of the bargain, the Jews were no longer obligated to abide by it either.[16] In effect, these disciples of the Gaon nullified the doctrine of the three oaths, even though it continued to dominate the thinking of much of the traditional Jewish world.[17]

Prompted in no small measure by the traumatic events of 1840, Judah Hai Alkalai (1798–1878), the rabbi of Semlin, in Serbia, reached the conclusion that the time had come for the Jewish people to take their destiny into their own hands. This obviously ran counter to the prevailing view among traditionalists that one must not attempt to force the end of days and thereby hasten the messianic redemption. Accordingly, in his book *Minhat Yehuda* (The offering of Judah), published in 1845, building on the work of the disciples of the Gaon, Alkalai undertook to revise fundamentally the long-accepted traditional conception of the character of the messianic redemption.

Grounding his argument in traditional sources, in typical rabbinic fashion, Alkalai asserted that the Messiah was not to be expected to appear suddenly, to be followed by a mass redemption of the Jewish people and their immediate transfer to the Holy Land, as had occurred in the days of Joshua. Because of Israel's sins, the coming redemption would necessarily be different in nature, requiring a number of steps that would have to be taken in advance of the momentous event. For one thing, the Land of Israel was largely uninhabited and uncultivated, without adequate shelter, food, and water to meet the needs that would be generated by the forthcoming ingathering of the exiles. Indeed, the current state of the country made a mass settlement there virtually impossible. Before such a settlement became feasible, houses would have to be built, wells dug, and crops planted. It was also necessary, Alkalai suggested, that some stay behind in the Diaspora to assist those who emigrated first. In this regard, the Lord "desires that this redemption be carried out properly and with dignity; therefore we are enjoined from emigrating en masse, so that we should not have to live like tent-dwellers all over the fields. Instead we are to go slowly until our Land is built up and prepared."[18]

Furthermore, Alkalai argued, there were also cultural factors that presented obstacles to the redemption, and this circumstance required that certain additional preparatory steps be taken. There was no question that "our greatest need is to gather our dispersed from the four corners of the earth to become a single society because, as a consequence of our transgressions we are very scattered and separated from one another, each Jewish community using a different language and script as well as different customs that divide the collectivity and impede the redemption." Consequently, even if all the Jews of the world were suddenly to be gathered together in the Land, they would be unable to communicate with one another and the enterprise would fail. Alkalai also rejected the suggestion that this problem might be solved miraculously at the time of the redemption by each person's being given knowledge of the language necessary for communication with all fellow Jews. Moreover, even though it seemed impossible that Hebrew, the historical language of the Jews, could be resuscitated by natural means, "we must not despair, but rather maximize our efforts to resurrect our language and make it the principal [means of communication]." In this manner, the groundwork for the redemption will be properly prepared. As Alkalai argued: "This sort of thing is not accomplished by a miracle, and it is almost impossible to imagine a true revival of our Hebrew tongue by natural means. But we must have faith that it will come . . . we must not despair. We must redouble our efforts to maintain Hebrew and strengthen its position. It must be the basis of our educational work."[19]

To justify this change from the long-standing interpretation of the manner of the messianic redemption, Alkalai invoked the ancient tradition of the two Messiahs. In this version of the tradition, the Messiah son of David is to be preceded by a forerunner, the Messiah son of Joseph. The latter will pave the way for *the* Messiah by reconquering the land from its occupiers, but he will fall in battle. Then, the Messiah son of David will appear and bring the children of Israel back to the Holy Land. Alkalai audaciously suggested that the appearance of the Messiah son of Joseph, whose work is of a prosaic nature, that is, the reconquest of the Land, is a symbolic reflection of the need for practical secular activity to prepare the conditions for the ultimate coming of the Messiah. In other words, the Messiah son of Joseph was not to be conceived as a heroic individual but rather as a historic process wherein the appointment of an assembly of elders would, in effect, initiate the "beginning of the redemption." These elders would eliminate the existing distinctions between the Ashkenazic and Sephardic communities, forging them into one coherent society. Thus, "this assembly of elders constitutes the Messiah son of Joseph for whom we aspire."[20]

The essence of the position taken by Alkalai on the nature of the coming redemption was also adopted by Zvi Hirsch Kalischer (1795–1874), rabbi of the community of Thorn, in the province of Posen. Like Alkalai, Kalischer, in his book *Drishat Zion* (Seeking Zion), published in 1862, sought to demystify at least the initial stages of the redemption. Thus, he wrote:

The Redemption of Israel, for which we long, is not to be imagined as a sudden miracle. The Almighty, blessed be His Name, will not suddenly descend from on high and command His people to go forth. Neither will He send the Messiah from heaven in the twinkling of an eye, to sound the great trumpet for the scattered of Israel and gather them into Jerusalem. He will not surround the Holy City with a wall of fire or cause the Holy Temple to descend from heaven. The bliss and the miracles that were promised by His servants, the prophets, will certainly come to pass—everything will be fulfilled—but we will not run in terror and flight, for the Redemption of Israel will come by slow degrees and the ray of deliverance will shine forth gradually.[21]

Kalischer insisted that this understanding of the redemptive process was already set forth in the prophecy of Isaiah: "And it shall come to pass in that day, that the Lord will set His hand again the second time to recover the remnant of His people, that shall remain from Assyria and from Egypt" (Isa. 11:11). Kalischer maintained that the prophet was surely telling us that there were to be two stages in the redemptive process: "The function of the first will be to pioneer the land, after which Israel will blossom forth to a most exalted degree."[22] He concluded his argument with a citation from the fourteenth-century treatise by Rabbi Meir Ibn Al-Dabi, *Shevilei Emunah* (Paths of faith):

> When many Jews, pious and learned in the Torah, will volunteer to go to the Land of Israel and settle in Jerusalem, motivated by a desire to serve, by purity of spirit, and by love of holiness; when they will come, by ones and twos, from all corners of the world; and when many will settle there and their prayers will increase at the holy mountain in Jerusalem—the Creator will then heed them and hasten the Day of Redemption.[23]

In this view, redemption was contingent upon Jewish resettlement in the Holy Land, and Kalischer was emphatic about the urgency of taking steps in this direction. Aware that strides were being made by other nations, he admonished the Jewish public:

> Why do the people of Italy and of other countries sacrifice their lives for the land of their fathers, while we, like men bereft of strength and courage, do nothing? Are we inferior to all other peoples, who have no regard for life and fortune as compared with love of their land and nation? . . . We should be ashamed of ourselves! All the other peoples have striven only for the sake of their own national honor; how much more should we exert ourselves, for our duty is to labor not only for the glory of our ancestors but for the glory of God who chose Zion![24]

While men like Noah, Alkalai, and Kalischer grappled with the need to modify the quietist attitudes that had dominated traditional Jewish thought since talmudic times, they also clearly laid the groundwork for a secular approach to the problem. That approach was more in keeping with the tenor of the latter part of the nineteenth century.

BEGINNINGS OF SECULAR NATIONALISM

The concept of a Jewish nationalism that was secular in nature struck a responsive chord in Moses Hess (1812–1875), a prominent pre-Marxian socialist and writer on politics and philosophy. Hess had been shocked by the Damascus affair into a recognition of the urgent need for the Jews to begin to take control of their own destiny. He undertook a critical appraisal of the national consequences of emancipation, which led him to a completely unanticipated conclusion. Hess, notwithstanding his deeply ingrained secularism, determined that the ceding of Jewish national identity in exchange for the benefits of civic emancipation was not a very good bargain. There was, he found, a fundamental and enduring value in the nationalist aspects of Judaism, which the Jewish people could ill afford to ignore or squander.

Hess wrote in 1840: "The proper understanding of this persecution of Jews must evoke a return to Judaism." He derided "our brothers, who for the sake of emancipation would like to persuade themselves and others that modern Jews no longer feel any trace of nationalism." Moreover, he argued: "As long as the Jew endured every persecution and every humiliation as God's punishment, confident of the future resurrection of his nation, his pride could not be hurt. His only mission was to preserve himself and his race for a future which will compensate his nation for all the injury it has suffered and reward for its faithfulness. But our enlightened Jews no longer possess this faith and this hope." It had been readily sacrificed by them as part of the price of emancipation. Hess, however, was convinced that the price was too high, and that the promise of civic progress would ultimately prove of little avail to the Jew. "As long as the Jew will deny his nationalism because he does not possess that altruism necessary to confess his solidarity with a persecuted and derided people, his false position must continually become more unbearable." Hess rejected the premise that the Jew would gain acceptance among the gentiles as a consequence of his readiness to abandon the nationalist traditions of his forefathers. He suggested instead that it was the traditional Jew, who clung to his faith, rather than the reforming modernist that had the truer grasp of reality.

> In spite of all enlightenment and emancipation, the Jew of the Diaspora who denies his nationalism will still not win the respect of the nations. He may well be able to become naturalized in their midst as a citizen but he will not be able to free himself from solidarity with his own nation. Not so the old pious Jew who would rather have his tongue torn out than misuse it to deny his nationalism! It is the modern Jew who is the contemptible one; it is he who denies his nationality, just when the hand of fate lies heavily upon his nation.[25]

The implications of his polemic against the complacency of his fellow enlightened Jews, especially in the face of the tragedy that was engulfing their coreligionists in Syria, contradicted much of Hess's earlier socialist values and ideas and caused him to undertake a fundamental reconsideration of his worldview. It was evidently a painful process for him. It would take another two decades before he once again turned to the question with renewed conviction, giving fuller expression to his own Jewish national consciousness.

In his *Rome and Jerusalem* (1862), Hess attempted to reinterpret the traditional messianic idea in terms of an idealistic nationalism. As part of this endeavor, he sought to elucidate a higher spiritual meaning of nationality in world history. Each people, he argued, has its own function or mission in the development of humankind. From the very outset, the Jews "conceived their historic mission to be the sanctification not only of man's individual life but also his social life. It was their aim to further the development of mankind and to prepare it for that harmony and unity of life which is the final aim of social evolution—a Messianic State which should measure up to the revealed divine essence of its spirit and be worthy of its holiness."[26] Hess thus conceived the goal of Judaism, in a manner fully consistent with traditional Jewish thought, as being the ultimate realization of the essential principles of social justice within the context of an organized and unified humanity. Accordingly, he asserted: "Judaism is no passive religion, but an active knowledge, which is organically related to Jewish nationalism. Judaism is, above all, a nationality whose history, outlasting millennia, goes hand in hand with that of humanity."[27]

Hess was vehemently opposed to both assimilation and the assimilationist tendencies of the growing movement for religious reform (see Chapter 7) in Judaism because of their perceived negative effects on the modern development of Jewish nationalism. In terms truly remarkable for a secularist, Hess wrote: "The pious Jew is before all else a Jewish patriot. The 'new-fangled' Jew who denies Jewish nationalism is not only an apostate, a renegade in the religious sense, but a traitor to his people and to his family. Should it prove true that the emancipation of the Jews is incompatible with Jewish nationalism, then the Jew must sacrifice emancipation." Hess went much further and conceptualized Judaism itself as the embodiment of Jewish nationalism. He asserted: "All the Jews' feasts and fasts, their reverence for traditions which amounts to an apotheosis of everything hebraic, the whole Jewish religion, and its complete dominance of the domestic life of the Jews, all these have their origin in the patriotism of the Jewish people. The Jewish religion is primarily Jewish patriotism." Because they rejected this fundamental notion, Hess expressed his contempt for the Jewish "Reformers" who "emancipated" themselves from the Jewish nation. Moreover, he insisted, the latter were quite aware of the cultural fraud they were perpetrating. "They are very wary of expressing their true sentiments frankly. Even in patriotism, which is a natural and simple sentiment, they seek a double meaning: an ideal (love for Judaism), and a reality (love for the adopted nation), advocating the one or the other according to circumstances."[28]

Hess disparaged the "enlightened" as playing a counterproductive role in Jewish life, and the "modern religion makers" as "Jewish 'Protestants'" and "sectarians without sects." Viewed from the perspective of such as these, he argued:

> I see for the existence of Judaism no valid reason at all. The Jew who does not believe in the national rebirth of his people can work only for the liquidation of his religion. What I understand still less is the startling suggestion that one should at the same time be enthusiastic about enlightenment and the "Mission of Justice" in the "Diaspora," i.e., at the same time about liquidation and continued existence. To conclude: humanity and tolerance, unity of law and life, these things only a nation which is organized as a state can make into reality in its social institutions.[29]

For Hess, there could be no question that the nation of Israel was capable of fulfilling its historic mission only through the restoration of its national independence in its ancient homeland. He fully understood that such a restoration could not be achieved overnight and would require commitment, patience, and preparation. "What we need to do today for the reestablishment of the Jewish nationality consists, first of all, of this: to keep alive the hope for our political rebirth. Then when world events, which are preparing themselves in the Orient, will permit a practical beginning for the reestablishment of the Jewish State, this beginning may first of all consist in the founding of Jewish colonies in the Land of the Fathers."[30] However, he cautioned, "The Jewish people must first show itself worthy of the rebirth of its world historic religion, first feel the necessity of its national rebirth, in order to achieve it."[31]

6

The Growth
of Secular
Nationalism

The themes sounded by the prophetic voices of Mordecai Manuel Noah and Moses Hess found little receptivity in Western Europe and the Americas. They were, however, more enthusiastically embraced in Eastern Europe, where the movement for Jewish emancipation had made only very limited inroads. Here far greater stress was placed on the cultural and spiritual significance of a Jewish national revival than was the case in the more progressive West. Some farsighted advocates of the Jewish enlightenment (*Haskalah*) placed little faith in the ability of the Jews to overcome the pervasive anti-Semitism that seemed to be so deeply imbedded in Russian and Slavic history and culture. At the same time, these advocates were no longer prepared simply to carry on with Jewish life in the Diaspora as that pattern of existence had been pursued in the past. Rejecting both of these approaches to the Jewish future as nonviable, they undertook a simultaneous struggle against traditional Judaism and contemporary assimilationism. They argued that the only acceptable course for the preservation and improvement of Jewish life, one that did not entail the sacrifice of the nation's very soul, was that of creating a Jewish national renaissance in the ancient Jewish homeland—the Land of Israel.

The principal advocates of this unabashedly nationalist position before 1881 were secular Hebrew writers such as David Gordon (1831–1886), who espoused the fundamental ideas of Jewish nationalism and a national revival in Palestine in essays written as early as 1860. Some of these intellectuals sought to forge a revitalized linkage between Jewish nationalism and what came to be known as Hebraism. To them the main goal of the national awakening that they were advocating was the conservation and rejuvenation of what they characterized as the genuine Hebrew spirit, which could only become fully manifest in the ancient land of the Hebrews. Such a Hebrew renaissance implied the rebirth of Hebrew as a living language and the eventual transplantation of the newly emerging modern Hebrew literature to its ancestral soil. In their writings, the Hebraists reflected a romantic enthusiasm for the past glory of the preexilic Jewish nation and people, as well as a determination to lay down the roots of a new and modern national culture; they became advocates of a Hebraic nationalism that bore only a superficial resemblance and connection to traditional Jewish nationalism.

The new secular nationalist movement became a significant factor in Jewish enlightenment circles as a result of the work of the popular Hebrew writer Peretz Smolenskin (1842–1885). Although he wrote a reasoned exposition of the idea of a modern Jewish nationalism in his *Am Olam* (The eternal people) in 1873, it was *HaShahar* (The dawn), the Hebrew journal that he began publishing in Vienna in 1868 that had the greatest impact. The journal's goal was to strike a new path between what its readers and supporters saw as the stultifying rigidity of the new Orthodoxy and the apparent national spinelessness of the more extreme advocates of enlightenment.

Smolenskin's position with regard to Judaism was unequivocally radical. He argued, in essence, that the Jewish religion was valid and worthy of public acceptance by Jews only to the extent that it contributed to the preservation of the nation; beyond this utilitarian purpose, it remained a strictly private affair. "Faith," he wrote,

is a matter for God alone, and He will quarrel with those who throw off His yoke. But the unity of the nation is given into the hands of men; those who are not strict in observing the divine commandments, but are faithful to the national covenant, are without doubt a thousand times more dear to us than those who are eager to perform the word of God, but in whose eyes the honor and happiness of their people are as nothing.[1]

Smolenskin became an indefatigable agitator for the development of a modern Jewish national consciousness, national unity, and a national renaissance, and religious traditionalists castigated him as a mortal danger to the community. As observed by Shmarya Levin (1867–1935):

In orthodox circles Smolenskin was regarded as a dangerous free-thinker, a revolutionary spirit who was corrupting the Jewish youth. The *Hashachar* had been banned from all the *Yeshivoth* [academies], and woe to the student who was caught with a copy: his dismissal took place on the spot. In spite of this, the influence of this periodical was perhaps greater among the students of the *Yeshivoth* than among any other class; for them Smolenskin became the prophet of those stormy times. . . . Smolenskin carried on the war with a double-edged sword and on two fronts. . . . He thundered alike against the obstinate conservatism of the Jewish people which led to petrification, and against assimilation which led to death.[2]

The fundamental thesis argued by Smolenskin was that the ultimate salvation of the Jewish people was grounded in their national distinctiveness. Consequently, the only possible solution to the persistent Jewish struggle for survival was the renationalization of the Jewish people. In his analysis, the root of the problem was not gentile disdain for Judaism or jealousy of the reputed wealth of the Jews; it was the simple fact that the Jews were weak and defenseless. This situation, he insisted, could be remedied only through the reestablishment of the Jewish nation in a land of its own.

The central issue for Smolenskin was the continued viability of the Jews as a nation. As far as he was concerned, the Jews had never ceased being a nation, "even after our kingdom was destroyed and we were exiled from our land, and whatever may yet come over us will not eradicate our national character." In arguing his nationalist brief, Smolenskin drew heavily on the biblical idea that the nation had originally been constituted independently of a territorial base. That is, the nation was first formed in the Diaspora. As a consequence of its extraordinary origin, the loss of state sovereignty in ancient times did not affect the continued existence of the nation, even though it was in exile. He wrote in this regard:

The foundation of our national identity was never the soil of the Holy Land, and we did not lose the basis of our nationality when we were exiled. We have always been a spiritual nation, one whose Torah was the foundation of its statehood. From the start our people has believed that its Torah took precedence over its land and over its political identity. We are a people because in spirit and thought we regard ourselves bound to one another by ties of fraternity.[3]

Because of this unique bond, those who sought relief from the national plight by assimilating were justifiably considered as traitors to their people.

Moreover, Smolenskin asserted, notwithstanding its many centuries of exile, the "eternal people" had never yielded its claim or denied its devotion to the Land of Israel. Hebrew had always remained the singularly national language of the Jews, while the basic precepts of traditional Judaism constituted their common religious heritage. These were the critical factors that conditioned Jewish existence, factors that could not be denied without indulging in gross self-delusion. He admonished the assimilationists with a touch of sarcasm:

> You wish to be like the other people? So do I. Be, I pray you, be like them. Search and find knowledge, avoid and forsake superstition, above all be not ashamed of the rock whence you were hewn. Yes, be like the other peoples, proud of your literature, jealous of your self-respect, hopeful, even as all persecuted peoples are hopeful, of the speedy arrival of the day when we, too, shall reinhabit the land which once was, and still is, our own.[4]

A FOCUS ON HEBREW

However, since the Land of Israel was inaccessible to the Jewish nation at the time, it was crucial that Hebrew, the national language, be ever more cherished and cultivated by the Jews of the Diaspora as their essential and indissoluble link with their ancient roots. Smolenskin wrote:

> You ask me what good a dead language can do us? I will tell you. It confers honor on us, girds us with strength, unites us into one. All nations seek to perpetuate their names. All conquered peoples dream of a day when they will regain their independence. . . . We have neither monuments nor a country at present. Only one relic still remains from the ruins of our ancient glory—the Hebrew language. Those, therefore, who discard the Hebrew tongue betray the Hebrew nation, and are traitors both to their race and their religion.[5]

The Hebrew writer and activist Eliezer Ben-Yehuda (1858–1923) was another major proponent of this general perspective. However, although he was fundamentally in accord with Smolenskin's Hebraic nationalism, Ben-Yehuda rejected much of his theorizing on the spiritual basis of Jewish nationality. Caught up in the secular currents of his time, he began to think in terms of modern political nationalism as well as of a Jewish national renaissance. In an 1878 article entitled "An Important Question," Ben-Yehuda pleaded not only for a Jewish revival in Palestine but also for the revival of the Hebrew language as a cultural factor that was critical to the survival of the Jews as a nation. In this latter regard, he became deeply concerned that it might not be possible to keep the language alive for much longer in the Diaspora, where, in the face of civic emancipation and cultural enlightenment, Hebrew was becoming increasingly less relevant to Jewish life. He gave expression to this fear in 1880 and proposed a nationalist solution to the dilemma. "We will be able to revive the Hebrew tongue only in a country in which the number of Hebrew inhabitants exceeds the number of gentiles. Therefore, let us increase the number of Jews in our desolate land; let the remnants of our people return to the land of their fathers; let us revive the nation and its tongue will be revived, too!"[6]

Ben-Yehuda was aware that his argument could be challenged on the grounds of reason. In a sense, he had stood the national idea on its head. After all, the essence of the nationalist dream was to reconstitute the nation in its ancient homeland, whereas he seemed to have made the Land of Israel a mere instrument for the renaissance of the Hebrew language, to which he appeared to accord highest priority. However, that this was not his intent is evident from the following argument:

> The heart of man is moved not by reason but by emotion. We may argue all day and cry aloud that we are a people, even though we are bereft of a homeland, but all this will be futile and meaningless. We can, however, appeal to people's feelings and address ourselves to the hearts of the Jews, saying: The land of our fathers is waiting for us; let us colonize it, and, by becoming its masters, we shall again be a people like all others.

Furthermore, he implicitly criticized those whose advocacy of Hebrew reflected a primarily cultural and linguistic nationalism, without significant political content. He wrote: "It is senseless to cry out: Let us cherish the Hebrew tongue, lest we perish! The Hebrew language can live only if we revive the nation and return it to its fatherland. In the last analysis, this is the only way to achieve our lasting redemption; short of such a solution, we are lost, lost forever!"[7]

IMPACT OF THE POGROMS

The majority of the "enlightened" or *maskilim*, however, rejected these nationalist arguments. Instead, they continued to profess an enduring faith in the possibility of Jewish emancipation in Russia and Eastern Europe. That this was an illusion was soon to be demonstrated: In 1881 the czarist regime supported devastating pogroms against the Jews. It then became clear to many that short of complete assimilation, including the total acceptance of Russian religion and culture, there was no longer hope of any significant improvement in the civil status of the Jew. An outspoken Jewish voice in the latter part of the nineteenth century, one that categorically rejected assimilation as a viable option for the Jews, was that of Moses Leib Lilienblum (1843–1910). He wrote in 1881: "All my life I had grieved over the decline of Jewish nationality and the thought that Jewry's existence as a nation was doomed. And now there lies before me a straight and sure path to the everlasting salvation of our people and its nationhood, a path to which the imperatives of life have brought me."[8] That path was the resettlement of the Land of Israel by the Jewish people and the restoration of Israel as a sovereign nation on its own soil. He demanded: "Work! Lay the foundation for a normal and healthy national life for the Jewish people, which has been persecuted in every time and place, but has never surrendered. Give it back its home, something which no people lacks, except the gypsies."[9]

Lilienblum scoffed at people who were opposed to Jewish nationalism on the basis of a presumed universal mission of the Jews to the world. He considered it absurd to hold such a view when those same Jews were almost everywhere suffering from persecution and in some instances being subjected to barbaric treatment. "We have not been able to teach mankind, in more than three thousand years, not to beat poor wanderers who are bereft of a home and of protection—shall we teach mankind love, brotherhood, peace, etc.?"[10] For Lilienblum, the Jews had three options for their future: They could remain in their present state, as objects of unrelenting oppression and persecution "and not be safe even against a major holocaust"; they could assimilate, that is, commit national suicide in the hope of achieving individual salvation; or they could initiate "efforts for the renaissance of Israel in the land of its forefathers, where the next few generations may attain, to the fullest extent, a normal national life."[11]

There was little doubt regarding which of these alternatives Lilienblum would choose. The first led to eventual self-destruction, whereas the second provided a possible solution for some individuals but surely not for the community as a whole. Only the third choice offered what could be considered a sound policy for the nation. Accordingly, Lilienblum became deeply involved in the work of the Hibbat Zion (Love of Zion) movement that emerged in Eastern Europe at the beginning of the 1880s to foster Jewish colonization in Palestine; he subsequently became an active supporter of Theodor Herzl and the Zionist movement in Russia.

It is noteworthy that both Ben-Yehuda and Lilienblum, like many others with a comparable secular nationalist orientation, made a significant point of expressing their hope of achieving national "normalcy," that is, the desire to be like the other nations. This should not be surprising: The traditional formulations of the Jewish national idea were quite alien to their way of thinking. Understandably then, their approach to Jewish nationalism was considered abhorrent by the traditionalists who unequivocally rejected the very notion of Jewish national normalcy as a moral aberration. The traditionalists had no wish to be like their gentile neighbors and saw the advocacy of normalcy as destructive of the ethos of Judaism and as undercutting the very basis for the autonomous existence of the nation.

The calamitous events of 1881 in Russia also took their toll on the illusions of the profoundly secular Leon Pinsker (1821–1891), an Odessa physician who had previously been one of the founders of the assimilationist Society for the Dissemination of Culture among the Russian Jews. Discarding his earlier optimism regarding the Jewish future in the Diaspora, in 1882 Pinsker published an anonymous pamphlet, written in German, entitled, *Auto-Emancipation: An Appeal to His People by a Russian Jew*. Firmly rejecting the quietism of the traditional Jewish community, Pinsker urged his compatriots to seize the moment and commit themselves to an activist nationalist enterprise. He cautioned his fellow Jews, "Close your eyes and hide your heads ostrich-fashion as you will; if you do not take advantage of the fleeting moments of repose, and devise remedies more fundamental than those palliatives with which the incompetent have for centuries vainly tried to relieve our unhappy nation, lasting peace is impossible for you."[12]

The essence of the Jewish problem, as Pinsker saw it, was the fact that "in the midst of the nations among whom the Jews reside, they form a distinctive element which cannot be assimilated, which cannot be readily digested by any nation. Hence the problem is to find a means of so adjusting the relations of this exclusive element to the whole body of the nations that there shall never be any further basis for the Jewish question."[13] The basic difficulty was that although the Jews were everywhere considered to be part of a distinct nation, notwithstanding the denials of the assimilationists and others, it was a nation without national sovereignty. This meant that the Jews were in no position to demand that they be treated the same as other alien nationals, as the ephemeral and stateless Jewish nation could not offer reciprocity for such treatment in their own land. The Jews therefore, not recognized in the usual sense of the term, found themselves in an anomalous and consequently precarious position in Russia. Presumably, once the generally accepted conditions of nationhood were achieved, the reasons for the persecution of the Jews would be undercut and a basis for their acceptance on equal terms with other nationalities would be established. In other words, the restoration of the Jewish state would make it feasible for the Jews to maintain a satisfactory existence in the Diaspora, one free of the disabilities that typified their lives, present as well as past.

Pinsker therefore rejected emancipation as a viable response to this complex historical dilemma. Emancipation was, of course, intrinsically highly desirable and, as such, was to be advocated strongly. But by itself it simply was not enough. Although it might improve the situation of some individual Jews, particularly those who were prepared to assimilate completely, emancipation alone was incapable of bringing about a general amelioration of the condition of the Jewish people. In Pinsker's view, the underlying premise of the movement for emancipation reflected the nature of the problem. His position was summarized by Shlomo Avineri: "Emancipation proceeds from an assumption that the Jews are a passive object of historical development. One has to liberate *them*, one has to award *them* rights, one has to treat *them* on the basis of equality and tolerance. The historical subject in these actions is always the non-Jewish majority culture; the Jews themselves remain a passive element."[14] However, acceptance of such a passive role was completely out of touch with the realities of the period, a time of national self-assertion, and placed the Jews at the mercy of historical forces over which they were unable to exercise even a small degree of control. Pinsker reminded his readers: "The nations never have to deal with a Jewish nation but always with mere Jews. The Jews are not a nation because they lack a certain distinctive national character, possessed by every other nation, a character which is determined by living together in one country, under one rule. It was clearly impossible for this national character to be developed in the Diaspora."[15] The evident solution to this problem was for the Jews to emancipate themselves, to take control of their own destiny. Therefore, "the proper and the only remedy would be the creation of a Jewish nationality, of a people living upon its own soil, the auto-emancipation of the Jews; their emancipation as a nation among nations by the acquisition of a home of their own."[16]

A completely secular Jew, Pinsker placed little value, beyond that of historic sentiment, on the significance of a Jewish national restoration in the Land of Israel. His principal concern was with the establishment of Jewish autonomy; where such took place was entirely a secondary consideration. If, as a practical matter, Palestine were not available for Jewish occupation and settlement, another territory would serve the secular nationalist purpose just as well, as long as it was "an extensive and productive place of refuge, a gathering place which is our own." The critical factor, as he saw it, was the establishment of the conditions for a normal national existence. He concluded that "no sacrifice would be too great in order to reach the goal which will assure our people's future, everywhere endangered. . . . Help yourselves, and God will help you!"[17]

HIBBAT ZION

Although Pinsker's pamphlet was generally ignored by the Jews of western Europe, to whom it was primarily directed, it clearly reflected the mood and sentiments of numerous groups of Russian Jews that began to gather to consider their options for the future. These spontaneous stirrings soon resulted in the emergence of the Hibbat Zion (Love of Zion) movement in 1881, which spread throughout the areas of Jewish settlement in southern Russia and Romania by the end of the following year. The Hibbat Zion, however, was fully committed to the support of Jewish settlement and colonization in Palestine; no other place was given serious consideration. Pinsker's ideas contributed significantly to setting the orientation of the movement, and he was elected chairman of its central committee at the first conference of the various Hibbat Zion societies, held in Kattowitz in November 1884.

The Hibbat Zion soon succeeded in establishing a tenuous but nonetheless significant Jewish agricultural presence in Palestine for the first time in some two millennia. However, it failed to attract a wide or particularly idealistic following. Although masses of Jews from Eastern Europe sought refuge from persecution in other lands, few made their way to the Land of Israel. The movement, deprived of the inspiration and support of a large following, before long lost its pioneering spirit and became, in effect, merely a medium of transmission for philanthropic donations directed to the support of the several settlements in Palestine that had been established under Hibbat Zion auspices. By 1889, the orientation of the movement had shifted from a focus on national revival in Palestine to a preoccupation with the support of individual resettlement there.

This basic change in the ideology of Hibbat Zion was subjected to the scathing criticism of the Hebrew writer Asher Ginzberg (1856–1927), better known as Ahad Ha'am. In an 1889 essay entitled "The Wrong Way," Ahad Ha'am suggested that the Hibbat Zion movement would fail to achieve permanent gains in Palestine because its adherents were not sufficiently imbued with the spirit of nationalism. He argued that the long and tragic history of the Jews had conditioned them to focus all their energies on the survival and well-being of individual Jews and their families. In practice, this imperative frequently was extended in scope to incorporate the immediate congregation as well but was rarely if ever extended to the wider Jewish community or to the survival of the Jewish people. "The national life of the people as a whole practically ceased to matter to the individual." Ahad Ha'am complained that even those who were still capable of feeling a sense of responsibility for the national well-being could only rarely overcome their individualism and subordinate their private interests to broader national needs. Therefore, he insisted in the essay, the highest priority of the Hibbat Zion movement should be to bring about a national revival, "to inspire men with a deeper attachment to the national life, and a more ardent desire for the national well-being."

He acknowledged that if the movement had adopted this orientation, the immediate practical settlement work that was being carried out in Palestine would undoubtedly have suffered; however, it would have better prepared the ground for the future leadership of the Jewish nation. "But," he lamented, such was not the policy of the first champions of our ideal. As Jews, they had a spice of individualism in their nationalism, and were not capable of planting a tree so that others might eat its fruit after they themselves were dead and gone. Not satisfied with working among the people to train up those who would ultimately work in the land, they wanted to see with their own eyes the actual work in the land and its results.

As a consequence, instead of laying a solid groundwork for the nation's future, they dissipated their efforts in the less-significant attempt to convince individuals of the merits of emigration to Palestine. Instead of directing their attention to the essential tasks of nation-building, they concentrated on calculations of benefit to the individual,

> so that anybody who wanted to do well and had the necessary capital should betake himself to the goodly land, where he and his family would prosper, while the nation too would benefit. An appeal on these lines did really induce some people to go to Palestine. . . . But these people, most of whom were by no means prepared to submit cheerfully to discomfort for the sake of a national ideal, found that when they reached Palestine that they had been taken in.[18]

In his view, this whole approach was a tragic error. "What wonder, then, that so great an ideal, presented in so unworthy a form, can no longer gain adherents; that a national building founded on the expectation of profit and self-interest falls to ruins when it becomes generally known that the expectation has not been realised, and self-interest bids men keep away? This, then, is the wrong way."[19]

However, Ahad Ha'am's pointed criticism of the Hibbat Zion movement had little tangible effect on its orientation or activity. A few of the movement's leaders may have entertained visions of an ultimate restoration of Jewish sovereignty in the Land of Israel, but the movement as a whole remained essentially apolitical. It continued to be concerned primarily with individual emancipation rather than national redemption. It also became increasingly secular in character, with many of its advocates downgrading the significance of Judaism as a central feature of Jewish existence. The growing tendency to define Jewish nationality in primarily secular terms drew a sharp response from Yehiel Michael Pines (1842–1912), who became a leader of the Jewish community of Jerusalem in 1878. Pines differed from earlier advocates of the primacy of religion in defining Jewish nationality; because he had a modern Western education, he was able to argue his case in the same intellectual genre as the secularists whom he attacked.

In an 1895 essay, Pines declared, "I have no sympathy with the currently fashionable idea, with the movement to make the Jewish people a pure secular nationality in place of the combination of religion with nationality that has enabled us to survive to this day." He was prepared to accept this idea, even though he considered it to be a distortion of Jewish history, in the cases of essentially assimilated Jews who were to be found on the fringes of the community. If such a secular national self-identification helped to keep them from breaking away entirely from their people, the idea evidently had utilitarian value. However, it was quite another matter to "impose the idea of secular nationalism on the whole Jewish people. . . . It is against this that I rise in vigorous opposition, for in the consequences of this doctrine I can see nothing but incalculable harm."[20]

Pines reminded his readers that the Jewish nation could not be defined by the conventions applied to other nationalities. The Jewish nation, in the first instance, was not simply a product of the territory and state within which it emerged. It was instead "a group professing a separate faith and bound in a mutual covenant to observe that faith." Accordingly, even after the Jewish people acquired a territory of its own and established a sovereign state therein, "it still did not look upon its statehood as the essence of its peoplehood." Throughout their history, he asserted, the Jews were generally prepared to accept loss of sovereignty but reacted with vehemence when their religion was threatened by foreign domination. "Conversely, when it was deprived of its homeland and was scattered abroad, and even ceased speaking its national language, the Jewish people continued to live as a national entity only by virtue of the Torah, which accompanied it in all its wanderings and lived with it in every country in which it settled."[21]

For Pines, there simply could be no such thing as a Jewish nationality divorced from the Jewish religion. He rejected the secularist argument that Jewish nationality is the product of a broader array of historical factors, or that it could be a mere consequence of the possession by the Jews of a common language, Hebrew. He declared unequivocally: "The nationalism I represent is the nationalism of Rabbi Yehudah Halevi and of Rabbi Moshe ben-Nahman, of blessed memory, a national sentiment organically integrated in faith, nationalism whose soul is the Torah and whose life is in its precepts and commandments."[22]

JEWISH SOCIALISM AND THE BUND

Parallel to the emergence of the first Jewish colonies in Palestine and the rise of the Hibbat Zion movement in Eastern Europe, there was a counter-nationalist movement composed primarily of Russian Jewish intellectuals who tried to imbue the Jewish masses with the revolutionary spirit of socialism. Rather than the restoration of the Jewish nation, these saw the universal adoption of socialism as the answer to the Jewish problem. They were convinced that by solving the general problems of society through socialist reconstruction, the Jewish problem itself would eventually disappear, as would all nationality problems. In essence, their argument was that socialism would obviate the need for the assimilation of one group into another by eliminating all the invidious social and economic distinctions that differentiated persons from one another. In other words, social and economic commonality would engender intergroup harmony.

One of this group of idealistic thinkers, Aaron Lieberman (1845–1880), became the founder of the Jewish socialist movement. A graduate of the rabbinical seminary in Vilna, Lieberman came under the influence of Aaron Zundelevich, a radical socialist, and soon became an ardent secularist, completely rejecting the Jewish religion. Lieberman nonetheless remained passionately devoted to the Hebrew language and stressed the need to publish socialist books and tracts in the ancient tongue in order to train propagandists from among Jewish students, whose knowledge of European languages was very limited. Although he was swept up in the general socialist ferment that was taking place in Russia at the time, he was concerned about the implications of a continuing Jewish national consciousness and the cultural uniqueness of the Jewish people: that seemed to make even Jewish socialists different from their gentile colleagues and ideological brethren.

Forced to flee Russia in 1875 because of his illegal underground activity, Lieberman went to Berlin where he tried unsuccessfully to establish a Jewish section within the Socialist International. He then went to England where, on May 20, 1876, he organized the first union of Jewish socialists (Agudat ha-Sotzialistim ha-Ivrim) in London, drafting the organization's manifesto in a scholarly Hebrew. Its credo declared, "We Jews are an integral part of humanity, and cannot be liberated except through the liberation of all humanity."[23] However, the organization seems to have had little appeal for Jewish workers in Britain and was disbanded in December of that same year. For a time, Lieberman contributed some articles to Smolenskin's *HaShahar*, but their differences over religion were such that Lieberman soon decided to publish his own Hebrew-language socialist periodical. In May 1876, he began publication of *Ha-Emet* (The truth) in Vienna. However, the periodical appeared only three times before it was suppressed by the Austrian authorities, and Lieberman was arrested and imprisoned for several years. He had no immediate successors, and his endeavors were ignored by later Jewish socialist leaders.

Not surprisingly, from the very beginnings of the socialist movement, it seemed clear that there was an incompatibility between the ideals of nationalism and those of socialism. Nationalism, fundamentally rooted in a national consciousness of historical continuity, is not principally concerned with the social and economic issues and conflicts that seem to be endemic in the life of a national community. Its primary interest is in the autonomy—if not sovereignty—of the national body, rather than the character of its internal structure. Socialism, in contrast, is predicated on the assumption of a universal commonality of economic interests among the working classes, irrespective of country or place of domicile. Through its appeal to class solidarity, socialism is supposed to transcend the traditional national and religious differences among the world's working classes. Socialism thus strives for a universal social order transcending national divisions as well as state borders. Consequently, from its very inception, the socialist movement was oriented toward cosmopolitanism, articulated in the notion of a homogeneous and undifferentiated humanity. Indeed, the early socialist thinkers belittled the significance of national distinctiveness, seeing it as a factor leading to artificial divisions among peoples who really harbored fundamentally common interests.

This latter perception was particularly prominent in the case of Marxism. According to Marx, factors such as individual will, national aspirations, and legal, ethical, and religious ideas are of secondary importance and do not play a decisive role in the drama of human history. At best, such factors merely contribute to the ideological superstructure of the prevailing socioeconomic system. However, the true motive power that drives history, with its endemic political, social, and spiritual conflicts, is inherent in the stage of a particular society's economic development and the prevailing pattern of control of the means of production. The social and political superstructure of society is thus critically dependent on the character of the existing economic substructure, which is itself a consequence of the dominant modes of production. The changes in the modes of production that result from the natural dynamics of the evolutionary process precipitate related changes in the character of the forces of production and a redistribution of economic functions within the social system. As seen from a Marxist perspective, the existing capitalistic societies are therefore composed essentially of two antagonistic classes, the bourgeoisie and the proletariat; that is, those who own the means of production are therefore in a position to exploit those who have to sell their labor to them as a commodity in exchange for the means of subsistence.

According to this theory, it is the unrelenting antagonism between these two economic classes that is the paramount factor shaping the development of modern history. The very character of this primal class conflict, which must ultimately result in the abolition of the prevailing capitalistic order, relegates all other conflicts between social groups to a position of relatively minor significance. In a capitalistic society, nationalism weakens the proletariat's class consciousness, thereby diverting its attention from revolution and the class struggle. This inevitably strengthens the position of the bourgeoisie. Therefore, the Marxist argues, it is essential that proletarian solidarity take precedence over national sentiments; the common universal interests of the proletariat must take precedence over the parochial interests of individual states and nations.

However, in practice, the contradictions between nationalism and socialism, particularly in its Marxist formulation, had to be resolved in some sort of compromise. The socialist rejection of nationalism, perhaps acceptable in theory, appeared overly simplistic and incapable of dealing adequately with the national sentiment that was flowering all over Europe. For all but the most committed Marxists, the pure theory of socialism was too abstract and one-sided to overcome nationalist feelings. Marxism had to yield much of its rigid dogmatism, to recognize the vitality of nationalism as a force in history, and to accommodate the growth of nationalist sentiments among its adherents. Indeed, particularly in the case of the Jews, to maintain that an irreconcilable antithesis existed between the ideals of nationalism and socialism was not credible.

The dominant vehicle for the expression of Jewish socialism was the Bund (Universal Jewish Workers' League in Lithuania, Poland, and Russia), which was founded in Vilna in 1897 under the leadership of Arkady Kremer (1865–1935), in order to extend the supranational socialist program to the Jews of Eastern Europe. The movement was essentially the product of the marriage of Haskalah rationalism and revolutionary Marxism. Having originated as a Russian socialist organization, the Bund was extremely hostile to both Hebraism and the general idea of Jewish nationalism. Although it reluctantly employed the Yiddish language in its publications and propaganda, the Bund made clear that this particularist deviation from socialist universalism was necessary because Yiddish was the only effective vehicle of communicating socialist ideas to the Jewish masses.

However, it was not long before the leaders of the Bund began to realize that the Jewish working class, in addition to their participation in the ongoing general class conflict, had to carry on a simultaneous struggle against anti-Jewish discrimination. It came as a shock to the Bundists that, notwithstanding the egalitarian convictions and pronouncements of the socialist leaders, there clearly existed a troubling strain of overt anti-Semitism among the rank and file of the gentile working class. As a consequence, many Jewish socialists felt compelled, at least as a matter of immediate practical necessity, to promote the national interests of their people. As observed in 1895 by Julius Martov (1873–1923), who was later to become a close—although temporary—collaborator of Lenin: "a working class, which is content with the lot of an inferior nation, will not rise up against the lot of an inferior class. . . . The growth of national and class consciousness must go hand in hand."[24] Similarly, Chaim Zhitlowsky (1865–1943) consistently attempted to harmonize Jewish nationalism with

Marxian internationalism. His basic ideas in this regard were first formulated in an essay, "A Jew to Jews" (1892), which gained wide currency in Bundist circles.

Vladimir Medem (1879–1923), who emerged as an outstanding Russian advocate of the role of social democracy in the solution of nationality questions, vigorously supported the right of Russian Jews to a national existence and self-determination, even though he was not personally an advocate of this latter approach to dealing with the Jewish problem. He was opposed to both assimilation and nationalism. It was his view that "the ideology of assimilation is the same as that of nationalism, only the other side of it. The assimilationist strives for a stranger's nationality and tries to make it his own. . . . While the [Jewish] nationalist tries to put his nationalist stamp on everything possible."[25] Caught in the apparent paradox of acknowledging the existence of a distinct Jewish nationality while opposing the further development of the Jewish national consciousness, Medem worked out a theoretical approach to resolving the contradiction. His approach came to be known as "neutralism" and was officially adopted by the Bund. In practice, this meant a refusal to take a stand or any political action on the matter of the future of the Jewish nation; in effect, it meant doing nothing that would either promote or retard the national survival of the Jews. Medem believed that the future of the Jewish people would be determined by the objective forces of history, and that one should merely observe the historical process and not attempt to interfere with it in any way. It is perhaps ironic that the same position was taken by most religious traditionalists, except that neutralism substituted the notion of a historical process for providence. Notwithstanding his adoption of neutralism as his formal theoretical position, Medem proved in fact to be a consistent advocate of the cause of Jewish national cultural autonomy; when put to the test, he was unwilling to submit the Jewish future entirely to the blind historical forces at work in the Russia of his day.

At its fourth conference in Bialystok in 1901, the Bund adopted a resolution demanding that Russia "be reconstituted as a federation of nationalities with complete national autonomy for each nationality, independent of the territory in which it is located."[26] However, this insistence on national autonomy was not intended as a vindication or acknowledgment of the international unity of the Jewish people and the validity of its national aspirations. The resolution was concerned with cultural autonomy, to which the Bund attached little intrinsic value but considered an element that would satisfy the cultural needs of the Jewish masses. The national program of the Bund was thus an attempt at a practical compromise in the face of the growing contemporary pressures for national self-determination. The program did not purport to provide a viable synthesis of socialism and Jewish nationalism.

Nonetheless, it was soon evident that the advocacy of cultural autonomy had failed to deal with the problem adequately. Cultural autonomy did not promise an end to discrimination in the workplace or in society generally. As a consequence, Jewish socialists found it increasingly difficult to deal with the peculiar problems resulting from the fact that the Jews, in practice if not in theory, constituted a landless nation.

In general, the problem faced by national groups living in their own historical homelands was primarily that of achieving national sovereignty over their territory or at least national autonomy within a broader political constellation. As a rule, at least in theory, such nationalist claims could be settled through a just delimitation of the political rights of contending national and social groups, including the elimination of the social and economic conditions within the country that favored the domination of one national group over others. Provided that the right of national self-determination was acknowledged, the realization of socialism within a state could be expected to lead to a just solution of existing nationality problems. For the Jews, however, the mere formal acknowledgment of their right to national self-determination solved nothing, because the very conditions for the existence of a sovereign or autonomous Jewish nation did not exist. The solution of the nationality problem of the Jews was dependent on the prior creation of the material conditions necessary for their autonomous existence. The Jewish socialists thus found themselves in a profound dilemma. In attempting to deal with the "Jewish problem," they increasingly found themselves confronted by the need to take a position on one of two fundamentally opposed options for the Jewish national future: They could accept the idea of assimilation and the gradual denationalization of the Jewish people, or they could undertake the struggle to establish the conditions necessary for a free and independent Jewish national existence. There simply was no way for them to conjure up an acceptable synthesis of the two that had any relevance to the issues of discrimination and persecution that demanded urgent resolution. It was a trap from which they never managed to extricate themselves successfully.

7

Affirmation
of the
Diaspora

At the same time that the new ideas of religious and secular nationalism were making inroads, in one form or another, on a broad spectrum of Jewish thinkers, others who rejected the nationalist response to the Jewish question began to focus anew on the problem of finding a viable intellectual accommodation with the realities of Jewish life in the Diaspora. There was, of course, nothing really new or exceptional about this. As we have seen, coming to terms with the Diaspora was a problem with which Jewish scholars and communal leaders had grappled since the Babylonian exile. What principally distinguished this modern endeavor from its ancient and medieval predecessors was its redefinition of the nature of the Jewish Diaspora. This new approach repudiated the traditional idea that the present Diaspora constituted an "exile."

There can be little question, as even a cursory examination of Jewish history will amply demonstrate, that the dispersion of the Jews throughout the world was a consequence of successive national disasters, beginning with the Babylonian exile of the sixth century B.C.E. That exile was different in one fundamental respect from the earlier exile of the eighth century B.C.E., which followed the destruction of the northern kingdom of Israel by Assyria. In the earlier instance, the exiles soon lost their national identity through total assimilation into the societies of their dispersion. In the case of the Babylonian exile, however, not only did many return to the Land of Israel when conditions permitted, but also those remaining behind in Babylonia continued to retain their national identity, even as they prospered. Indeed, over time, the large Jewish community of Babylonia underwent a national cultural renaissance that rivaled and eventually surpassed that of the parent community in Palestine. However, as repeated political and military disasters struck both the Palestinian and Babylonian Jewish communities, the dispersion became more widespread, extending to new lands and locations. This pattern was replicated again and again as the Jewish communities of these countries were similarly struck by disaster and dislocation. It was not long before the Jewish people as a whole became homeless, in the sense of not having a central national home, its communities being repeatedly compelled to dissolve and reconstitute as they were forced to move from one country or place to another.

From a national perspective, perhaps the most significant aspect of the Diaspora was that throughout this long period of adversity the Jews consistently considered themselves as exiles. That is, even during the periods when Jewish communities flourished and thrived in their various Diasporas, they saw themselves as being in exile (*galut*) from their natural homeland, which was the Land of Israel. The commonly held conception of being a nation in exile, over a period of centuries and in some cases of millennia, had long since become an integral element of the Jewish national consciousness. Israel's enforced state of exile was seen throughout the history of the Diaspora as a fulfillment of the warnings of the prophets regarding the consequences of Israel's disobedience to the will of God. Exile was understood as a continuing punishment from which relief would come with the ultimate restoration of the nation in its land under the leadership of the Messiah.

Jewish self-consciousness of exile and national homelessness fluctuated in intensity during different periods of history and in various countries, depending upon the particular political and social circumstances in which the Jews found themselves. However, it was always present to a significant degree, even when conditions were favorable. In fact, the sense of awareness of being in exile had always received positive reinforcement through the liturgy of Judaism and its commemorative practices. The Jewish people were thus always encouraged to remember with sorrow and despair, even on joyous occasions, the destruction of their ancient state and the massacres and persecutions that ensued, and to pray for national redemption and restoration.

In the nineteenth century, as Jews were increasingly granted legal equality with other citizens in the relatively "enlightened" countries of Western Europe and the United States, with an accompanying improvement in their general economic and social status, a radical change in attitude toward the idea of exile began to take shape among some segments of the world Jewish community. The pursuit of the struggle for emancipation in the country of one's domicile, and the opportunities this presented—or seemed to present—for integration and assimilation into the national majority within the state, made many feel it was impolitic or otherwise undesirable to continue to nurture a Jewish nationalist orientation that was directed elsewhere.

As a consequence, parallel to the renaissance of Jewish nationalism and the rejection of the Diaspora in modern times, there emerged a countermovement dedicated to the affirmation of the significance of the Diaspora in its own right. Advocates of this tendency categorically rejected the notion that authentic Jewish nationalism required autonomous political expression. This was a radical departure from the traditional position, which stated that Jewish life in the Diaspora was a temporary aberration from Israel's historic destiny, an anomaly that would be rectified with the arrival of the messianic era that would usher in a new period of sovereign Jewish national existence in the Land of Israel. Instead, protagonists of the new approach argued that the true essence of Jewish nationalism was principally cultural and religious in nature and therefore was not indissolubly linked to the notion of a political renaissance of the Jewish people in their ancient homeland.

The advocates of this argument advanced what amounted, at least in traditional Jewish terms, to a revisionist reconstruction of biblical history, particularly with regard to the proper understanding of the views and teachings of the prophets. This may be seen most clearly in the work of the historian Simon Dubnow (1860–1941), who wrote:

> In the face of the growing power of the aggressive empires of Assyria and Babylonia and the danger of the impending political destruction of the weak Kingdom of Israel, the Prophets acted energetically to shift the center of gravity of national survival from the political sphere to the social and spiritual spheres. They taught that political weakness or even the loss of statehood were no danger as long as the people were united and bound together by inner spiritual energy, for the state was merely the shell placed around the kernel, which is the nation.[1]

In other words, Dubnow argued that the nation could have a valid continued existence even in the absence of a territory of its own in which it lived. In effect, Dubnow affirmed the historic national abnormality of the Jews: no other nation had continued to thrive under such conditions of homelessness.

Similarly, Salo W. Baron argued that the singular achievement of the prophets was their conception of a universal ethical monotheism, which was predicated on their acknowledgment of the transcending importance of religion over temporal circumstances such as statehood and possession of territory.

Under the stress of an extraordinary world situation and peculiar domestic tensions, the prophets severed the fate of their people, which they extolled as the chosen bearer of God's universal message, from the destinies of its country. . . . With an enthusiasm often called disloyal but tested by subsequent history as the main safeguard for Jewish survival, these immortal leaders viewed the victorious enemy as but a "rod of God's anger" and the downfall of their country as part of the divine guidance of history.

It is noteworthy that this argument implies that the prophets did not believe that the loss of sovereignty and national exile were punishments for the transgressions of Israel, but that it was foreordained as part of the divine plan for the world—a rather dubious proposition at best. Baron continued:

In this way Israel's prophets, lawgivers and priests came to preach also "historical monotheism," i.e., the doctrine that God revealing himself and operating through the history of mankind and their own people teaches them to overcome the forces of nature. . . . Similarly, these teachers taught, the nation's ethnic and religious loyalties ought to surpass its "natural" attachments to state and territory. Of course, they did not object to their people's political self-determination. . . . The Israelitic prophets and priests may thus be designated the first exponents of a religious and cultural nationalism, in which culture was equated with religion but in which all political aspirations were considered secondary.[2]

The inevitable corollary to views such as these is a rejection of the very notion of the Diaspora as exile, that is, as something extraordinary or unnatural. Instead, the Diaspora came to be viewed by a wide variety of advocates of this general perspective as a natural state of affairs for the Jewish people. Among those who held this view were to be found Jews who aspired to assimilate within the dominant society of the country in which they were domiciled, as well as some who found themselves more comfortable on the fringes of assimilation than within the confines of the traditional Jewish community. Because of the intimate historic intertwining of Jewish religion and nationalism, traditional Judaism itself became the principal battlefield on which the ideological struggle over the affirmation of the Diaspora was fought.

In 1812, a spokesman for the new orientation, David Friedlander (1750–1834), published a pamphlet in Prussia in which he urged the abolition of all prayers that reflected messianic aspirations and expectations. "I stand here before God," he wrote, "I invoke blessings and prosperity upon my king, my compatriots, myself, and my family; I pray not for a return to Jerusalem, for the restoration of the Temple and its sacrificial cult, I entertain no such desire in my heart, their fulfillment will not make me happy, my mouth shall not utter them."[3] The pamphlet was presented to Frederick William III by the Prussian chancellor, Prince Karl August von Hardenberg, along with an endorsement that stated in part:

> It is not surprising that the Jews long for a restoration to Palestine, since they are so much oppressed by the peoples among whom they live. But when equal rights have been granted to them, they will no longer pray for their renationalization in Palestine, but rather for the peace and prosperity of the Prussian government; they will give up the hope of the coming of a Messiah, and will pray for the welfare of the king whom they love and respect with all their souls.[4]

There is little reason to doubt that Hardenberg's argument accurately reflected the views of many of the new crop of religious reformers of Judaism.

THE REFORM MOVEMENT

At first, even those who regarded the civic emancipation of the Jews as the signal event through which Jewish life throughout the world would become stabilized and then normalized dared not tamper with the messianic aspirations contained in the prayer book that had been part of the Jewish liturgical tradition for such a long time. Initially, they merely sought to reform the liturgy and practices of the religion so as to make it appear more compatible with the enlightened societies into which they aspired to gain entry. Thus, although the first public Reform worship service took place in 1815, it was to take another quarter of a century before a new Reform prayer book, one that omitted all references to Zion and Jerusalem as well as to the coming of the Messiah, was introduced in 1841. Having crossed that frontier, some leading reformers subsequently became fully determined to purge the rites and liturgy of Judaism of all vestiges of traditional Jewish nationalism. And in this latter regard, they considered the very conception of the Diaspora as exile to reflect an anomalous perspective that was best suppressed completely.

This latter approach may be seen as expressed rather clearly in the work of Abraham Geiger (1810–1874), one of the major figures of the religious Reform movement. Writing of the period following the destruction of the Jewish state by the Romans, Geiger observed:

> Where religion and people coincide, where religion and state institutions remain in constant reaction upon each other, there the state is, of course, consecrated in its laws and institutions by the religious life breathed into it; but vice versa, the religious institutions become at the same time commands

of the state and popular custom, they penetrate and color the ideas of right which the state is called upon to materialize; they wear the garment of nationality which that people has to form.

Such indeed was the situation of Israel prior to the destruction of its central national institutions. However, Geiger argued, once the Jewish state, along with the realistic possibility of any autonomous national political existence, was destroyed by the Romans, the Jewish people had to find a new means of continuing its existence as a religious confession.

As long as people and religion, state and doctrine progressed within Judaism with hands joined, isolated clouds might arise out of such commingling, but the junction was a natural one. But now the people's bands were dissolved, nationality was to cease, the state was broken up, the confessors of Judaism became and should become members of that people among whom they lived and citizens of the state within the sovereignty of which they resided.

The challenge before the Jewish leaders of the day was to find the means by which the Jews could integrate into the societies among which they lived, without succumbing to the religion of the majority, as they went about their universalist task of bringing the true understanding of God's wishes for man to all humankind.

How will this religion now accomplish its new task within this new position? Is Judaism really so completely permeated by nationality that it cannot exist without the same, is its real task exhausted as soon as nationality has disappeared? Or does this religion (Judaism) stand higher than nationality, will it dissolve the national ties by which it was swathed, and try to respond to the call of becoming common property of mankind?[5]

Geiger's own response to the final question was affirmative. In his view, Judaism was fully capable of adaptation to the new environment in which its purposes were to be realized. He wrote:

The strength of Judaism lies precisely in the fact that it has grown out of a full national life and that it possesses both a language and a history as a nation. The idea of Judaism was an all-embracing one. Hence, if it was not to be a drifting shadow, it had to find expression in a healthy national individualism which, on the one hand, saw all of mankind epitomized within itself, but, on the other hand, sought to embrace all the world of mankind beyond its own confines. Thus it is a strong point of Judaism that it originally revealed itself in a language which was entirely imbued with the idea and which was the noblest fruit of a full national life. Judaism was not, however, dependent upon language and nationality; indeed, it has survived in all its vitality even after being deprived of both. When its vessel was smashed, its survival was not affected thereby. Because it always had to engage in violent struggle, Judaism remained a closed and separate entity; and yet it has succeeded in transmitting its basic ideals to mankind as a universal heritage. And when the artificial barriers fall, it will continue to retain its universality throughout the course of history. Let us, therefore, look back with joy on our former life as a nation, as being an essential transitional era in our history, and on our language, through which the life of that Jewish nation had taken root in spiritual soil![6]

It is clear that Geiger offered a vision of Judaism that was radically different from that which had prevailed until his time; his Judaism was shorn of all its particularist national features. As summarized by Geiger's biographer, Max Wiener:

To him Judaism in its ideal form was religion *per se*, nothing but an expression of religious consciousness. . . . Since Judaism was destined to be a universal religion, he felt that it had to divest itself of all nationalistic elements. It never occurred to the adherents of this view that they might ever wish to form a political entity such as Judaism had been prior to the fall of the Second Commonwealth. To them, the nation whose citizens they were, or desired to become, was their sole Fatherland.[7]

These radical views were clearly reflected in the statement of principles adopted by the Philadelphia Rabbinical Conference of 1869, which also redefined the concept of the Messiah in a manner that stripped it of all nationalist implications.

The Messianic aim of Israel is not the restoration of the old Jewish State under a descendant of David, involving a second separation from the nations of the earth, but the union of all children of God in the confession of the unity of God, so as to realize the unity of all rational creatures and their call to moral sanctification.

We look upon the destruction of the Second Jewish commonwealth not as a punishment for the sinfulness of Israel, but as a result of the Divine purpose revealed to Abraham, which, as has become ever clearer in the course of the world's history, consists in the dispersion of the Jews to all parts of the earth, for the realization of their high-priestly mission, to lead the nations to the true knowledge and worship of God.[8]

VARIOUS INTERPRETATIONS OF THE JEWS' MISSION

There is a certain irony in the fact that, with the exception of an affirmation of the belief in the Messiah as it had been traditionally understood, the essence of Geiger's vindication and affirmation of the Diaspora was also argued by his principal Orthodox opponent, Samson Raphael Hirsch (Chapter 5) (1808–1888). The latter set forth a theory of the Jewish national mission that completely excluded any role for the nation reconstituted as an autonomous political entity on its ancient land. For Hirsch, as for Geiger, the national mission of the Jews was to serve as religious missionaries to the nations of the world. Hirsch did not conceive of this mission as a national model of the ideal society that could be emulated by the nations of the world, but rather as the model of a religious community devoted to fulfilling the will of God. He wrote:

> Because men had eliminated God from life . . . it became necessary that a people be introduced into the ranks of the nations which through its history and life should declare God the only creative cause of existence, fulfillment of His will the only aim of life. . . . This mission required for its carrying out a nation, poor in everything upon which the rest of mankind reared the edifice of its greatness and power; externally subordinate to the nations armed with proud reliance on self, but fortified by direct reliance on God.

This universal mission was assigned to Israel, which "was to receive from the hands of its Creator all the means of individual human and national prosperity, in order that it might dedicate all its wealth of resources to the one purpose—fulfillment of the Divine will." However, Hirsch continued:

> Such a mission imposed upon it another duty, the duty of separation, of ethical and spiritual isolation. It could not join in the doings of the other peoples in order that it might not sink to their level and perish in the abyss of their worship and pleasure. It must remain alone and aloof, must do its work and live its life in separation, until, refined and purified by its teachings and its example, universal humanity might turn to God and acknowledge in Him the only Creator and Ruler. That attained, Israel's mission will have been accomplished.[9]

For Hirsch, then, the continued existence of the Jews as a national community served a purely instrumental purpose, namely, that of preventing their individual assimilation into the societies and cultures among which they were destined to bear witness to their religious message.

Another approach to the matter was that argued by the religious philosopher Salomon Ludwig Steinheim (1789–1866) who, although never developing a following of any consequence, nonetheless contributed an interesting perspective to the ideological debate. Steinheim suggested that the decay of the Jewish nation served to make the ground fertile for the growth of the Jewish religion. In his view, the nation fulfilled its particularist historic mission by laying the foundation for the universal mission of the Jews as the bearers of the gospel of Judaism. Judaism, he wrote, "began to blossom fully only with the cessation of the nation; the people arose in spirit even as it perished physically." With regard to messianism, Steinheim argued:

> Possibly, someone might get the notion that there still remained a political center for national preservation, namely, the idea of the Messiah, which followed the people into exile and has been maintained to the present time. Although up to a certain time the messianic belief sustained for many the prospect of a political unification in the future and, thereby, provided for the present a bond and focal point for the people, it actually did not function as such.[10]

The "fathers of the synagogue" had long since wisely relegated political messianism to the ever-distant future, in view of the endless troubles caused to the people by pseudomessiahs from Bar Kokhba to Shabbatai Zevi.

Steinheim saw assimilation as the natural destiny of the Jewish people once it was detached from its national moorings in the Land of Israel.

> By all criteria with respect to the national principle of the Jews and other nations, this people ended its normal career. . . . Unmistakably, we see that each and every nation-building element having to do with nationality, history, politics, and family life was extinguished long ago. Therefore, the Jewish people, quite in keeping with the laws of human nature, yields to the irresistible powers of attraction and assimilation of large masses of people.

Indeed, he observed with no little disdain:

> Wherever freedom rules in the full sense of the word, the Jew turns into one of the aborigines with all the ill manners of an over-active, arrogant nationalist. . . . He is overcome everywhere by that egotism that transcends individual limits to manifest itself with fire and sword as so-called "patriotism," even where he may hardly claim a homeland, let alone a fatherland as his own. . . . And yet—there is a spiritual essence that grows within every Jew, which he imbibes with his mother's milk, which enters his soul as part of child's play, animates and penetrates it with all its power, and stamps it with its signature.

This spiritual essence, of course, is the motive power of Judaism. "It is the pure imprint of a spiritual power upon the religious consciousness and the expression of a spiritual citizenship in transcendental regions."[11] Accordingly, Steinheim insisted: "Every individual member of this people remains a participant in its great mission in the Diaspora as long as he has not solemnly separated and voluntarily excluded himself from its community. Every member is, wherever he may be and merely by his own personal existence, a part of that great missionary enterprise."[12] In the last analysis, in his view:

> The element that built and maintained the nation is revelation. It is the confidence and certainty of faith, humble as it is exalted, which neither shuns nor spurns the judgment seat. In it lies indestructible vitality, the eternal youth of the people, the permanence of the ineradicable house of Judah. Accordingly, every individual member of this people belongs to the holy covenant as a religious person exclusively, since religion alone is its nationality.[13]

DIASPORA NATIONALISM

In sharp contrast to those who openly advocated assimilation, or who like Steinheim suggested that assimilation was indeed a natural and therefore possible option for the Jews, there also emerged a number of advocates of a rather different approach to the issue of the reaffirmation of the Diaspora. Their formulation became known as "diaspora nationalism" or "autonomism," the most prominent spokesman for which was Simon Dubnow. Like the ideas of those religious reformers whose principal concern was to find an acceptable place within society for the Jews as a religious denomination rather than as an ethnic-national community, diasopra nationalism was predicated on a fundamental rejection of the concept of the Diaspora as exile. For the advocates of this perspective, the very idea of the Jews being in exile from their homeland was considered to be a counterintuitive anachronism. At the same time, however, the diaspora nationalists firmly rejected the proposition that there was no longer any basis for considering the Jews as a distinct nation.

The Diaspora nationalists insisted that the Jews were and would always remain a distinct nationality. They therefore categorically rejected—as a conscious self-delusion—the idea that the Jews could assimilate in the nations among whom they lived. Dubnow argued that it was absurd to imagine that a Jew living in France or Germany, by virtue of his having been emancipated, could become a Frenchman or a German, that is, the bearer of French or German nationality. Dubnow scoffed at the suggestion that a Jew could take on French nationality while continuing to profess Judaism. For Dubnow, the idea of "a Frenchman of the Mosaic faith" could at best mean that the Jew in question was a citizen or resident of France but certainly not that he could become a Frenchman in the sense of being a member of the French nation. On the contrary, he argued, the

Jew's nationality would necessarily remain Jewish. In essence, Dubnow insisted that a person cannot be *made* a member of one nationality or another. Just as the word "nation" derives from the verb *nasci* (to be born), one must be born into a national group in order to bear its stamp of nationality. "One may become a member of some artificial, legal or social-political grouping, but it is impossible for a person 'to be made' a member of a natural collective group, of a tribe, or people, except through mingling of blood (through marriage) in the course of generations, through the prolonged process of shedding one's national individuality."[14] But if the Jewish citizen of France does not take on French nationality by virtue of the grant of citizenship, what nationality does he have? Dubnow's answer, of course, is that he remains a Jew, the bearer of Jewish nationality. As for those who rejected the idea of Jewish nationality in favor of the concept of the Jews' merely constituting a "religious group," Dubnow dismissed their position as one that "is rooted in assimilation and represents merely an attempt of certain parts of Diaspora Jewry to fuse with the ruling people."[15]

Dubnow maintained that it was a simple fact that the Jewish people existed as a cultural nationality in the consciousness of the majority of its members. They continued to think of themselves as a "religious nation" because their national culture was so closely identified with the religion that dominated the life of the people throughout its history. But what of the Jew who is indifferent to or rejects the ideals and practices of the Jewish religion? What can the retention of Jewish nationality mean for him as a practical matter? In Dubnow's view, the answer is that Judaism is more than a mere religion; it is a vast body of culture that evolved to its present form primarily as a consequence of the unique historical trials through which the Jewish nation had passed. Thus, although the fundamental character of the Jewish nation was originally determined by its religion, its subsequent history resulted in the transformation of Judaism from a merely tribal creed into an all-encompassing world view. Judaism, as we have come to know it, is therefore composed not only of religious elements but also of political, social, messianic, ethical, and philosophical components. In contrast to the traditional religious perspective, which considers Judaism as essentially fixed in its fundamental elements and perspectives from the very beginning, Dubnow viewed Judaism as basically evolutionary in character, having reached its present state by passing through various formative stages and continuing to be open to new and unprecedented developments. He conceived of the Bible, Talmud, rationalist Jewish theology, and Jewish mysticism not merely as various aspects of a central religious teaching but also as different and distinct stages in the evolutionary development of Judaism. Viewed from this perspective, Judaism may be understood as offering a broad and variegated religious prospectus from which every Jew may draw sustenance in accordance with his outlook and spiritual needs. Accordingly, one may choose what he will from the accumulated treasures of the Jewish thought of three millennia. Indeed, one may choose the barest minimum and still remain a Jew, "as long as one does not reject entirely the national idea, which is not a matter of theory but a historical fact."[16]

Dubnow, however, although he readily acknowledged and accepted the importance of Judaism as an essential although not necessarily critical factor defining the nation, rejected the idea that the religion should serve as the dominant influence in determining the future course of the nation. He predicted an inevitable secularization of the national idea that would eventually transform the traditional religious consciousness into a historical evolutionary consciousness. At the same time, he also rejected the notion of a Jewish national "mission." He would "subordinate the Jewish national idea neither to a 'mission' idea nor to the traditional forms of the Jewish law, but bind it to the free growth of the nation on its spiritual soil."[17] He considered the future of the nation to be critically dependent on the unimpeded growth and development of its autonomous culture, which would of necessity contribute to the flowering and perfection of everything the nation created in the course of its history.

Having rejected the idea of the Diaspora as exile and consequently the notion of a forthcoming political restoration of the Jewish nation in its ancient homeland as advocated by the proponents of the emerging Zionist movement, Dubnow sought to infuse a new and metapolitical content into the concept of Jewish nationalism. He argued the proposition that a nationality, considered from the standpoint of its overall historical development, is a historical-cultural collectivity whose members are united in the first instance by common descent, language, territory, and political organization. Subsequently, the nationality evolves toward a spiritual unity that is predicated on a common cultural heritage, historical traditions, common spiritual and social ideals, and other characteristics typical of national development. A nationality that has undergone these fundamental developmental stages in its past, that reflects a store of common ideas, sentiments, and needs in the present, and which gives expression to aspirations for future independent development has earned universal recognition as an autonomous body, whether political, social, or cultural in character, among the nations of the world. For Dubnow, then, "a nation may be defined as a historical-cultural group which is conscious of itself as a nation even though it may have lost all or some of the external characteristics of nationality (state, territory or language), provided it possesses the determination to continue developing its own personality in the future."[18] And in his opinion, it is the Jews that reflect the highest type of the historical-cultural or spiritual nation. The Jewish nation was forged through a long and unique development process that toughened it, giving it the fortitude to survive even though it had neither a unified state nor a territory of its own. As it had emerged successfully from the ordeals of its history, there was every reason to believe that it would continue to thrive as a nation, further strengthening its national will to exist, as it has done in the past.

The theory of diaspora nationalism, as expounded by Dubnow, was therefore predicated on the assumption that national self-consciousness is the essential element of a nation, the primary criterion of its existence. Dubnow wrote, " 'I think of myself as a nationality—therefore I am' is the formula of the national-cultural group."[19] This collective self-consciousness is visibly manifested in the determination of the nationality to protect and defend its autonomy. A nationality such as that of the Jews, which lacked the important attributes of state and territory, was forced to compensate for this deficiency through the development of powerful internal defense mechanisms. These are devoted to the consolidation and strengthening of the social and spiritual forces for unity that serve as weapons in the struggle for national survival. Moreover, Dubnow insisted, the truth of this assertion is amply demonstrated by the historical fact that the Jewish nation has proven itself able to preserve and develop its own distinctive culture during the many centuries of its existence without a state or territory. The Jewish nation has successfully survived and flourished as a culturally autonomous and internally self-sufficient body even within an alien and frequently hostile social and cultural environment.

What is the nature of the forces that have enabled the dispersed nation of Israel to maintain its national identity over the course of its long and troubled history? There are, of course, many contributing factors, not the least of which are the biblical laws, the teachings of the Talmud, the decisions of the rabbis, and the irrepressible faith in the coming of the messianic era and the ultimate national redemption and restoration. Of considerable importance was the long isolation of the Jew behind the walls of the ghetto, which facilitated the nation's continued autonomous cultural development. For Dubnow, however, although these factors had great intrinsic significance and contributed to Jewish national survival, they were in themselves insufficient to account for the historical outcome.

> Quite apart from these, the source of vitality of the Jewish people consists in this: that this people, after it had passed through the stages of tribal nationalism, ancient culture and political territory, was able to establish itself and fortify itself in the highest stage, the spiritual and historical-cultural, and succeeded in crystallizing itself as a spiritual people that draws the sap of its existence from a natural or intellectual "will to live."[20]

According to this view, although the Jewish nation had long since failed to satisfy the objective conditions of nationhood, the Jews remained a nation in the full meaning of the word and may even be perceived as constituting the highest spiritual type of nation. For Dubnow, the prospect of achieving an independent political existence for the nation, as sought by the Zionists, represented a reversion to a distinctly lower-order form of national life.

As a higher-order spiritual or historical-cultural nation, one that essentially harbored neither the political ambition nor the potential for seeking physical control of any given territory or for subjecting any other nation to its cultural domination, the Jewish nation posed no threat to any existing political entity. "It has no aggressive national aspirations even of the kind found among other peoples that lack political independence but live on their own soil and show the tendency to wipe out the national minorities living in their midst."[21] Consequently, the nation's only "political" concern was with the protection of its national individuality and the safeguarding of its autonomous cultural development. Reflecting the traditional Jewish self-image, Dubnow considered the historical-cultural Jewish nation as a manifestation of the highest sense of social justice, a nation that seeks nothing from any state or nation other than the recognition of its inherent rights of cultural self-determination and self-preservation.

However, Dubnow observed, a nation's instinct for self-preservation naturally grows stronger as the dangers that threaten it increase. Therefore, in a nation without a state or a territory, one in danger of being absorbed by other peoples, the national instinct for survival takes on the form of "eternal vigilance," putting its stamp on all aspects of the life of the community and its members.

> As the pressure from without increases, each member of a cultural nationality, not protected by state frontiers or armed might, must reaffirm the moral imperative: "Act in such a way as to preserve the autonomy of your people and its perfection!" This imperative must become the supreme criterion in the life of Jewry, exposed as it is to dangers from every side. This imperative must rouse and strengthen the national will.[22]

Any within the nation whose ideas or actions served to weaken that collective will, such as those who advocated assimilation, were to be considered as diseased members of the national organism and destructive of its capacity for survival.

Dubnow, employing a clearly Hegelian terminology, although he explicitly denied any connection between his use of the terms and the German philosopher's dialectics, argued that the solution of the Jewish problem in modern times required a higher synthesis of the traditional medieval thesis of national isolation and that of the contemporary antithesis of assimilation. The Jews, through acceptance of their isolation in the societies within which they lived, had been able to preserve intact that which they held to be of the greatest value for them—their national life. This was especially the case where they were able to actualize communal self-government behind the ghetto walls. This pattern was disrupted in the new era introduced by the French Revolution, with its promise of liberty and equality for all. These ideals were embraced with wild enthusiasm by many Jews who felt they were suffocating from the limitations of the ghetto and soon led to the emergence of an antithetical drive to end the isolation of the past through the process of assimilation. However,

> assimilation was bound to expose itself as a doctrine of national suicide.
> . . . Experience has demonstrated that both the thesis and antithesis are one-sided. . . . The way is open for a broad synthesis which must unite in itself all the solid and vital elements of the two previous stages of development and, once extremism has been overcome, create from them the basis for a new order of life . . . the synthesis is called "autonomism."[23]

Dubnow argued that recognition of Jewish cultural autonomy by the countries in which the masses of the Jews were concentrated would secure both the singularity of the nation and its harmonious collaboration with others in furthering the progress of humanity. Moreover, as a historical-cultural or spiritual nation, it would be anachronistic for the Jews to aspire once again for territorial or political segregation. The Jews had finally arrived at a stage in their long history where their need was for nothing other than national autonomy, and such autonomy had but three fundamental requirements: communal self-determination, legal recognition of Yiddish—the language spoken by the masses—as the Jewish national language, and the freedom to provide national education for Jews.

Dubnow attempted to take practical political steps toward achieving recognition of Jewish autonomy through organization of the Folkspartei in Russia in 1906. The program of the Folkspartei was based on two principles: "the recognition of the common needs of all sections of Jewry in the political, civic, and national-cultural fields," and "the recognition that the Jews must carry on their fight for existence as members of one indivisible Jewish nationality, which, in the Diaspora, is divided into parts of different states, but not into parts of other nationalities."[24] Accordingly, each local Jewish communal organization was to have the responsibility for establishing schools to provide an education that was intrinsically Jewish in both orientation and spirit. The local communities were to be organized into a larger council that would represent the broader Jewish community to the authorities and would have the power to tax its constituents in order to meet its internal resource needs. Dubnow also envisioned the founding of a world Jewish congress that would concern itself with the problems of Jewry as a whole, settlement in Palestine and other countries, and the struggle for emancipation in those countries where it remained to be achieved. However, the Folkspartei failed to attract a significant following and achieved little of any consequence. The party lingered on for a number of years and finally disintegrated in the late 1930s under the pressures of growing anti-Semitism and nationalism. A parallel party, which had a short-lived popularity, was organized in Poland during World War I. However, it too was unable to compete effectively with the Zionists and Bundists for influence among the Jewish masses.

8

Political Zionism
and
Territorialism

Despite its generally apolitical orientation, the Hibbat Zion movement constituted the principal manifestation of Jewish nationalist thinking until the middle of the 1890s. As a practical matter, however, the movement's nationalist activities were limited almost exclusively to seeking ways and means of circumventing the restrictions imposed by the Ottoman government on Jewish immigration and settlement in Palestine. The Hibbat Zion demonstrated no inclination whatever to work for the elimination of those arbitrary constraints through organized political activity and contributed little to the increasingly vigorous debate concerning nationalism and its alternatives that was taking place within the broader Jewish community. Its limited perspectives on the nationality question, and its promotion of the notion that Jewish national aims in Palestine would ultimately be achieved through the steady infiltration of small numbers of settlers into the country, were dismissed as completely unrealistic by the movement's many critics.

ORGANIZED POLITICAL ACTIVITY
AND THEODOR HERZL

It was clear to Theodor Herzl (1860–1904), a prominent secular Viennese author and journalist, that the only viable solution to the perennial "Jewish question" was the re-creation of a Jewish state, and that this could only be achieved through unequivocally political means. In an article published in the London *Jewish Chronicle* on January 17, 1896, Herzl argued that "the Jewish Question is no more a social than a religious one, even if it sometimes assumes such and other tinges. The Jewish Question is a national question, which can only be solved by making it a political world question to be discussed and solved in the councils of the civilized nations."[1] That is, the political restoration of the Jews would take place when the nations of the world were convinced that it was in their interest to facilitate it. It would not result from the emigration of small numbers of Jews to Palestine. In a sense, this argument was but a reformulation of the earlier traditional view that a Jewish restoration in the Land of Israel would take place only as a result of divine intervention, which would be actualized through the actions of the gentile nations, much as the Second Commonwealth was brought into being through the good graces of the Persians.

Herzl insisted repeatedly that modern anti-Semitism was no longer a product of traditional medieval motivations. He argued that, in the age of nationalism, anti-Semitism had taken on a new national dimension. It was caused by the dissonance that resulted from the Jews' recent emancipation and the popular perception of them as a rootless and therefore abnormal nation in their midst. Given this formulation of the problem, the solution obviously lay in a Jewish national renaissance, one that would reconstitute the Jews as a nation in the same sense that the term applied to other peoples and not in the manner employed by the different schools of apologists for the Diaspora.

In developing this theme, Herzl called attention to the fact that for hundreds of years the European powers had granted charters to particular groups, enabling them to settle legally as virtually autonomous bodies in various parts of the world. Indeed, it was the judicious use of such charters that had facilitated the colonization and settlement of the European empires from the Americas to East Asia. Accordingly, Herzl proposed that if the Jews wanted to reestablish their presence in Palestine in a manner that would assure their future national autonomy there, they would have to seek to obtain such a charter from the Ottoman Sultan; in Herzl's view, this could only be accomplished through carefully orchestrated international political action.

He set forth his ideas on how such a new Jewish state should be founded and organized in a pamphlet that was published in February 1896, *The Jewish State: An Attempt at a Modern Solution of the Jewish Question*. In the preface to the work, Herzl declared:

> The idea which I have developed in this pamphlet is a very old one: it is the restoration of the Jewish State. . . . It depends on the Jews themselves whether this political pamphlet remains for the present a political romance. If the present generation is too dull to understand it rightly, a future, finer

and a better generation will arise to understand it. The Jews who wish for a State shall have it, and they will deserve to have it.[2]

As had his nationalist precursors, Herzl argued that assimilation was not a realistic solution to the Jewish question. He conceded that it might seem to offer a way out of the dilemma for those individuals who were prepared to submerge themselves in the surrounding society even if such meant the loss of national identity. However, it was not a viable option for the Jewish people as a whole. As far as he was concerned:

> Whoever can, will, and must perish, let him perish. But the distinctive nationality of Jews neither can, will, nor must be destroyed. It cannot be destroyed, because external enemies consolidate it. It will not be destroyed; this is shown during two thousand years of appalling suffering. It must not be destroyed. . . . Whole branches of Judaism may wither and fall, but the trunk will remain. . . . Thus, whether we like it or not, we are now, and shall henceforth remain, a historic group with unmistakable characteristics common to us all.[3]

As an immediate practical measure to further the nationalist cause, he proposed the establishment of a Society of Jews that would "be authorized to confer and treat with Governments in the name of our people. The Society will thus be acknowledged in its relations with Governments as a State-creating power. This acknowledgement will practically create the State."[4] The principal aim of the society was to be the achievement of sovereignty over a suitable portion of the globe. Herzl was therefore opposed to the efforts being made by Hibbat Zion to infiltrate settlers into Palestine. In his view, infiltration was not a viable long-term policy for achieving Jewish national aims. He argued that infiltration could succeed in advancing the national goal only up to the "inevitable moment when the native population feels itself threatened, and forces the Government to stop a further influx of Jews. Immigration is consequently futile unless we have the sovereign right to continue such immigration."[5] The future of the Jewish state was not to be held hostage to the approval of the indigenous population.

As a completely secular nationalist, with little sentimental attachment to the Land of Israel, Herzl considered the question of where the Jewish state should be located a matter of secondary concern. Like Pinsker, Herzl stressed that the Jews must be granted the sovereign power over an autonomous political entity. He was not necessarily committed to the restoration of the Jewish state in its ancient homeland, although he readily acknowledged that "Palestine is our ever-memorable historic home" and would therefore have a far greater attraction for the Jewish people than any other location.[6] It was, however, only one possible option. He was equally ready to accept Argentina as an alternative site. It was there that Baron Maurice de Hirsch (1831–1896) had financed a scheme for the resettlement of thousands of European Jews, and Herzl was quite prepared to see the Jewish national aim fulfilled there instead of in the ancient Land of Israel. Indeed, he was willing to consider any territory offered that would be found acceptable to the proposed Society of Jews.

Using the term "Zionist" in its strict meaning, Herzl was not one; he was really a "territorialist." The primary aim of his Jewish nationalism was the reconstitution of the Jews as a sovereign nation, and he did not equate the achievement of that goal with a national restoration in Palestine, even though he was fully aware that for most Jews a Jewish state would have been inconceivable anywhere else. As it turned out, Herzl's fundamental territorialism was to become a contentious issue and would soon threaten the internal cohesion of the emerging Jewish national movement.

Herzl's *Jewish State* received a mixed, but mostly negative, reception among the Jews of Central and Western Europe. For one thing, as he had anticipated, some people worried that his call for Jewish autonomy could jeopardize the gains in civil status and social preference that had been achieved with great difficulty and effort throughout the preceding century. Stefan Zweig (1881–1942), who was a student in Vienna at the time of the publication of the pamphlet, later recalled:

> I can still remember the general astonishment and annoyance of the middle class Jewish elements of Vienna. What has happened, they said angrily, to this otherwise intelligent, witty, and cultivated writer? What foolishness is this that he has thought up and writes about? Why should we go to Palestine? Our language is German and not Hebrew, and beautiful Austria is our homeland. Are we not well off under the good Emperor Franz Josef? Do we not make an adequate living, and is our position not secure? . . . Why does he, who speaks as a Jew and who wishes to help Judaism, place arguments in the hands of our worst enemies and attempt to separate us, when every day brings us more closely and intimately into the German world?[7]

In an attempt to rebut Herzl's argument in *The Jewish State*, the chief rabbi of Vienna, Moritz Gudemann (1835–1918), published a brochure, *National-Judentum* (National Judaism). Gudemann suggested that Herzl had erred in his assertion that the Jewish problem was fundamentally a national one. Taking the same position as the religious reformers, Gudemann insisted that the Jews had long ago ceased to be a distinct nation and were linked solely by their common religious affiliation.

In England, where the reception to Herzl's pamphlet was somewhat warmer, a split on the matter developed between Hermann Adler (1839–

1911), chief rabbi of the United Hebrew Congregations of the British Empire, and Moses Gaster (1856–1939), the chief rabbi of the Sephardic communities of England. Adler was in favor of continued Jewish settlement in Palestine but was quite opposed to Herzl's political program, whereas Gaster was an active proponent of political Zionism.

The reaction to Herzl's ideas among the activists and supporters of the Hibbat Zion movement was also mixed, although generally far more positive than openly negative. There was an understandable reluctance on their part to abandon the movement's long-standing emphasis on individual emigration and resettlement in the Land of Israel. However, for those who despaired of the piecemeal approach taken by Hibbat Zion with regard to the resettlement of Palestine and its lack of any clear political orientation, Herzl's radically different approach to the problem infused new life into the dream of a national return to Zion. Moreover, Herzl had challenged the practicality of Hibbat Zion's approach even on strictly economic grounds. As he told Max Bodenheimer (1865–1940) in May 1896: "What the Zionists have hitherto achieved evokes my grateful admiration, but I am a confirmed opponent of infiltration. If this method continues unchecked, land will increase in value and it will become progressively harder for us to buy it." Furthermore, he argued:

The idea of a Declaration of Independence "as soon as we shall be strong enough over there" is to my mind impracticable, for the Great Powers would certainly not recognize it, even if the Porte had weakened enough. My program, far more preferable, is to stop infiltration and concentrate all our strength upon an internationally-sanctioned acquisition of Palestine. To achieve this, we require diplomatic negotiations . . . and propaganda on the largest scale.[8]

Chaim Weizmann (1874–1952), who was at the time a student in Berlin, later recalled that Herzl's pamphlet "was an utterance which came like a bolt from the blue." It was not that Herzl had propounded some brilliant new concept that had eluded all earlier thinkers. It was more the impact of the charismatic personality of Herzl himself, the urbane Western man of affairs, that made the Jewish public sit up and take notice. As Weizmann observed:

Fundamentally, *The Jewish State* contained not a single new idea for us; that which so startled the Jewish bourgeoisie, and called down the resentment and derision of the Western Rabbis, had long been the substance of our Zionist tradition. . . . Yet the effect produced by *The Jewish State* was profound. Not the ideas, but the personality which stood behind them appealed to us. Here was daring, clarity and energy.[9]

OPPOSING POSITIONS

Early in 1897, Herzl took the next step and proposed the convening of an international Zionist Congress to set forth the nationalist agenda. His proposal quickly evoked widespread concern in the Jewish communities of Western Europe and the United States. The principal concern, once again, was that the call for Jewish autonomy would jeopardize the gains that many Jews had achieved through emancipation. In New York, a Jewish group adopted a formal resolution expressing opposition to "any formation of a Jewish State in Palestine in such a manner as may be construed as casting a doubt upon the citizenship, patriotism, and loyalty of Jews in whatever country they reside."[10] Then, on July 6, 1897, the Executive Committee of the Association of Rabbis in Germany, composed of both Orthodox and Liberal members, including the rabbis of Berlin, Frankfort, Breslau, Halberstadt, and Munich, whom Herzl dubbed the "Protest Rabbis," issued a joint declaration against the forthcoming Zionist conference that reflected a strong hint of virtual hysteria. Indeed, it is difficult to believe that the signatories—religious antagonists—all took seriously the arguments against Zionism that they dredged up in the effort to find common ground among them. The document proclaimed:

1. The endeavors of so-called Zionists to found a Jewish national state in Palestine run counter to the Messianic prophecies of Judaism as contained in the Holy Writ and in later religious sources.
2. Judaism obligates its adherents to serve the fatherland to which they belong with full devotion and to further its national interests with all their heart and all their strength.
3. However, those noble endeavors which are directed toward the settlement of Palestine by Jewish farmers are not inconsistent with these obligations, because they have no relation whatever to the founding of a national state.

Religion and patriotism thus equally impose upon us the duty to ask all those who have the welfare of Judaism at heart to stay away from the aforementioned Zionist endeavors and most particularly from the Congress, which, despite all the warnings against it, is still being planned.[11]

A rather different position was reflected in the views of Rabbi Samuel Mohilever (1824–1898), a prominent Orthodox leader who was fully supportive of the proposed Zionist objectives and program. Writing in 1897, he observed:

Of late certain orthodox rabbis have arisen in western Europe, among whom one has even declared that the promises of future bliss and consolation made by our seers were in the form of symbols and parables. The coming of the Messiah, they say, will not be to bring Israel back to the Land of its Fathers and put an end to its long dispersion and many sorrows, but will be to establish the Kingdom of Heaven for all mankind, while Israel continues in exile as a light to the gentiles. Others of these rabbis assert, without qualification, that nationalism is contrary to our belief in the advent of the Messiah. I am therefore constrained to declare publicly that all this is not true. Our hope and faith has ever been and still is, that our Messiah will come and gather in all the scattered of Israel, and, instead of our being wanderers upon the face of the earth, ever moving from place to place, we shall dwell in our own country as a nation, in the fullest sense of the word. Instead of being the contempt and mockery of the nations, we shall be honored and respected by all the peoples of the earth. This is our faith and hope, as derived from the words of our prophets and seers of blessed memory and to this our people clings![12]

Mohilever went even further and insisted that Zionists "must be completely convinced and must believe with a perfect faith that the resettlement of our country . . . is one of the fundamental commandments of our Torah. Some of our ancient sages even say that it is equivalent to the whole Law, for it is the foundation of the existence of our people."[13]

The issue of Zionism was clearly creating a split within the ranks of the religious leadership as other rabbis rallied to Herzl's support. After much wrangling, the First Zionist Congress was finally convened on August 29, 1897, in Basel, Switzerland. In his address to the assembly, Herzl demonstrated that he was acutely aware of and sensitive to the strains and fears that the secularity of the political Zionist approach generated within the religious community, and he took steps to alleviate that situation. He observed that Jewish solidarity had been in the process of disintegration for some time, presumably as a direct consequence of the extension of civil emancipation, but was currently being resuscitated as a result of the new inroads of anti-Semitism, a trend that was exemplified by the Dreyfus Affair and its aftermath. Shaken by the vehemence of modern anti-Semitism, Jewish solidarity had been significantly strengthened.

We have returned home, as it were. *Zionism is a return to Jewishness even before there is a return to the Jewish land.* We, the sons who have returned, find in our father's house many things in urgent need of improvement; above all, we have brothers who have sunk deep into misery. However, we have been made welcome in an old home, because it is well known that we do not harbor the presumptuous notion of undermining what is time-honored.[14]

Herzl's deft handling of the delicate question of the place of religion in the Zionist enterprise succeeded in allaying the concerns of many of the attendees. Thus the assembly was able to reach agreement on a set of principles that would govern the future agenda of political Zionism. The official Zionist program approved by the congress declared:

> The aim of Zionism is to create for the Jewish people a home in Palestine secured by public law. The congress contemplates the following means to the attainment of this end:
>
> 1. The promotion, on suitable lines, of the colonization of Palestine by Jewish agricultural and industrial workers.
> 2. The organization and binding together of the whole of Jewry by means of appropriate institutions, local and international, in accordance with the laws of each country.
> 3. The strengthening and fostering of Jewish national sentiment and consciousness.
> 4. Preparatory steps toward obtaining Government consent, where necessary, to the attainment of the aim of Zionism.[15]

It is particularly noteworthy that Herzl's concept of the "Jewish State" is mentioned nowhere in this declaration. This, of course, was the result, not of an oversight, but rather of a necessary compromise. At that time, given the reality of Ottoman control of Palestine, even Herzl recognized that it was probably premature to speak publicly of a "Jewish State," and that to do so might raise additional and unnecessary complications for the fledgling movement. Indeed, there was little reason to believe that the sultan was prepared to contemplate the emergence of a sovereign Jewish state in territory under his domination. Accordingly, the central concept of the Zionist movement was reformulated in terms of Jewish autonomy rather than sovereignty. The formulation, "a home in Palestine secured by public law," which was finally arrived at after considerable debate, was deemed to be sufficiently vague to permit a variety of conflicting interpretations. Most significant, the elimination of the term "state" and its replacement by "home" avoided, so the authors of the formula wished to believe, the troubling issue of national sovereignty. The "home in Palestine" could be taken as meaning nothing more than an internally autonomous region within the Ottoman Empire, something that might be less offensive to the sultan than a program publicly dedicated to achieving sovereign independence at his expense.

Despite the evident weaknesses in the statement of the aims of the new movement, as far as Herzl was concerned the actions of the Zionist Congress constituted a turning point in the history of the world. He noted in his diary entry for September 3, 1897: "If I were to sum up the Congress in a word—which I shall take care not to publish—it would be this: at Basel I founded the Jewish State. If I said this out loud today I would be greeted by universal laughter. In five years perhaps, and certainly in fifty years, everyone will perceive it." He had unquestionably succeeded in transforming the principally philanthropic Hibbat Zion movement into a national political movement—Zionism. As Israel Cohen later described what had occurred: "Hitherto the national idea had meant that Western Jews helped Eastern Jews to settle in Palestine; henceforth it was to mean that Western Jews were to work together with their eastern brethren for the restoration of Jewish national life in Palestine, in which not a section of the people but the whole people should be represented."[16]

As noted earlier, Herzl was fundamentally a "territorialist" rather than a "Zionist"; that is, his primary interest was the re-creation of a sovereign Jewish state. The geographical location of the future state was a matter of secondary importance.

NEGOTIATIONS WITH THE OTTOMANS AND THE BRITISH

Herzl's initial attempts at Zionist diplomacy were not at all encouraging; there appeared to be little hope that the sultan could be induced to allow the Jews to establish an autonomous national home in Palestine. Although Herzl never quite gave up on the idea of reaching an accommodation with the Ottomans, their resistance to Zionist overtures caused him to redirect his diplomacy toward Great Britain. It occurred to him that if he could not get Palestine for the Jews, perhaps he might be able to obtain a foothold for them elsewhere in the immediate vicinity, perhaps in Sinai or Cyprus, both of which were under British control. Once established there, he thought it might be possible to spill over into Palestine at such time as objective circumstances permitted.

This idea had originally been raised with the Zionist leadership following the Third Zionist Congress in 1899 but was dropped because of the vehement opposition by the majority to considering it. However, Herzl, faced by the reality of a total unwillingness of the sultan to reach an accommodation with the Zionists regarding a national home in Palestine, met in 1902 with the British colonial secretary, Joseph Chamberlain, to discuss the possibility of establishing a self-governing Jewish colony at El Arish in the Sinai. Chamberlain indicated that the plan was agreeable to him but would also require the approval of Lord Cromer, the viceroy of Egypt. After several months of study, the project was ultimately rejected by Cromer in May 1903, primarily because of the shortage of adequate water supplies in the area to support the contemplated settlement. In anticipation of such an outcome, Chamberlain had already suggested to Herzl a month earlier the possibility of establishing a Jewish colony in British East Africa (Uganda). Herzl originally dismissed the latter idea out of hand. It seemed quite clear to him that the proposed Jewish colony would have to be established in the vicinity of Palestine if he was to entertain any hope of obtaining the necessary support from the Zionist movement for such a project. However, as the grim reports of the extensive pogroms that struck the Jews of Russia that year reached the West, Herzl became desperate to find a place of refuge for the masses of Jews that were now streaming out of Russia and Eastern Europe. As a result, he indicated a renewed interest in the Uganda scheme suggested by Chamberlain. His active consideration of this possibility soon precipitated a major crisis within the Zionist movement that threatened to tear it apart.

Just prior to the start of the Sixth Zionist Congress, in August 1903, a message was received from the British Colonial Office indicating that the British government was prepared to assist a Zionist commission that might go to East Africa to study the feasibility of establishing a Jewish colony there. Herzl made it clear to the assemblage during his opening address that, of course, Uganda could never be considered as a substitute for Palestine. However, it could well serve as an emergency haven for the increasingly desperate Jews of Eastern Europe. He emphasized that the congress was not being asked to make a decision for or against establishing a colony in Uganda, as the British had not yet formally made such an offer. What was at issue before the assembly was the question of whether to send a study mission there. Because of his immense personal prestige, Herzl eventually succeeded in obtaining a favorable vote on the question. However, it is noteworthy that the principal opposition to his proposal came overwhelmingly from the delegates from Russia and Eastern Europe, who represented the very communities for which an African colony was being considered as a safe haven.

Interestingly, and perhaps somewhat surprisingly, the proposal received the support of most of the religious delegates. On the one hand, they were in general accord with the idea that finding even a temporary place of asylum for the oppressed Jews of Eastern Europe was a matter of the highest importance. On the other hand, they considered the use of Africa for this purpose as clearly preferable to other possible places of refuge. This was so for strictly ideological reasons. These were expressed in their monthly publication, *HaMizrah* (The East):

> Emigration to Africa, as an organized settlement with civil rights and absolute religious freedom, is of greater value and more desirable than emigration to America or Australia, where the danger of assimilation is greater. The settlement in Uganda will not have an individual character, but will have a political basis, and a Jewish state even outside of the Land of Israel would be something very significant.[17]

Notwithstanding the favorable delegate vote of 295 to 177, the geographical distribution of the votes contained a clear message. The Western Jews might have the votes to decide to establish a colony in Africa, but the Russian Zionists would accept only Palestine, regardless of the pressure of events in the czarist empire. Although the turbulent Sixth Congress ended on a note of ostensible harmony, with a resounding reaffirmation of Palestine as *the* Jewish national homeland, the impassioned debate over the territorial issue left deep wounds in the movement which were soon to be reopened.

Herzl died before the Seventh Zionist Congress convened in July 1905, when the Uganda question came up once again for a final determination. Without Herzl to lend his prestige and personal support to the scheme, the opposition, under the leadership of Menahem Ussishkin and Chaim Weizmann, was able to prevail and the proposal was rejected. Nonetheless, some of the advocates of the Uganda scheme refused to accept the majority decision and precipitated a split in the movement. A minority led by Israel Zangwill (1864–1926) seceded from the Zionist organization and formed an independent Jewish Territorial Organization (ITO) to continue the quest for a Jewish state anywhere on the surface of the earth. Although some extreme territorialists rejected Palestine entirely as a potential site, because of its inadequate natural resources and its large indigenous Arab population, Zangwill himself merely argued his belief that the Jews would benefit substantially from the initial period of self-preparation for eventual independent statehood that could be realized in an intermediate self-governing community located elsewhere.

LABOR ZIONISM

Herzl's approach to Jewish nationalism and the achievement of Zionist goals was completely and avowedly political, but other, competing approaches soon dominated Zionist affairs. The most historically significant of these was reflected in the general ideological perspective of the Socialist-Zionist, or Labor Zionist, movement, which rose to great prominence in the Zionist world under the leadership of Nahman Syrkin (1868–1924). The movement emerged about the same time as the Bund, in 1897. However, whereas the Bund was vehemently opposed to Zionism, which it saw as a device for distracting the Jews away from the critical need to bring about basic reforms in Russian society. The Labor Zionists were fully committed to a Zionist solution. That is, they saw the answer to the Jewish question in the creation of an autonomous Jewish social-democratic state in Palestine. It is important to bear in mind the significance of this formulation. The Zionist program they were committed to was not the creation of a Jewish state in Palestine; they wanted only a Jewish "social-democratic" state, and they sought to transform the Zionist movement as a whole into an instrument for achieving their aim. Accordingly, Syrkin vehemently attacked the bourgeois and religious elements that dominated the Zionist movement up to that time. In his view, Zionism meant only Socialist Zionism; all other perspectives were illegitimate. Thus, he wrote in a 1898 polemic, *The Socialist Jewish State*:

> No other class is as morally bankrupt as the bourgeoisie. It lives in an atmosphere of falsehood and fraud. . . . Outwardly, they parade their love of country and government, inwardly they are cynical. Zionism removes the mask and presents them as they are—people without honor and dignity, whose sole purpose is the accumulation of money. Because Zionism arouses the Jews to protest, it forces them to understand their own worthless and miserable existence.

Similarly, Syrkin had little regard for religion, which he saw as a reactionary force for the preservation of the status quo in society. "The modern synagogue," he asserted, "is partner to the Jewish bourgeoisie. Zionism comes into sharp collision with it. At no time in history was the church so pliable to the demands of the ruling class as is the Jewish synagogue of the present time. The synagogue prostituted itself to the Jewish bourgeoisie."[18]

Syrkin's demand for a Socialist-Jewish state was absolutely unequivocal. Any other form of Zionist fulfillment was for him unthinkable. He insisted that "the form of the Jewish state is the only debatable issue involved in Zionism. . . . Zionism must of necessity fuse with socialism, for socialism is in complete harmony with the wishes and hopes of the Jewish masses. Sociological and technical factors make any other form of Jewish state impossible."[19]

The rapidly growing Labor Zionist movement soon encompassed a broad spectrum of socialist thought and belief, including that of classical Marxism. Syrkin's socialism, however, was thoroughly non-Marxist in character. He maintained that the abnormalcy of the economic situation of the Jews throughout the world, exacerbated by their constant need to migrate, could only be rectified through the aims of Socialist, or Labor, Zionism; that is, only in a socialist Jewish state would the Jewish masses feel secure enough to abandon their typically nonproductive middle-class occupations and become productive workers and builders of a new egalitarian society. Syrkin thus laid the theoretical basis for a conception of Zionism that had little in common with the ideals of his predecessors. He was not interested in transplanting the traditional social and economic patterns of Jewish life from Europe to Palestine; he wanted to create an entirely new type of Jewish existence. Indeed, for Syrkin the primary task of Zionism was to create such a new type of Jew. The geographical location where this metamorphosis was to be achieved, whether it took place in Palestine or in some other land, was a matter of only secondary significance. The main thing was to establish a Jewish national home, somewhere, anywhere. Syrkin's essentially "territorialist" position was by no means accepted by all in the Socialist-Zionist movement. One group of socialists who rejected his territorialism, to draw a sharp distinction between their views on the issue and those of Syrkin and to emphasize their stance, subsequently adopted the name of Zionei Zion (Zionists of Zion). For them, the Jewish future could only be fully realized in the Land of Israel.

One of the most prominent spokesmen for the Zionists of Zion in Russia was Ber Borochov (1881–1917), who was also perhaps the socialist movement's preeminent advocate for the synthesis of Marxism and Zionism. In a document prepared for the movement in 1906, entitled "Our Platform," Borochov set forth his version of the fusion of Marxism and Zionism, making it clear that "Proletarian Zionism is possible only if its aims can be achieved through the class struggle; Zionism can be realized only if proletarian Zionism can be realized." There was to be no question whatever about the end goal of the movement; the realization of Zionist aims was preliminary to the higher purpose of achieving a truly socialist society. "Our ultimate aim, our maximum program, is socialism—the socialization of the means of production. . . . Our immediate aim, our minimum program, is Zionism." For Borochov, the Land of Israel was essential not because of any intrinsic value that it represented. It was necessary for the Zionist purpose only because of the historic connection to it of the Jewish people, who were desperately in need of a national territory of their own.

> The necessity of a territory in the case of the Jews results from the unsatisfactory economic strategic base of the Jewish proletariat. The anomalous state of the Jewish people will disappear as soon as the conditions of production prevailing in Jewish life are done away with. . . . Parallel with the growth of economic independence will come the growth of political independence. The ideal of political autonomy for the Jews will be consummated by political territorial autonomy in Palestine. Political territorial autonomy is the ultimate aim of Zionism. For proletarian Zionists, this is also a step toward socialism.[20]

It was not very long before the Labor Zionists took effective control of the Zionist movement, setting the ideological tone for future Jewish state. It is important to recognize that the socialist approach to Zionism essentially argued that economic "normalcy" was the critical step toward creating the "new Jew," although it never clearly articulated just what such a new Jew would be like in a positive sense. As a practical matter, the ideological goal of creating such a "new Jew" really amounted to nothing more than a modern secular reformulation of the long-standing aspiration for national normalcy, a desire that had been a matter of controversy in Jewish life and thought since biblical days.

9

The National Idea in the Twentieth Century

In a series of lectures given in Berlin in the winter of 1899–1900, reviewing the history of the Jews and Judaism during the nineteenth century, the popular writer Gustav Karpeles (1848–1909) took note of the rise of the new secular Jewish nationalism. "In my opinion," he stated, "Zionism is not a main current of Jewish history, but undeniably it has the importance of an underset accompanying the main current. . . . Zionism is the expression of despair. It seeks the solution of the Jewish problem and the end of all confusion, not in the steady, victorious advances of humanity and liberty, but solely and alone in the restoration of Jewish nationality, that is, in self-liberation."[1]

A SPIRITUAL RETURN

Karpeles, and many who shared his views, perceived Zionism as a counterproductive approach to dealing with the vicissitudes of Jewish existence, an ideology that tended to distort the true history of the Jews and their reason for being. In his opinion, the Jews simply were not a nation, and the effort being expended to evoke a sentiment of Jewish nationalism was therefore quite misguided. On the contrary, he argued: "Israel is still what it always was, a religious brotherhood. Herein lies its peculiarity, its individuality." Since remote antiquity, Israel had conceived its special universal role, as indicated by the prophet Isaiah, to be that of serving as a "light to the Gentiles" (Isa. 49:6).

141

Indeed, Karpeles asserted, "it is *par excellence* the historical task of Judaism to combat the tendency toward national particularism," a mission that was completely at odds with Zionist aspirations. He suggested further that given this understanding of Israel's reason for being,

> there can logically be but one conclusion: were Judaism to revive the national sentiment in its adherents, it would commit suicide. The lowest stage of religious development is the stage of a national religion, the highest the stage of a world-religion. We Jews having mounted from step to step, now being close to the desired goal of a world-religion, Zionism would have us return to the primitive stage of a national religion.

In his view, the nationalism represented by Zionism was counterhistorical and therefore anachronistic.

> Since the overthrow of the Temple, Israel's vocation consists in influencing mankind spiritually, and hastening the Messianic age of reconciliation between nation and nation. . . . From this point of view the history of the Diaspora is one of the most glorious portions of Jewish history, for during the long dispersion Judaism has demonstrated its indestructibility, and proved itself far more than a mere national formation.[2]

Karpeles's viewpoint was unquestionably deeply influenced by the ideas of the contemporary Reform movement in Judaism. However, it was also reflective of the position adopted by many other Jewish intellectuals. In essence, the same argument was made by the philosopher Hermann Cohen (1848–1918). Responding to an open letter that Martin Buber addressed to him, asking him to support Zionism, Cohen asserted that modern Judaism had derived its self-identity from its historical development, which had been "given its inner direction by prophetism and its lofty concept of a Messianic mankind. We interpret our entire history as pointing to this Messianic goal. Thus we see the destruction of the Jewish state as an exemplification of the theodicy of history." In other words, whatever purpose it may have served initially, the very notion of the rebirth of a Jewish state had become antithetical to Judaism's universal aims. Cohen thus forcefully reasserted the concept of the affirmation of the Diaspora as an essential element in Israel's mission to the gentiles. He wrote:

> We are proudly aware of the fact that we continue to live as divine dew among the nations; we wish to remain among them and be a creative force for them. All our prophets have us living among the nations, and all view "Israel's remnant" from the perspective of its world mission. And it is from that perspective alone that the natural desire of the remnant to return to the

land of its origin must be understood. For hardly ever is it stated that the remnant is to return all by itself. There is almost always a reference to "many" or to "all peoples" which will be flocking to the light of God.[3]

That is, the notion of a "return" no longer had any exclusive reference to the Jews; in its new and expanded content it encompassed all mankind. Accordingly, Cohen insisted, the idea of a "return" no longer bore any physical connotation or implications; it certainly did not refer to a mass movement of the peoples of the world to the Land of Israel. It quite evidently had become a purely spiritual notion.

Consistent with this approach, Cohen proceeded to redefine the very meaning of the terms "Holy Land" and "Promised Land" so as to deprive them of any connection to the tangible Land of Israel. He wrote:

> Palestine is not merely the land of our fathers; it is the land of our prophets, who established and perfected the ideal of our religion. Hence, we consider it indeed the Holy Land, though only in the sense that our timeless, sacred heritage originated there. But by the same token by which we regard our religious present as a projection of the future we regard the moral world as it unfolds throughout history as our real Promised Land.

Accordingly, Cohen concluded, there was no longer any real nexus between the Jews and Palestine. On the contrary, "we therefore see the entire historical world as the future abode of our religion. And it is this future alone which we acknowledge as our true home."[4]

This entire argument, which was essentially predicated on the drawing of a clear distinction between Jewish nationalism and Judaism, did not go unchallenged. Indeed, it was categorically rejected by the Zionist writer Ahad Ha'am. In a letter written in 1910, the latter declared: "Judaism is fundamentally national, and all the efforts of the 'Reformers' to separate the Jewish religion from its national element have had no result except to ruin both the nationalism and the religion. Clearly, then, if you want to build and not to destroy, you must teach religion on the basis of nationalism, with which it is inseparably intertwined."[5]

Nonetheless, the thrust of Cohen's argument was developed further by the philosopher Franz Rosenzweig (1886–1929), who similarly stripped the notion of the national home of its territorial content. He wrote: "To the eternal people, home never is home in the sense of land, as it is to the peoples of the world who plough the land and live and thrive on it, until they have all but forgotten that being a people means something besides being rooted in a land."[6] The Jews, in this formulation, are necessarily different from other peoples, to whom such a notion would be largely incomprehensible. It seems clear that Rosenzweig probably would have agreed wholeheartedly with the Spanish writer Salvador de Madariaga, who declared: "The Jews have no roots in space. Their roots are in time; their soil is made of twenty centuries of tradition. They differ from all the peoples of the earth in that their fatherland is history itself."[7] Rosenzweig too saw the Jews as eternally rooted in the flow of history rather than in a particular geographical space. "The eternal people has not been permitted to wile away time in any home. It never loses the untrammeled freedom of a wanderer who is more faithful a knight to his country when he roams abroad, craving adventure and yearning for the land he has left behind, than when he lives in that land. In the most profound sense possible, this people has a land of its own only in that it has a land that it yearns for—a holy land." He suggested further that this was not simply a consequence of Israel's peculiar history. It was, in his view, an essential aspect of the divine design. "And so," he wrote, "even when it has a home, this people, in recurrent contrast to all other peoples on earth, is not allowed full possession of that home. It is only 'a stranger and a sojourner.'" The Land, he agreed, is the Lord's, and the very holiness of the Land makes it elude Israel's permanent grasp. At the same time,

> this holiness increases the longing for what is lost, to infinity, and so the people can never be entirely at home in any other land. This longing compels it to concentrate the full force of its will on a thing which, for other peoples, is only one among others yet which to it is essential and vital: the community of blood. In doing this, the will to be a people dares not cling to any mechanical means; the will can realize its end only through the people itself.[8]

For Rosenzweig, then, it is the perseverance of the Jewish people that becomes the issue of paramount concern; there is no place in his conception for Israel as a viable national force in the unfolding of history. Indeed, as he understood it, by its very definition Jewish nationalism represents a negation of Israel's universal mission to the nations.

The issue of the incompatibility between Jewish nationalism and Jewish universalism was addressed by Eliezer Berkovits in a work published in 1943, at a time when the extent of the catastrophe that was engulfing European Jewry had not yet become a matter of general public knowledge. Berkovits sought to draw a distinction between a properly Jewish nationalism and the sort of "national egotism" that had created international anarchy during the preceding century.[9] In his view, there was no fundamental antithesis between authentic Jewish nationalism and Jewish universalism, which were in effect the two sides of a common coin. Discussing the intimate relation between the two, Berkovits wrote:

The Jewish national unit is an instrument serving a higher purpose that in its very essence is anational. But, in order to be an effective working instrument, the national unit must control its own life. This means that for Jews to live dispersed all over the world in the midst of strange surroundings, necessarily moving to the rhythm of a life different from that of the Jewish national unit, is an unnatural form of "judaistic" existence. Galut may at times be an historic necessity, it may produce its own great values, but it must always be looked upon as a period of transition, something temporary, not only from the national point of view but also from that of the realisation of Judaism.[10]

RELIGIOUS ZIONISM

The antithesis drawn between Jewish particularism and Jewish universalism in the works of Cohen and Rosenzweig, as well as by the Reformers and other advocates of the affirmation of the Diaspora, was challenged most forcefully by Abraham Isaac Kook (1865–1935), the first chief rabbi of Palestine, who sought to synthesize the two perspectives. In his view, the national deliverance and restoration of Israel would constitute the necessary prelude to the universal salvation of humankind from paganism and agnosticism. The fulfillment of Jewish national aspirations was therefore an essential and intrinsically positive aspect of Israel's universal mission, the achievement of which was otherwise inconceivable. From this standpoint, Jewish nationalism and Jewish universalism were intimately interrelated rather than antithetical.

Pursuing the thrust of this argument, Rabbi Kook insisted that the Land of Israel itself possessed a unique attribute that inextricably bound the people of Israel to it. "Eretz Israel," he wrote, "is not something apart from the soul of the Jewish people; it is no mere national possession, serving as a means of unifying our people and buttressing its material, or even its spiritual, survival. Eretz Israel is part of the very essence of our nationhood; it is bound organically to its very life and inner being." He acknowledged that this was a metarational conception but insisted that this in no way invalidated the essential truth of the proposition. He suggested that

human reason, even at its most sublime, cannot begin to understand the unique holiness of Eretz Israel; it cannot stir the depths of love for the land that are dormant within our people. What Eretz Israel means to the Jew can be felt only through the Spirit of the Lord which is in our people as a whole, through the spiritual cast of the Jewish soul, which radiates its characteristic influence to every healthy emotion.

Accordingly, he considered the idea that the Land of Israel should be regarded as a mere instrument in the service of the achievement of national unity, or even as a point of common reference for sustaining Judaism in the Diaspora, to be a sterile concept. It was, in his view, a notion "unworthy of the holiness of Eretz Israel." On the contrary, he argued: "A valid strengthening of Judaism in the Diaspora can only come from a deepening attachment to Eretz Israel. The hope for the Return to the Holy Land is the continuing source of the distinctive nature of Judaism. The hope for the Redemption is the force that sustains Judaism in the Diaspora; the Judaism of Eretz Israel is the very Redemption."[11]

The strong nationalist views of Rabbi Kook facilitated an alliance between religious and secular Zionists on the common ground of devotion to the land and people of Israel, but they failed to redirect the secularists toward a new synthesis of traditional and modern Jewish nationalism. As a consequence, the dominant role in the Jewish nationalist movement asserted by the secular Zionists evoked expressions of concern from a variety of sources that extended well beyond the ambit of the religious traditionalists. Notable among these was the philosopher Martin Buber (1878–1965). One issue of particular concern to him was the emphatic advocacy by the secular Zionists of the goal of achieving national "normalcy," a goal that attacked the traditional conception of Israel and Judaism.

It seemed clear from the traditional perspective that if the Jews were to become a nation like all others, they would thereby forfeit their very reason for being. In support of this position, Buber declared:

Israel is not a nation like other nations, no matter how much its representatives have wished it during certain eras. Israel is a people like no other, for it is the only people in the world which, from its earliest beginnings, has been both a nation and a religious community. In the historical hour in which its tribes grew together to form a people, it became the carrier of a revelation. The covenant which the tribes made with one another and through which they became "Israel" takes the form of a common covenant with the God of Israel.

Because of this, "Israel was and is a people and a religious community in one, and it is this unity which enabled it to survive in an exile no other nation had to suffer." Buber therefore concluded that "he who severs this bond severs the life of Israel."[12]

Buber saw it as an anomaly that although, as a result of the pioneering work done in Palestine by the Zionists to restore the national homeland, the nation seemed to be on the mend, the national religion appeared to be in a state of unrelenting decline. In essence, Judaism had been relegated almost exclusively to the synagogue and seemed to have little significance or relevance for the developing cultural life of the people. He considered this condition deplorable, and a grave danger to the future of the nation. Buber insisted that

a Jewish nation cannot exist without religion any more than a Jewish religious community without nationality. . . . According to the ideas current among Zionists today, all that is needed is to establish the conditions for a normal national life, and everything will come of itself. This is a fatal error. We do, of course, need the conditions of normal national life, but these are not enough—not enough for us, at any rate. We cannot enthrone "normalcy" in place of the eternal premise of our survival. If we want to be nothing but normal, we shall soon cease to be at all.[13]

Nonetheless, the desire for national "normalcy" continued to dominate much Zionist thought and aspiration throughout most of the present century.

The establishment of the reborn State of Israel in May 1948 (the circumstances of the establishment are not within the scope of this book) raised a peculiar dilemma for Jewish nationalism. Was the creation of the state itself the culmination of Zionism, or did there still remain a national mission that had yet to be achieved? This question, of course, goes beyond the matter of Israel's immediate survival as a state within the hostile environment of the contemporary Middle East. It is in essence not a political issue but a philosophical one, the roots of which reach far back into Jewish antiquity. Today, the issue is often couched in terms of the relationship of Israel to the Diaspora, where Zionism has come to mean, almost exclusively, the rendering of political and financial support to the struggling Jewish state.

To the disappointment of many, it soon became abundantly evident that the creation of a Jewish state in the ancient Jewish homeland did not bring an end to the "Jewish problem," as had been widely anticipated. That problem still persists. Nor did the Jewish state bring an end to anti-Semitism, which today appears once again to be on the rise. As suggested by Immanuel Jakobovits, chief rabbi of the British commonwealth, in 1962:

Israel certainly has not "solved the Jewish problem." Jews today are as uniquely different as they had always been. . . . The dangers of anti-Semitism today are as great as they were before the establishment of Israel. . . . The Jewish problem has remained unsolved and will remain so in the foreseeable future. Jewish statehood has not "normalized" Jewish life in the Diaspora. On the contrary, in some ways Israel has added for Jews many new problems which never existed before.[14]

One evident consequence of this has been a significant loss of confidence in the continuing significance of secular Jewish nationalism, as it has been professed for a century, both in Israel and in the Diaspora. Zionism is no longer the evocative conception that spurred Jewish nationalists to extraordinary accomplishments against enormous odds. It is of course true that Israel, by virtue of its Law of Return, continues to remain a Zionist state, committed to serving as the national home of all the Jewish people. However, as a resonating ideology predicating the nation's direction into the future, Zionism appears to have run its course.

NORMALIZING THE STATE

In the view of many of the remaining adherents and advocates of Zionism, the principal task of secular Jewish nationalism is that of "normalizing" the state, that is, transforming modern Israel into a state like all other states. To achieve this, according to those Zionists, the people of Israel must first become a nation like all others; a position that has been consistently and categorically rejected by religious traditionalists and nationalists since biblical days. As a consequence, the issue of "normalization" continues to be a major bone of contention among Israelis and thoughtful Jews everywhere. Rabbi Joseph B. Soloveitchik, perhaps the most authoritative contemporary voice of religious nationalism, suggested that the singular failing of secular Zionism lay in its adoption of the specious proposition that by becoming "like all the nations," the new State of Israel would bring an end to the historic isolation of the people and nation of Israel.[15]

The Israeli religious philosopher and statesman, Yaacov Herzog (1921–1972), epitomized the traditional nationalist perspective on this question in his argument affirming the historical validity of the idea of Jewish uniqueness among the nations of the world. He wrote:

Three thousand years ago Balaam the Prophet described the Children of Israel as "a people that dwells alone." This is a very strange concept, one that cannot be explained in terms of any mythology of the ancient world. . . . The problem is whether this concept denotes a privilege—not an escape from society as a whole, but a unique role within it—or whether it is an anomaly, which must be denied and discarded. This is *the* question of Jewish history.[16]

The answer of Herzog and the traditionalists, as already indicated, is a strong reaffirmation of the conviction that the Jews were and remain intended to be a unique people within the universal framework of the divine purpose. Indeed, for Herzog this national uniqueness is neither an abnormality nor a curse. It is, as one contemporary writer suggested, "the sign of a Jewish spiritual mission, which should be regarded as a blessing, a paramount moral imperative, and the raison d'être of Israel's international existence."[17] Herzog recalled that the sages held Balaam in the highest esteem as a prophet, and he explained this as follows:

> All prophecy relates to events as they will unfold, but Balaam's prophecy was even higher in that it related to the nature of a people until the end of time, which lies beyond any possible human concept. A human being with wisdom, with insight, with intuition may see ahead a year or two, or perhaps ten or twenty, and conceive of the unfolding of events in some form. If this reaches a perception over thousands of years, it is clearly Divine Providence that has been given to the man. . . . Therefore his prophecy was put above all other prophecy except that of Moses.[18]

In other words, he suggested that the prophecy of Balaam has eternal validity—Israel is destined to be "a people that dwells alone"; that is the essential condition of its existence—to be unlike all other nations.

This view is given powerful expression by Rabbi Soloveitchik, who argued that unless this uniqueness becomes the overriding characteristic of the Jewish state, the very significance of the state becomes dramatically diminished. Discussing this question from the standpoint of the human costs of statehood in the face of the unrelenting hostility of the Arab world, Soloveitchik asserted:

> If the State of Israel is a part of the Divine covenant with Abraham . . . if the State of Israel will be a link in the golden chain of Jewish tradition . . . then all the sacrifices are worthwhile, all the altars that we have built to found the State are sacred and precious. . . . But if the State of Israel will become a secular kingdom, without Torah, without sanctity, . . . a state in which Jewish uniqueness will be erased, then the price we are paying for her in blood and tears is too heavy.[19]

Accordingly, as far as the traditionalists are concerned, the essential tasks of Jewish nationalism were not accomplished with the creation of the modern Jewish state and still remain to be addressed. As a consequence of this deeply held conviction, it is the religious nationalists of modern Israel who have become the most assertive nationalist force in the country, particularly as secular nationalism slides increasingly into disrepute as an ideology capable of stirring the people to self-sacrifice for a higher and selfless cause. Although it is difficult for many to accept, secular Zionism, having made the principal contribution to the re-creation of an independent Jewish state, seems no longer to be a viable concept, having exhausted its content in the process of its victory in the political and military struggle to bring the state into being. Indeed, viewed with some detachment from Israel's ongoing struggle against the unrelenting enmity of its neighbors, the saga of the Zionist movement and Zionism may with some justice be seen as no more than a critical, albeit brief, episode in the multimillennial history of Jewish nationalism. Now that the state has been created, the question of its national purpose has once again become the crucial issue, and on this question there is a sharp dichotomy between secularists and religious traditionalists.

From the standpoint of the new generation of religious nationalists, the establishment of the State of Israel can only be understood properly as the beginning of the ultimate restoration of the nation and national redemption, rather than as its culmination. This school of contemporary Jewish nationalist thought takes its immediate inspiration from the work of Rabbi Zvi Yehuda Kook (1891–1982). Rooting his position in traditional perspectives, he wrote:

> Just as the Galut [Exile] constituted the destruction of the nation's life in its severance from its own place . . . so the Redemption, which is the cancellation of the Galut, is the reconstruction of the nation's life and restoration to its own place. Just as the plan of the first Redemption ends with the arrival in the land given to the patriarchs as a heritage . . . so the plan of the latter Redemption is to be accomplished upon our restoration to this inheritance of ours.[20]

Arguing that the creation of the State of Israel is itself evidence of God's intervention in history and the beginning of the redemption, he insisted: "The State of Israel was created and established by the council of nations by order of the Sovereign Lord of the Universe so that the clear commandment in the Torah 'that they shall inherit and settle the Land' would be fulfilled."[21]

But, Zvi Yehuda Kook cautioned, no one should conclude that the emergence of the modern State of Israel in itself represents the ultimate redemption. In making this argument, he put forward a notion that helps explain the continuing role of the Diaspora in the unfolding of the divine scheme in history. He suggested that the restoration of the Jewish state represents a necessary preliminary stage in the redemptive process, which necessarily follows a gradual course toward its culmination.

> This basic concept of gradual progress is indeed implicit in the lowest stage of Redemption—a stage which is not the Redemption in the true sense of a complete cessation of the Exile, but in the sense of a "deliverance" that occurs during the period of Exile but which is accompanied by its own particular troubles. . . . The advance by gradual stages in the process of this

"Redemption" within the period of the Exile in itself represents a revelation of the stages by which the true and absolute Redemption of the Land of Israel will be directed.[22]

The restoration of the nation of Israel in its land is clearly intended to serve a higher purpose, one that transcends nationalism as an end in itself. Israel has a cosmic mission that can only be carried out when it is reconstituted as the unique nation it was intended to be at its formation. Accordingly,

> this true Redemption must gradually end our people's state of being "scattered abroad and dispersed" among hostile nations, and restore it to its pristine state of being "one nation on earth" on its own soil, just as it must fulfill the words of the Torah and establish the Shekhina when Israel returns to its own place and to its national revival there . . . so this Redemption must renew Israel's vital existence in all its true perfection, in the pleasantness of God and in the light of His ordinance, by renewing the strength of its settlement in the Land and of its inheritance thereof.[23]

Moreover, he insisted, "the true Redemption, which is to be manifested in the complete resettlement in the Land and the revival of Israel in it, is thus seen to be a continuation of renewed settlement in the Land accompanied by the ingathering of the captive exiles within its boundaries." Rabbi Kook went even further and effectively asserted that the redemptive process demands that the Land in its entirety be under the unequivocal control of Israel. Only then will the restoration reflect

> the peak of the actual fulfillment of our inheriting the Land, of its being in our possession and not "in that of any other of the nations nor in a state of desolation," of the rule of our own government in it, and of the adherence of our group behavior to its real holiness. Hence, when this State of ours is in full control, both internally and externally, then the fulfillment of this mitzva of the Inheritance can be truly revealed—the mitzva that is the basis and essence of all the mitzvot relating to settlement in the Land. It is these mitzvot that, by means of our rule, can accomplish the act of Redemption, and it is by their means that the vision of Redemption must be progressively fulfilled according to the word of the Universal King.[24]

Viewed from this perspective, secular Jewish nationalism may serve a utilitarian purpose in helping to advance the redemptive process but cannot in itself fulfill Israel's destiny as a nation. As Shlomo Goren, the former chief rabbi of Israel, put it: "The State of Israel cannot shirk the nation's historical obligation to preserve the eternal heritage of Torah and the ethics of the prophets, values which have represented, from the very beginning, the meaningful content of our lives and our national and spiritual image." Consistent with the traditional nationalist understanding of Judaism, Rabbi Goren emphatically rejected the secular arguments for achieving national "normalcy" as a primary goal of the new Jewish state. In his view, the very notion that "'the house of Judah is like all the nations' undermines our very right to existence as a nation and a state and is injurious to our eternal rights to the Land of Israel."[25] Or, as this same point is made by Immanuel Jakobovits: "The one thing the Jewish State could not, and must not, and never will achieve is to turn us into a nation like all other nations, losing our historic identity as a unique people."[26]

Rabbi Goren carried his argument further by also rejecting the notion that one can successfully distinguish between religious and national goals, which he considers to be inextricably bound together, at least as far as Judaism and Israel are concerned.

> From time immemorial the absolute identity between Israel's uniqueness and its Torah was taken for granted by the Jewish people and the world at large. . . . Similarly, the national goals of the Jewish people have always been identified with those of the Torah of Israel. . . . *Neither the Torah nor the Prophets recognize the possibility of divorcing our national goals from religion.* Nationhood and religion have been linked throughout our glorious, heroic history, complementing each other and even overlapping.

Indeed, he argued, "The values of faith, ethics and society contained in the Torah determined the foundations of our nation's uniqueness." Consequently, he concludes, "any separation between religion and the state detracts from the nation's completeness and oneness and deprives the state of its special meaning."[27]

The lines of the ideological conflict over the nature of Jewish nationalism, and how this shall be manifested in the purposes and aims of the State of Israel, are thus being drawn ever more sharply within the broader Jewish community. It would be premature to suggest how this issue will be resolved, if indeed it is susceptible to resolution. In the short run, however, an implicit marriage of convenience has taken place between a significant segment of the religious nationalists and the "right-wing" secular nationalists in Israel, the point of convergence of their common interests being the disposition of the territories of Judea, Samaria, and Gaza, the former two often referred to as the "West Bank."

To understand the nature of this temporary alliance, it is necessary to bear in mind that what the religious nationalists consider to be the Land of Israel is not limited to the land that was included within the borders of the State of Israel, as they were defined by the United Nations partition plan and the subsequent adjustments made in the armistice agreements of 1949. For the religious nationalists, the Land of Israel encompasses all of biblical Israel, which clearly includes Judea and Samaria where most of the significant events in ancient Israel's national history took place. Moreover, this land—all of it—is considered to be basically inalienable. Thus, in a recent article discussing the biblical concepts of the sabbatical years and the Jubilee, Rabbi Shlomo Riskin wrote: "In fact, the land belongs to God, and He determines in what way and for how long it is to be used. But there is another equally important element; God has determined that the land will belong eternally to the Israelites who conquered it. . . . The land is eternal, linked to an eternal God who gives an eternal inheritance, one which can't be lost or whittled away."[28]

The religious nationalist position is thus one that would limit the authority of the government of Israel to make any political concessions for the sake of peace that would entail the alienation of any part of the Land of Israel, which by religious definition includes Judea and Samaria. In this regard, the chief rabbi of Israel, Avraham Shapira, declared: "Matters concerning the Land of Israel are above politics. . . . And we are commanded to defend in its entirety the land granted to us by the Holy One, blessed be He. It is impossible that the Jewish people should concede in any manner whatever with regard to its boundaries, and any such concession, if there should be such, has no significance."[29]

The political importance of the religious nationalist position became highly evident in early 1990 when, following an inconclusive national election in Israel, the attempt by the Labor Coalition to form a government was effectively scuttled because of the opposition of Rabbi Menachem Mendel Schneerson of New York, the grand rabbi of Lubavitch, to its policy calling for the exchange of "land for peace." In this instance, two members of religious parties critical to the formation of a legislative majority reneged on their prior agreement, in apparent response to the wishes of Rabbi Schneerson, who had issued a ruling declaring it to be contrary to Jewish law to surrender any part of the Land of Israel, even in exchange for peace. Rabbi Schneerson's rationale for such a position is simply that "the Land of Israel belongs to each and every one of the children of Israel, wherever they may be, both those who may be found in the Land of Israel and those who may for the time being be found outside the Land. Clearly, no one has the authority to give to the nations of the world any part of the territories of the Land of Israel that belongs to the entire people of Israel."[30] In other words, no government of the State of Israel would be considered to have the legitimate authority to dispose of any portion of the Land of Israel, since it is the divinely granted patrimony of the entire Jewish people, which has not empowered the Israeli government to act on its behalf for such purpose. Moreover, even if it were so empowered, Rabbi Schneerson would surely insist that the Israeli government still could not legitimately alienate the Land permanently, an act that would constitute a unilateral abrogation of the fundamental covenant between God and the children of Israel.

This political intervention by a powerful religious leader, on an issue of immense importance from the religious nationalist perspective, had the net result of preventing a Labor government from coming to power in Israel and permitting the right-wing Likud to form a ruling coalition in its stead. However, as already suggested, this affair reflects what is clearly a temporary marriage of political convenience, one that is based solely on a coincidence of interests with respect to a single—albeit vitally important—issue. It is therefore reasonable to expect that once the status of Judea and Samaria is resolved, this alliance between the religious nationalists and the secular nationalist Right will dissolve. At such time, if not before, the fundamental differences between these groups over the essential character of their diverse and conflicting nationalist perspectives will rise to prominence once again.

Whereas some secularists would like to consider this resurgent Jewish religious nationalism as a "fundamentalist" aberration that will soon run its course, that seems, at least to me, to be wishful thinking. As this study has sought to demonstrate, Jewish nationalism is deeply embedded within Judaism, and with the reemergence of a sovereign Jewish state, the reasons for the repeated efforts throughout history to suppress or transform it are no longer considered valid by a growing number of religiously committed people. Why, they ask, should Israel not be the ideal state predicated in Scripture and tradition? At this particular time, it is much too early to venture a guess about whether and to what extent the religious nationalists will be able to shape the future course of the nation and state of Israel. The only thing that seems certain is that they will continue to make a major effort to do so in the years ahead.

NOTES

INTRODUCTION

1. Hans Kohn, *The Idea of Nationalism*, p. 36.

CHAPTER 1

1. Henry Tudor, *Political Myth*, pp. 138–139.
2. W. D. Davies, *The Territorial Dimension of Judaism*, pp. 8–9.
3. Mircea Eliade, *The Sacred and the Profane*, pp. 20–21.
4. Ibid., p. 26.
5. Ibid., p. 34.
6. Hans Kohn, *The Idea of Nationalism*, pp. 36–37.
7. Martin Buber, *Israel and Palestine*, p. xi.
8. *Shabbat* 88a: *Avodah Zarah* 2b.
9. Maimonides, *The Commandments*, pt. 2, #246. See also Aaron haLevi of Barcelona, *Sefer haHinukh*, #525.
10. Maimonides, *Hilkhot Geneivah*, 7:11 (Maimonides citations beginning with "*Hilkhot*" refer to books of the *Mishne Torah*). Translation used here is by Hyman Klein, *The Book of Torts,* p. 81. See also Joseph Karo, *Shulhan Arukh: Hoshen Mishpat* #376.
11. *Sifre: A Tannaitic Commentary on the Book of Deuteronomy*, Piska 188, pp. 207–208.
12. Buber, *Israel and Palestine*, p. xi.

CHAPTER 2

1. Joseph Grunblatt, *Exile and Redemption*, p. 78.
2. See Jonathan A. Goldstein, "Even the Righteous Can Perish by His Faith," *Conservative Judaism* 41 (3), Spring 1989.
3. Grunblatt, *Exile and Redemption*, p. 91.

CHAPTER 3

1. Bernard Joseph, *Nationality: Its Nature and Problems*, p. 239.

2. *Yoma* 9b.

3. See discussion of this point in Joseph Grunblatt, *Exile and Redemption*, pp. 45–49.

4. *Sanhedrin* 74a. See also *Ketuvot* 19a.

5. *Yoma* 9b.

6. See Isaac Hirsch Weiss, *Dor Dor veDorshav*, vol. 2, p. 37, especially n. 1.

7. *M. Pesahim* 10:6.

8. *Sifre Deuteronomy*, Piska 1. See also *Pesikta de-Rab Kahana*, Piska 20:7; *Song of Songs Rabbah* 7:5:3.

9. *Kelim* 1:6.

10. *Leviticus Rabbah* 13:2. See also *Midrash Tanhuma*, "Re'eh," 8.

11. *Numbers Rabbah* 3:7. See also *Yalkut Shimeoni*, "Ekev," #860.

12. Joseph Klausner, *The Messianic Idea in Israel*, p. 404.

13. *Berakhot* 34b; *Shabbat* 63a; *Pesahim* 68a; *Sanhedrin* 91b, 99a.

14. *J. Ma'aser Sheni* 5:2.

15. *Avodah Zarah* 9b.

16. *Sanhedrin* 97b.

17. This episode is chronicled in Socrates, *Historia Ecclesiastica*, vol. 7, p. 36 (Bohn's ed.) and is cited by Julius H. Greenstone, *The Messiah Idea in Jewish History*, p. 110.

18. Ibid.

19. *Sanhedrin* 97b.

20. *Pirke de Rabbi Eliezer*, chap. 35, near end; *Midrash Shoher Tov*, Ps. 91; *Yalkut haMakhiri al Tehillim*, Ps. 91:23. Note also the *Targum of Palestine* regarding "the foundation stone wherewith the Lord of the world sealed up the mouth of the great deep at the beginning" (Exod. 29).

21. "Seder Arkin," in J. D. Eisenstein, ed., *Otzar Midrashim*, vol. 1, p. 70.

22. "Midrash HaShem beHokhmah Yassad Aretz," in Eisenstein, *Otzar Midrashim*, vol. 1, p. 104. The point is also found in "Midrash Konen," in *Otzar Midrashim*, vol. 1, p. 254: "And He took the 'foundation stone' and shot it into the place of the Holy Temple, and founded the world upon it." See also teaching of R. Yose in *Tosefta Yoma* 2:12, and discussion in *Yoma* 54b.

23. *Pirke de Rabbi Eliezer*, chap. 11, chap. 12.

24. *Ketuvot* 111a; *Tosefta Avodah Zarah* 5:2.

25. This is based on the following exegesis: "And, behold, the glory of the God of Israel came from the east; and His voice was like the sound of many waters; and the earth did shine with His glory (Ezek. 43:2). Now, 'His glory' is nought else but the Temple, as you read: Thou throne of glory, on high from the beginning, Thou place of our sanctuary (Jer. 17:12)." *Genesis Rabbah* 3:4; also in *Leviticus Rabbah* 31:7. See also *Pesikta de-Rab Kahana*, Piska 21:5; *Midrash Shoher Tov*, Ps. 104:4.

26. *Pesikta de-Rab Kahana*, Piska 21:5, p. 341; *Leviticus Rabbah*, 31:7. See also *Midrash Tanhuma*, Rosen ed., "Tetzaveh," 7.

27. *Genesis Rabbah* 55:7. See also *Midrash Tanhuma*, Buber ed., "VaYerah," 45.

28. *Berakhot* 30a.

29. *Gittin* 45a.

30. *Makkot* 7a. See also *Tosefta Sanhedrin* 3:11 and *J. Makkot* 1:8. The latter sources indicate that the sanctuary offered is limited, that is, the merit of the Land merely entitles the fugitive from abroad to a new trial.

31. *Megillah* 14a.

32. Abraham Hirsch Rabinowitz, *The Jewish Mind*, pp. 131–132, in reference to the Responsa, *Tzofenat Pa'aneah*, #143.

33. *Yevamot* 64a.

34. *Sifra*, "Kedoshim," 12:14.

35. *Yalkut Shimeoni*, "Bo," #187; *Midrash Tanhuma*, Buber ed., "Bereshit," 11; *Midrash Lekah Tov*, "Bereshit," 1.

36. *Yalkut Shimeoni*, "Eikhah," #1038.

37. *Ketuvot* 110b. See also *Tosefta Avodah Zarah* 5:2.

38. Explanation offered by Samuel Eidels (Maharshah), *Hiddushei Aggadot* (printed in standard rabbinic editions of Babylonian Talmud). Reference is to *Ketuvot* 110b.

39. *Sifra*, "BeHar," 5:4.

40. *Midrash Shoher Tov*, Ps. 99:1.

41. *Sifre Deuteronomy*, Piska 80; *Tosefta Avodah Zarah* 5:2.

42. Simon Federbusch, "Yesodot Tziyonut haTorah," in S. Federbusch, ed., *Hazon Torah veTziyon*, p. 15, n. 40.

43. *Baba Kamma* 80b.

44. *Ketuvot* 110b–111a; *Shabbat* 41a.

45. *Ketuvot* 111a.

46. Ibid.

47. *Song of Songs Rabbah* 2:7:1.

48. *Ketuvot* 111a. It should be noted that the Talmud records a statement by R. Eleazar made in connection with his support of proselytization that could be interpreted as implying that the exile was not entirely a punishment for Israel's sins, but that it also served a positive purpose. "The Holy One, blessed be He, did not exile Israel among the nations save in order that proselytes might join them." This view was also shared by R. Johanan. See *Pesahim* 87b.

49. *Genesis Rabbah* 96:5; *Midrash Tanhuma*, Rosen ed., "VaYehi," 4; *Midrash haGadol*, "Bereshit," 47:29, p. 809.

50. *Ketuvot* 111a. See also *Yalkut Shimeoni*, "Yehezkel," #366.

51. *Genesis Rabbah* 96:5; *Midrash Tanhuma*, "VaYehi," 4.

52. *J. Ketuvot* 12:3; *J.Kilayim* 9:3; *Yalkut Shimeoni*, "Tehillim," #142.

53. *Ketuvot* 111a.

CHAPTER 4

1. Joseph Klausner, *K'sheUmmah Nilhemet al Herutah*, pp. 298–307.

2. Saadia Gaon, *The Book of Beliefs and Opinions*, p. 290.

3. Ibid., pp. 294–295.

4. Commentary on *Berakhot* 59a. Quoted by Salo W. Baron, *A Social and Religious History of the Jews*, vol. 6, p. 46. Hananel's commentary does not appear in standard editions of the Talmud and is cited from a manuscript published by B. M. Lewin in his "R. Hananel's Commentary on Berakhot 59a" (Hebrew), *Ginze Kedem*, 1, 26–45.

5. Abraham bar Hiyya, *Megillat haMegalleh*, p. 110.

6. Abraham bar Hiyya, *The Meditation of the Sad Soul*, p. 146.

7. Ibid., p. 142.

8. Ibid., p. 147.

9. Judah Halevi, *Selected Poems of Jehudah Halevi*, p. 15.

10. Judah Halevi, *Book of Kuzari*, p. 78.

11. Ibid., p. 80.

12. Ibid., p. 78.

13. Ibid., p. 258.

14. Ibid., pp. 258–259.

15. *Makkot* 2b.

16. Halevi, *Kuzari*, p. 259.

17. Ibid., p. 261.

18. Maimonides, "Hakdama lePerek Helek," *Hakdamot lePerush haMishnah*, pp. 129–130. See also Abraham Maimonides, *Milhamot haShem*, p. 64, where his father's position is explicated and defended.

19. Maimonides, *Hilkhot Melakhim* 11:1.

20. David Kimhi, *Perush haRadak*, on Ps. 146:3.

21. *The Bahir*, #130, p. 48.

22. Quoted in *The Early Kabbalah*, p. 134.

23. Gershon Scholem, *Kabbalah*, pp. 165–166.

24. Quoted by Moshe Idel, "Some Conceptions of the Land of Israel in Medieval Jewish Thought," in his *A Straight Path*, p. 130.

25. Nahmanides, *Perushei haTorah*, on Gen. 19:5.

26. Ibid., on Lev. 18:25.

27. Ibid., on Num. 33:53.

28. Ibid., on Lev. 26:16.

29. For Maimonides' position, see his *The Commandments*, #187; *Hilkhot Melakhim* 6:1; and *Guide of the Perplexed* 1:54. For Nahmanides, see his *Hasagot al haSharashim uMinyan haMitzvot*, addition #4, to Maimonides' *Sefer haMitzvot*. For discussion of entire issue, see Shlomo Goren, *Torat haShabbat vehaMoed*, pp. 338–356; J. David Bleich, *Contemporary Halakhic Problems*, pp. 5–9; Isaac Herzog, *Tehukah leYisrael al pi haTorah*, vol. 1, app. 1.

30. Nahmanides, commentary on *Song of Songs* 8:12, quoted in Yosef Tirosh, *Religious Zionism: An Anthology*, p. 22.

31. Nissim Gerondi, *Shnaim Assar Derushim*, Lecture #4, p. 25.

32. Idel, "Some Conceptions of the Land of Israel," p. 133.

33. *Sefer haZohar—Midrash haNe'elam*, "Vayera," p. 113b.

34. Ibid., p. 136b.

35. Quoted by Joseph R. Hacker, "Links Between Spanish Jewry and Palestine, 1391–1492," in Richard I. Cohen, ed., *Vision and Conflict in the Holy Land*, pp. 114–115.

36. *Perush al haTorah: Meyuhas leTalmid HaRan*, p. 95.
37. Ibid.
38. Ibid., p. 37.
39. Isaac Aboab, *Menorat haMaor*, #100.
40. Quoted by Scholem, *Kabbalah*, p. 167.
41. Quoted by Idel, "Some Conceptions of the Land of Israel," p. 135.
42. Ibid.
43. André Neher, *Moses and the Vocation of the Jewish People*, p. 162.
44. Judah Loew ben Bezalel (Maharal), *Netzah Yisrael*, chap. 1, p. 4.
45. Ibid., chap. 10, p. 39.
46. Ibid., chap. 24, p. 76.
47. Ibid., chap. 1, p. 5.

CHAPTER 5

1. Quoted by E. I. Bromberg, "MeHolelei haTziyonut haDatit beTekufat Shivat Tziyon," in S. Federbusch, ed., *Hazon Torah veTziyon*, p. 28.
2. Quoted by Abraham Hirsch Rabinowitz, *The Jewish Mind*, pp. 136–137.
3. Elijah of Vilna, *Aderet Eliyahu*, on Deut. 8:1, p. 390.
4. *Moses Mendelssohn: Selections from His Writings*, p. 85.
5. *Transactions of the Parisian Sanhedrim*, pp. 133–134.
6. Franz Kobler, *Napoleon and the Jews*, pp. 143–144.
7. *Transactions of the Parisian Snadhedrim*, pp. 180–181.
8. Quoted by Kobler, *Napoleon and the Jews*, p. 152.
9. Simon Dubnow, *Nationalism and History*, p. 112.
10. Quoted by Isaac Goldberg, *Major Noah: American-Jewish Pioneer*, pp. 139–141.
11. Ibid., pp. 240–242.
12. Ibid.
13. Ibid., p. 262.
14. Samson Raphael Hirsch, *The Nineteen Letters of Ben Uziel*, pp. 161–162.
15. Quoted by Arie Morgenstern, "Messianic Concepts and Settlement in the Land of Israel," in Richard I. Cohen, ed., *Vision and Conflict in the Holy Land*, p. 148.
16. Ibid., p. 149.
17. See discussion of approaches to this issue in J. David Bleich, *Contemporary Halakhic Problems*, pp. 13–15.
18. Judah Alkalai, *Kitvei haRav Yehudah Alkalai*, vol. 1, pp. 202–203.
19. Ibid., pp. 246–247.
20. Ibid., p. 249.
21. Quoted by Arthur Hertzberg, *The Zionist Idea*, p. 111.
22. Ibid., p. 112.
23. Ibid., pp. 112–113.
24. Ibid., p. 114.
25. Moses Hess, *Rome and Jerusalem*, pp. 32–34.
26. Ibid., p. 18.

27. Ibid., p. 12.
28. Ibid., pp. 27–28.
29. Ibid., pp. 57–59.
30. Ibid., p. 75.
31. Ibid., p. 82.

CHAPTER 6

1. Quoted by Ehud Luz, *Parallels Meet*, p. 22.
2. Shmarya Levin, *Childhood in Exile*, pp. 273ff.
3. Arthur Hertzberg, *The Zionist Idea*, p. 147.
4. Quoted by Jacob S. Raisin, *The Haskalah Movement in Russia*, p. 263.
5. Ibid., p. 264.
6. Hertzberg, *The Zionist Idea*, pp. 164–165.
7. Ibid.
8. Ibid., p. 170.
9. Ibid., p. 176.
10. Ibid.
11. Ibid., p. 177.
12. Ibid., p. 182.
13. Ibid.
14. Shlomo Avineri, *The Making of Modern Zionism*, p. 74.
15. Hertzberg, *The Zionist Idea*, p. 183.
16. Ibid., p. 198.
17. Ibid.
18. Ahad Ha'am, *Nationalism and the Jewish Ethic*, pp. 40–42.
19. Ibid., p. 43.
20. Hertzberg, *The Zionist Idea*, p. 411.
21. Ibid., p. 412.
22. Ibid., p. 414.
23. Quoted by Nora Levin, *While Messiah Tarried*, p. 42.
24. Ibid., p. 247.
25. Ibid., p. 337.
26. Quoted by Salo W. Baron, *Modern Nationalism and Religion*, p. 226.

CHAPTER 7

1. Simon Dubnow, *Nationalism and History*, p. 82.
2. Salo W. Baron, *Modern Nationalism and Religion*, pp. 213–214.
3. Quoted by Julius H. Greenstone, *The Messiah Idea in Jewish History*, p. 247.
4. Ibid., p. 248.
5. Abraham Geiger, *Judaism and Its History*, pp. 219–220.
6. Abraham Geiger, "Preface" to *A General Introduction to the Science of Judaism*, excerpted in Geiger, *Abraham Geiger and Liberal Judaism*, p. 151.
7. Wiener, "Biography," in Geiger, *Abraham Geiger and Liberal Judaism*, p. 42.
8. Quoted by Greenstone, *The Messiah Idea*, p. 263.

9. Samson Raphael Hirsch, *The Nineteen Letters of Ben Uziel*, pp. 66–69.

10. Salomon L. Steinheim, *The Revelation: According to the Doctrine of Judaism*, in Joshua O. Haberman, *Philosopher of Revelation: The Life and Thought of S. L. Steinheim*, p. 80.

11. Ibid., pp. 81–82.

12. Ibid., p. 83.

13. Ibid., p. 86.

14. Dubnow, *Nationalism and History*, p. 102.

15. Ibid., p. 99.

16. Ibid., p. 92.

17. Ibid., p. 95.

18. Ibid., pp. 86–87.

19. Ibid., p. 98.

20. Ibid., pp. 84–85.

21. Ibid., p. 97.

22. Ibid., pp. 97–98.

23. Ibid., pp. 134–135.

24. Ibid., pp. 224–225.

CHAPTER 8

1. Theodor Herzl, *Zionist Writings*, vol. 1, p. 23.

2. Theodor Herzl, *The Jewish State*, pp. 69, 72.

3. Ibid., pp. 80, 92.

4. Ibid., p. 94.

5. Ibid., p. 95.

6. Ibid., p. 96.

7. Quoted by Howard M. Sachar, *A History of Israel*, p. 42.

8. Theodor Herzl, *The Diaries of Theodor Herzl*, ed. Marvin Lowenthal, pp. 133–134.

9. Chaim Weizmann, *Trial and Error*, p. 43.

10. Quoted by Jacob de Haas, *Theodor Herzl*, vol. 1, p. 154.

11. Quoted by Herzl, *Zionist Writings*, vol. 1, pp. 119–120.

12. Samuel Mohilever, "Message to the First Zionist Congress," quoted by Arthur Hertzberg, *The Zionist Idea*, p. 404.

13. Ibid., p. 402.

14. Herzl, *Zionist Writings*, vol. 1, p. 133.

15. Nahum Sokolow, *History of Zionism*, vol. 1, p. 268.

16. Israel Cohen, *Jewish Life in Modern Times*, p. 329.

17. Quoted by Shlomo Eidelberg, "Givush haRaayon ad Milhemet haOlam haRishonah," in S. Federbusch, ed., *Hazon Torah veTziyon*, p. 185.

18. Quoted in Marie Syrkin, *Nachman Syrkin: Socialist Zionist*, pp. 282–283.

19. Ibid., p. 283.

20. Ber Borochov, *Nationalism and the Class Struggle*, pp. 191, 196, 203.

CHAPTER 9

1. Gustav Karpeles, *Jews and Judaism in the Nineteenth Century*, p. 62.

2. Ibid., pp. 63–64.

3. Hermann Cohen, *Reason and Hope: Selections from the Jewish Writings of Hermann Cohen*, p. 168.

4. Ibid., pp. 169–170.

5. Ahad Ha'am, "On Nationalism and Religion," quoted by Arthur Hertzberg, *The Zionist Idea*, p. 262.

6. Franz Rosenzweig, *The Star of Redemption*, p. 300.

7. Salvador de Madariaga, *Essays with a Purpose*, p. 135.

8. Rozenzweig, *Star of Redemption*, p. 300.

9. Eliezer Berkovits, *Towards Historic Judaism*, p. 67.

10. Ibid., p. 73.

11. Abraham Isaac Kook, *Orot*, quoted by Hertzberg, *The Zionist Idea*, pp. 419–420.

12. Martin Buber, *Israel and the World: Essays in a Time of Crisis*, pp. 248–249.

13. Ibid., p. 252.

14. Immanuel Jakobovits, *"If Only My People . . ." Zionism in My Life*, p. 160.

15. Joseph B. Soloveitchik, "Kol Dodi Dofek," in his *Ish haEmunah*, p. 103.

16. Yaacov Herzog, *A People That Dwells Alone*, p. 129.

17. Ofira Seliktar, "The New Zionism," *Foreign Policy*, Summer 1983, p. 128.

18. Herzog, *A People that Dwells Alone*, p. 149.

19. Joseph B. Soloveitchik, *Five Addresses*, p. 79.

20. Zvi Yehuda Kook, "Zionism and Biblical Prophecy," in Yosef Tirosh, ed., *Religious Zionism: An Anthology*, p. 167.

21. Zvi Yehuda Kook, "On the Genuine Significance of the State of Israel," homily delivered in March 1978, published in *Artzi*, vol. 1 (1982), p. 5, quoted by Ian S. Lustick, *For the Land and the Lord*, p. 35.

22. Z. Y. Kook, "Zionism and Biblical Prophecy," p. 175.

23. Ibid., pp. 175–176.

24. Ibid., pp. 176–177.

25. Shlomo Goren, "Problems of a Religious State," in Tirosh, *Religious Zionism: An Anthology*, p. 183.

26. Jakobovits, *"If Only My People . . ."*, p. 161.

27. Goren, "Problems of a Religious State," pp. 183–184.

28. Shlomo Riskin, "In the Eternal Land, There Is Only One Landlord," *Jerusalem Post International*, Week ending May 4, 1991.

29. Cited in "HaRabanim haRashiyim leYisrael al haRav Ovadiah Yosef: haKol Politika," *Israel Shelanu*, March 3, 1990. This article deals with a controversy set off by a former chief rabbi, Ovadia Yosef, who attempted to stipulate conditions under which it might be halakhically permissible to alienate some of the "occupied territories" in order to avoid continued bloodshed. His arguments were roundly repudiated by his colleagues.

30. Cited in "HaRabbi miLubavitch al Divrei haRav Shakh," *Israel Shelanu*, April 6, 1990.

BIBLIOGRAPHY

Aaron haLevi of Barcelona (ca. 1300). *Sefer haHinukh*. Edited by Charles B. Chavel. Jerusalem: Mossad Harav Kook, 1966.

Aboab, Isaac. *Menorat haMaor*. Jerusalem: Mossad Harav Kook, 1961.

Abraham bar Hiyya. *Hegyon haNefesh*. Leipzig: 1860; facsimile edition, Jerusalem, 1967.

———. *Megillat haMegalleh*. Berlin: Mekitze Nirdamim, 1924; facsimile edition, Jerusalem, 1968.

———. *The Meditation of the Sad Soul* (Hegyon haNefesh). Translated by Geoffrey Wigoder. London: Routledge & Kegan Paul, 1969.

Abraham Maimonides. *Milhamot haShem*. Edited by Reuven M. Margoliot. Jerusalem: Mossad Harav Kook, n.d.

Abramsky, Yehezkel. *Eretz Yisrael Nahlat Am Yisrael: BaAspeklariah shel haMasoret*. B'nai B'rak: Netzah, 1969.

Ahad Ha'am. *Nationalism and the Jewish Ethic: The Basic Writings of Ahad Ha'am*. Edited by Hans Kohn. New York: Schocken Books, 1962.

Alkalai, Judah. *Kitve haRav Yehudah Alkalai*. 2 vols. Edited by Isaac Raphael. Jerusalem: Mossad Harav Kook, 1974.

Altmann, Alexander. *Moses Mendelssohn: A Biographical Study*. Philadelphia: Jewish Publication Society, 1973.

Avineri, Shlomo. *The Making of Modern Zionism: The Intellectual Origins of the Jewish State*. New York: Basic Books, 1981.

———. *Moses Hess: Prophet of Communism and Zionism*. New York: New York University Press, 1985.

The Babylonian Talmud. 18 vols. Translated under editorship of I. Epstein. London: Soncino Press, 1978.

The Bahir. Translated by Aryeh Kaplan. York Beach, Maine: Samuel Weiser, 1979.

Baron, Salo W. *Modern Nationalism and Religion*. New York: Harper, 1947.

———. *A Social and Religious History of the Jews*. Vol. 6. New York: Columbia University Press, 1958.

Berkovits, Eliezer. *Towards Historic Judaism*. Oxford: East and West Library, 1943.

Berlin, Isaiah. *The Life and Opinions of Moses Hess*. Cambridge: W. Hefer and Sons, 1959.

Bleich, J. David. *Contemporary Halakhic Problems*. New York: Ktav Publishing House, 1977.

Borochov, Ber. *Nationalism and the Class Struggle*. New York: Young Poale Zion Alliance of America, 1937.

Buber, Martin. *Israel and the World: Essays in a Time of Crisis*. New York: Schocken Books, 1948.

————. *Israel and Palestine: The History of an Idea*. London: East and West Library, 1952.

Cohen, Hermann. *Reason and Hope: Selections from the Jewish Writings of Hermann Cohen*. Translated by Eva Jospe. New York: W. W. Norton, 1971.

Cohen, Israel. *Jewish Life in Modern Times*. New York: Dodd, Mead, 1914.

Cohen, Richard I., ed. *Vision and Conflict in the Holy Land*. Jerusalem: Yad Izhak Ben-Zvi, 1985.

Davies, W. D. *The Territorial Dimension of Judaism*. Berkeley: University of California Press, 1982.

de Haas, Jacob. *Theodor Herzl: A Biographical Study*. 2 vols. Chicago: Leonard, 1927.

de Madariaga, Salvador. *Essays with a Purpose*. London: Hollis & Carter, 1954.

Dubnow, Simon. *Nationalism and History: Essays on Old and New Judaism*. Edited by Koppel S. Pinson. Philadelphia: Jewish Publication Society, 1958.

Duvernoy, Claude. *Le Sionisme de Dieu*. Paris: Editions S.E.R.G., 1970.

The Early Kabbalah. Edited by Joseph Dan. New York: Paulist Press, 1986.

Eisen, Arnold M. *Galut: Modern Jewish Reflection on Homelessness and Homecoming*. Bloomington: Indiana University Press, 1986.

Eisenstein, J. D., ed. *Otzar Midrashim*. 2 vols. Israel, 1969.

Eliade, Mircea. *The Sacred and the Profane: The Nature of Religion*. New York: Harper & Row, 1961.

Elijah of Vilna. *Aderet Eliyahu*. Tel Aviv: Sinai Publishing, n.d.

Federbusch, Simon, ed. *Hazon Torah veTziyon*. New York: Moriah Publishers, 1960.

Finkelstein, Louis. "Some Aspects of Early Rabbinic Nationalism," in *The Brandeis Avukah Volume of 1932*. Edited by Joseph S. Shubow. New York: American Student Zionist Federation, 1932.

Geiger, Abraham. *Abraham Geiger and Liberal Judaism: The Challenge of the Nineteenth Century*. Compiled, with a biographical introduction by Max Wiener. Translated by Ernst J. Schlochauer. Philadelphia: Jewish Publication Society, 1962.

————. *Judaism and Its History: In Two Parts*. Lanham, Maryland: University Press of America, 1985.

Goldberg, Isaac. *Major Noah: American-Jewish Pioneer*. Philadelphia: Jewish Publication Society, 1936.

Goren, Shlomo. *Torat haShabbat vehaMoed*. Jerusalem: World Zionist Organization, 1982.

Greenstone, Julius H. *The Messiah Idea in Jewish History*. Philadelphia: Jewish Publication Society, 1906.

Grunblatt, Joseph. *Exile and Redemption: Meditations on Jewish History*. Hoboken, N.J.: Ktav Publishing House, 1988.

Haberman, Joshua O. *Philosopher of Revelation: The Life and Thought of S. L. Steinheim*. Philadelphia: Jewish Publication Society, 1990.

Halevi, Judah. *Selected Poems of Jehudah Halevi*. Translated by Nina Salaman. Philadelphia: Jewish Publication Society, 1928.

———. *Book of Kuzari*. Translated by Hartwig Hirschfeld. New York: Pardes Publishing, 1946.

Heller, Joseph. *The Zionist Idea*. New York: Schocken, 1949.

Hertzberg, Arthur. *The Zionist Idea: A Historical Analysis and Reader*. New York: Harper and Row, 1966.

———. *The French Enlightenment and the Jews*. New York: Columbia University Press, 1968.

Herzl, Theodor. *The Jewish State: An Attempt at a Modern Solution of the Jewish Question*. New York: American Zionist Emergency Council, 1946.

———. *The Diaries of Theodor Herzl*. Edited by Marvin Lowenthal. New York: Dial Press, 1956.

———. *Zionist Writings: Essays and Addresses*. 2 vols. New York: Herzl Press, 1973–1975.

Herzog, Isaac. *Tehukah leYisrael al pi haTorah*. Vol. 1. Jerusalem: Mossad Harav Kook, 1989.

Herzog, Yaacov. *A People that Dwells Alone: Speeches and Writings of Yaacov Herzog*. London: Weidenfeld and Nicolson, 1975.

Heschel, Abraham J. *The Prophets*. Philadelphia: Jewish Publications Society, 1962.

Hess, Moses. *Rome and Jerusalem*. Translated and edited by Maurice J. Bloom. New York: Philosophical Library, 1958.

Hirsch, Samson Raphael. *The Nineteen Letters of Ben Uziel*. Translated by Bernard Drachman. New York: Bloch Publishing, 1942.

Idel, Moshe. *A Straight Path: Studies in Medieval Philosophy and Culture*. Editor-in-Chief: Ruth Link-Salinger. Washington, D.C.: Catholic University of America Press, 1988.

Jakobovits, Immanuel. *"If Only My People . . ." Zionism in My Life*. Washington, D.C.: B'nai B'rith Books, 1986.

Joseph, Bernard. *Nationality: Its Nature and Problems*. London: George Allen & Unwin, 1929.

Judah Loew ben Bezalel (Maharal). *Netzah Yisrael*. Tel Aviv: Pardes Books, n.d.

Karo, Joseph. *Shulhan Arukh*. 10 vols. New York: Otzar Hasefarim, 1959.

Karpeles, Gustav. *Jews and Judaism in the Nineteenth Century*. Philadelphia: Jewish Publication Society, 1905.

Kimhi, David. *Perush haRadak: Tehillim*. (Printed in standard editions of rabbinic bibles).

Klausner, Joseph. *K'sheUmmah Nilhemet al Herutah*. Tel Aviv: Medinit, 1952.

———. *The Messianic Idea in Israel*. New York: Macmillan, 1955.

Kobler, Franz. *Napoleon and the Jews*. New York: Schocken, 1976.

Kohn, Hans. *The Idea of Nationalism: A Study in Its Origins and Background*. New York: Macmillan, 1951.

Levin, Nora. *While Messiah Tarried: Jewish Socialist Movements 1871–1917*. New York: Schocken, 1977.

Levin, Shmarya. *Childhood in Exile*. New York: 1929.

Livneh, Eliezer. *Yisrael uMashber haTzivilizatzis haMaaravit*. Tel Aviv: Schocken Publishing House, 1972.

Lustick, Ian S. *For the Land and the Lord: Jewish Fundamentalism in Israel*. New York: Council on Foreign Relations, 1988.

Luz, Ehud. *Parallels Meet: Religion and Nationalism in the Early Zionist Movement, 1882–1904*. Translated by Lenn J. Schramm. Philadelphia: Jewish Publication Society, 1988.

Maimonides. *The Book of Judges*. Translated by A. M. Hershman. New Haven: Yale University Press, 1949.

———. *The Book of Torts*. Translated by Hyman Klein. New Haven: Yale University Press, 1954.

———. *Hakdamot lePerush haMishnah*. Edited by Mordekhai Dov Rabinowitz. Jerusalem: Mossad Harav Kook, 1961.

———. *Mishne Torah*. 16 vols. Edited by Mordecai Dov Rabinovitz. Jerusalem: Mossad Harav Kook, 1962.

———. *The Guide of the Perplexed*. Translated by Shlomo Pines. Chicago: University of Chicago Press, 1963.

Midrash haGodol. 5 vols. Edited by Mordecai Margaliot. Jerusalem: Mossad Harav Kook, 1975.

Midrash Lekah Tov. 2 vols. Edited by Solomon Buber. Vilna, 1880; facsimile edition: Jerusalem, 1986.

Midrash Rabbah. 10 vols. 3rd edition. Translated and edited by H. Freedman and Maurice Simon. London: Soncino Press, 1983.

Midrash Shoher Tov. Edited by Solomon Buber. Vilna, 1891; facsimile edition: Jerusalem, 1977.

Midrash Tanhumah. 2 vols. Edited by Solomon Buber. Vilna, n.d.; facsimile edition: Jerusalem, 1964.

Midrash Tanhumah. 2 vols. Edited by Abraham M. Rosen. Warsaw, 1878; facsimile edition: New York, 1970.

The Mishnah. Translated by Herbert Danby. Oxford: Clarendon Press, 1967.

Moses Mendelssohn: Selections from His Writings. Edited and translated by Eva Jospe. New York: Viking Press, 1975.

Nahmanides. *Hasagot al haSharashim uMinyan haMitzvot*. (Printed in *Sefer haMitzvot lehaRambam*. New York: Jacob Shurkin, 1956).

———. *Perushei haTorah*. 2 vols. Jerusalem: Mossad Harav Kook, 1959.

Neher, André. *Moses and the Vocation of the Jewish People*. Translated by Irene Marinoff. New York: Harper and Brothers, 1959.

Nissim Gerondi. *Shnaim Assar Derushim*. Jerusalem, 1959.

Our Mandate on Palestine: The Bible on Israel's Right to the Holy Land. Compiled by Max Pritzker. New York: Eastern Publishers, 1944.

Patai, Raphael. *Man and Temple*. 2nd enlarged edition. New York: Ktav Publishing House, 1967.

Perush al haTorah: Meyuhas leTalmid HaRan. Edited by Leon A. Feldman. Jerusalem: Shalem Institute, 1970.

Pesikta de-Rab Kahana. Translated by William G. Braude and Israel J. Kapstein. Philadelphia: Jewish Publication Society, 1975.

Pinson, Koppel S. "Arkady Kremer, Vladimir Medem and the Ideology of the 'Bund,'" *Jewish Social Studies* 7 (1945).

Pirke de Rabbi Eliezer. Translated and annotated by Gerald Friedlander. 4th edition. New York: Sepher-Hermon Press, 1981.

Prinsker, Max. *Our Mandate on Palestine*. New York: Eastern Publishers, 1944.

Rabinowitz, Abraham Hirsch. *The Jewish Mind: In Its Halachic Talmudic Expression*. Jerusalem: Hillel Press, 1978.

Raisin, Jacob S. *The Haskalah Movement in Russia*. Philadelphia: Jewish Publication Society, 1913.

Rosenzweig, Franz. *The Star of Redemption*. Translated by William W. Hallo. New York: Holt, Rinehart and Winston, 1971.

Saadia Gaon. *The Book of Beliefs and Opinions*. Translated by Samuel Rosenblatt. New Haven: Yale University Press, 1948.

Sachar, Howard M. *A History of Israel*. New York: Alfred A. Knopf, 1976.

Safran, Alexander. *Israel dans le temps et dans l'espace*. Paris: Payot, 1980.

Scholem, Gershom. *Kabbalah*. New York: Quadrangle/New York Times, 1974.

Schulman, Mary. *Moses Hess: Prophet of Zionism*. New York: Thomas Yoseloff, 1963.

Schweid, Eliezer. *Leumiyut Yehudit*. Jerusalem: S. Zack, 1972.

Sefer haZohar. 3 vols. Jerusalem: Mossad Harav Kook, 1970.

Seliktar, Ofira. "The New Zionism," *Foreign Policy*. Summer 1983.

Sifra or *Torat Kohanim*. Hosiyatin: Dovevei Siftei Yeshainim, 1908; facsimile edition: Israel, 1968.

Sifre: A Tannaitic Commentary on the Book of Deuteronomy. Translated by Reuven Hammer. New Haven and London: Yale University Press, 1986.

Sokolow, Nahum. *History of Zionism, 1600–1918*. 2 vols. New York: 1969.

Soloveitchik, Joseph B. *Ish haEmunah*. Jerusalem: Mossad Harav Kook, 1968.

_____. *Five Addresses*. Jerusalem: Tal Orot Institute, 1983.

Syrkin, Marie. *Nachman Syrkin: Socialist Zionist*. New York: Herzl Press, 1961.

Talmud Bavli veYerushalmi. 20 vols. New York: Otzar Hasefarim, 1959.

Talmud Yerushalmi. 3 vols. Zhitomer, 1866; facsimile edition, Jerusalem: Torah MiZion, 1968.

Tirosh, Yosef, ed. *Religious Zionism: An Anthology*. Jerusalem: World Zionist Organization, 1975.

Tosefta. (Printed in standard editions of the Talmud.)

Transactions of the Parisian Sanhedrin, or Acts of the Assembly of Israelitish Deputies of France and Italy. Translated by M. Diogene Tama. London: C. Taylor, 1807; Reprinted, Lanham, Md.: University Press of America, 1985.

Tudor, Henry. *Political Myth*. New York: Praeger, 1972.

Weiss, Isaac Hirsch. *Dor Dor veDorshav*. 5 vols. Jerusalem: Ziv Publishers, n.d.

Weizmann, Chaim. *Trial and Error*. New York: Harper and Brothers, 1949.

Yalkut Shimeoni. 2 vols. New York: Pardes Publishing, n.d.

ABOUT THE BOOK
& AUTHOR

This book provides unique insights into the profound religious and cultural issues underlying the increasingly ideological divisions within Israeli society over the questions of territorial concessions and the future character of the state. It explores the significant distinctions between modern Zionism, a primarily secular nationalist movement modeled after the European movements of the nineteenth century, and the much older traditional Jewish nationalism, which is deeply rooted in ancient religion and culture. Dr. Sicker offers a concise overview of the 3,000-year intellectual history of Jewish nationalism, within which modern secular Zionism represents a relatively brief—although immensely important—interlude that may be entering its final stage as other more traditional religious nationalist concepts seek to take its place as the national ideology of the State of Israel.

An analysis of how Jewish religious nationalism has shaped the history of the Jews, this book examines the national and territorial dimensions of classical Judaism, explains the survival of the nationalist idea despite the repeated loss of independence and the exile of the majority of the people from their homeland, and demonstrates how the nineteenth-century religious reform movement sought to counter both the growth of Zionism and the resurgence of traditional Jewish nationalism. The book concludes with a discussion of the new ideological synthesis of Judaism, nationalism, and the Land of Israel and its implications for the future of the Jewish state.

Martin Sicker is a writer, lecturer, and consultant on international strategic and political affairs, specializing in the Middle East. He is the author of *Israel's Quest for Security* and *The Genesis of the State*.

INDEX